DANCING

DANCING

THE PLEASURE, POWER, AND ART OF MOVEMENT

GERALD JONAS

PREFACE BY RHODA GRAUER

ABRAMS, NEW YORK
IN ASSOCIATION WITH THIRTEEN/WNET

Opposite: Ballet class, United States, c. 1914

Dancing is a companion book to an eight-part public television series. The series was produced with the generous support of the following funders and the editorial contributions of the following consultants:

Series Funders

Lila Wallace–Reader's Digest Fund

National Endowment for the Humanities
National Endowment for the Arts
Corporation for Public Broadcasting
Public Broadcasting Service
The Ford Foundation
The Rockefeller Foundation
Rosalind P. Walter
The JCT Foundation
Ballet Makers, Inc.
The Charles Evans Hughes
    Memorial Foundation
The Japan Foundation
The Hosa-Bunka Foundation
The Frederick W. Richmond Foundation
Marie G. Dennett Foundation
Felice H. Francis
Eugenia and Henri G. Doll

Series Core Consultants

Elizabeth Aldrich, Diane Apostolos-Cappadona, Brenda Dixon-Gottschild, Adrienne Kaeppler, Joann Keali'inohomoku, Elizabeth Kendall, Judy Mitoma, Cynthia Novack, Allegra Fuller Snyder

Series Advisors

Najwa Adra, Omofolabo Soyinka Ajayi, Daniel Ampousah (Ko Nimo), Sally Banes, Karin Barber, Eileen Blumenthal, Virginia Brooks, Noel Carroll, Curtis Carter, Selma Jeanne Cohen, Roger Copeland, Beate Gordon, David Gordon, Peter Grilli, Camille Hardy, Millicent Hodson, Indrani, Pamela Takiora Ingram, Angana Jhaveri, Deborah Jowitt, Father Thomas Kane, Amna Kusumo, Samuel L. Leiter, Bella Lewitsky, Sophia Lokko, Bruce Marks, Morton Marks, Maria Messina, Barbara Stoler Miller, Jane Freeman Moulin, Joseph Nketia, Constance Old, Albert Opoku, Benito Ortolani, Eiko Otake, Naima Prevots, Pearl Primus, Nancy Reynolds, Enid Schildkrout, Marcia Siegel, Sally Sommer, Jeanelle Stovall, Twyla Tharp, Robert Farris Thompson, Kapila Vatsyayan, Anmol Vellani, Sheila Walker, Dianne L. Woodruff

Production team for the *Dancing* book:

For Thirteen/WNET

Project Director: David Wolff
Picture Editor: Alexandra Truitt
Editorial Supervisor: Licia Hurst
Research Supervisor: Beth Pollack
Editorial Assistants: Elisabeth Keating, Diane Boardman

Special Editorial Consultant: Joann Keali'inohomoku

For ABRAMS

Editor: Eric Himmel
Art Director: Samuel N. Antupit
Designers: Maria Miller, Anne Winslow

Library of Congress Cataloging-in-Publication Data

Jonas, Gerald, 1935
  Dancing / Gerald Jonas; preface by Rhoda Grauer.
        p.   cm.
  This is a companion volume to an eight-part television series.
  Includes bibliographical references and index.
  ISBN 978-0-8109-2791-9
  1. Dancing. 2. Dancing—Social aspects. 3. Dancing—History. I. Title.
GV1594.J66   1922   92–8038
792.8—dc20

The *Dancing* series is a production of Thirteen/WNET in association with RM Arts and BBC-TV

Printed and bound in Italy
30 29 28 27 26 25 24 23 22

Abrams books are available at special discounts when purchased in quantity for premiums and promotions as well as fundraising or educational use. Special editions can also be created to specification. For details, contact specialsales@abramsbooks.com or the address below.

ABRAMS
The Art of Books

195 Broadway
New York, NY 10007
abramsbooks.com

To Barbara, Phoebe, Sarah, James, and Peter

C O N T

E N T S

Preface

y earliest dance memory is of the Ditmar sisters sitting through gym class whenever we square danced in grade school. They said it was against their religion to dance. At the time I took this as just one of those strange things about religion: I wasn't allowed to eat pork, my friend Barbara had to eat fish on Fridays, the Ditmar sisters couldn't dance.

Another vivid memory is of a class in ballroom dancing my parents sent me to. Here we were forced to embrace boys we had never met, breathe into each other's faces, and drag around the floor in a series of steps that we were told would leave us looking and feeling like Fred Astaire and Ginger Rogers. Well, I had seen them on television, and you couldn't fool me. What we did in dance class was completely embarrassing. Who would have guessed that only a few years later I would use what I had been taught to conquer the cutest boy at the prom in a steamy tango which left my friends in shock, the teachers frozen in place, and me confined to my room for three weekends?

Dance was mysterious. Sometimes you did it, and it was good—like square dancing in gym class—unless, of course, you were the Ditmar sisters. Sometimes you did it really well, and it was bad—like applying the intimate rhythms of the tango to "seduction" instead of "socializing." Although they were not always intuitively clear, dance had its rules; and there were serious consequences if you got them wrong.

Dancing, both the television series and the book, takes a close-up, cross-cultural look at the rules, messages, and meanings embodied in dance around the world. Dance, like language, is found in all human societies. And like language, dance has power. The universality of dance is easily explained: the human body itself is its vehicle. All societies acknowledge its power and harness it according to their fundamental values, aesthetics, and mores. You can learn a lot about a society from its dances, but reading the culture-specific "languages" of dance can be tricky.

For example, rules concerning gender identity, often expressed as ideals of modesty, are embedded in the traditional dances of most societies: women's movements are generally more restricted than men's; men can do high leg extensions but women can't; male dancers do not touch the legs of female dancers, and so on. In the classical ballet of the West, however, women extend their legs, reveal their bodies, and are lifted by men who hold them firmly by the legs. Does this mean that Western society is somehow less "modest" than other societies? Hardly. In fact, the Judeo-Christian West, where ballet developed, has often been more puritanical about the body—its physical functions, its erotic power—than many other parts of the world. What classical ballet tries to do is transcend the physicality of the dancers' bodies by creating the illusion that the dancers are ethereal beings—nymphs and sylphs and such—for whom the rules of touch and extension do not apply. Ironically, classical ballet, often considered the height of elegance and beauty in the West, has shocked people elsewhere in the world who might go naked but who would not dream of touching someone of the opposite sex while dancing.

To comprehend a dance, we must open ourselves to the culture from which it springs; conversely, as we begin to gain insight into a dance, we are on a path to understanding the culture that produced it. This is the basic premise of *Dancing*.

The idea for *Dancing* was born in Hawaii in 1978. Perched in a gallery of the Bishop Museum in Honolulu, I watched a small group of musicians and dancers perform a series of traditional hulas. Pua Kanahele, seated on a pandanus mat, beat out a rhythmic pattern on a large gourd shaped like an hourglass, while she chanted ancient songs in the Hawaiian language honoring the goddess of the volcanoes, Pele. The dance itself, performed by four students of Pua Kanahele and her mother Edith Kanaka'ole, startled me. As director of the dance program of the National Endowment for the Arts, I was in Hawaii to attend the annual meeting of the American Dance Guild/Conference on Research on Dance. I had spent most of my career in the American professional dance scene, and had seen literally hundreds of dance performances from the largest ballet companies to small avant-garde groups performing in drafty lofts and overheated garages. But nothing in my experience had prepared me for this.

To begin with, the space allotted for the dancing was about fifteen square feet, hardly room enough for a small leap. In any case, the dancers' feet never left the ground. This hula was utterly unlike the "hulas" I had seen in Hollywood movies. Instead of rapid hip gyrations, the dancers' movements evolved naturally and gracefully out of

a complex stepping-in-place motion in which the knees were slightly bent and the feet rocked gently from a flat-on-the-ground position to a heel-lift with the weight resting on the ball of the foot. Instead of a Dorothy Lamour sarong or grass skirt, the dancers wore loose-fitting skirts and tops. Finally, they were both—by the standards that had informed my own life—very, very big women (each weighed more than two hundred pounds). I had no idea of what I was seeing, but I was determined to find out.

During the rest of the conference I saw many kinds of dance from the Pacific region, ranging from the exquisitely refined Balinese wayang wong, with its articulated finger movements, highly expressive eyes, and glorious costumes of red, green, yellow, and gold brocade, to a ceremony called Obon led by members of the Japanese community in Hawaii. Obon is an annual event to honor the souls of ancestors. The dancers form a large circle and perform simple steps more or less in unison to the beat of a single large drum. I have never felt more a part of something than when I fell in step with about two hundred other people dancing in homage to the generations that came before us.

Before I left Hawaii, I learned that the dances I had seen served many functions beyond entertainment. The aesthetics of each were completely strange to my Western eyes. Though the large hula dancers initially appeared to be unattractive, I learned that their shape is, in fact, a highly desirable sign of beauty and status in traditional Hawaiian culture. Clearly, there was a lot to learn. Upon my return home,

I quickly contacted my brother, Victor, an ethnomusicologist. He sent me off in a direction of exploration that led to this book and series.

Until recently, serious dance scholarship in the West took forms that proceeded in isolation from one another: dance criticism/history (which tended to evaluate dance qualitatively according to aesthetic judgments) and dance ethnology/anthropology (which tended to focus on the larger cultural functions that dance serves). The former disciplines were usually applied to the dances of the Western world, the latter to the dances of the non-Western world. The challenge of *Dancing* was to combine these two approaches and apply them to dance throughout the world. In pursuit of this goal, we have avoided the typical presentation organized historically or geographically. Instead, we have identified a number of important ways in which dance functions in human societies—always keeping in mind that while dance is a universal human activity it does not play the same role in every culture. The functions we settled on were each allotted a chapter in this book:

Dance as an emblem of cultural identity, with a focus on clashes between societies;

Dance as an expression of religious worship, with a focus on Nigeria and Europe;

Dance as an expression of social order and power, with a focus on royal courts;

Dance as an expression of cultural mores, with a focus on gender-specific behavior;

Dance as a classical art, with a focus on ballet in the West and kabuki in Japan;

Dance as a medium of cultural fusion, with a focus on the intertwining of African and European dance traditions in the Americas;

Dance as the creation of individual artists, with a focus on the twentieth century in America;

Dance as an indicator of who we are today and where we are going, with a focus on electronic media.

From the corpus of world dance, we have selected examples that offer cross-cultural comparisons between theatrical and nontheatrical dance forms as well as insights into important historical issues, such as the evolution of dances, the struggle to preserve traditional dances, and the adaptation of old dances to new purposes. Though our examples represent only a small fraction of world dance, they were chosen because they shed light on larger, more universal issues. By delving deeply into specific examples, we hope to generate an understanding that can be applied to dances and cultures worldwide.

Dance today is not simply cross-cultural but pan-cultural and planetary; dances are borrowed, degraded, adapted, and transformed at rates unparalleled in the past, with consequences that cannot be predicted. There has never been a more exciting time to be part of the dance world—and anyone who has ever danced, watched a dance, or wondered why someone else was dancing is part of it. Which includes, most definitely, the Ditmar sisters.

One final note: Over the years that I worked on this project, I learned that the dynamics of dance are as close to the dynamics of life as any art I can imagine. Dance changes with every body that dances; it changes with the time, the country, even the weather; it does not have one history but many. *Dancing*, the series and the book, present one set of stories about dance. There are many more to be told.

Rhoda Grauer

Chapter I
The Power of Dance

Under a father's eager palm, the taut skin of a mother's belly ripples once, then again, prodded from within by a force that only a mother and father could identify: "It's a hand, no, a foot, an elbow, maybe a knee. . . ." Whatever the limb, the happy parents take its stirring as a sure sign of new life; they attribute to the quickening fetus a command, however rudimentary, of a basic human impulse: the thrusts and flexions and twists and turns of self-generated movement.

The impulse to move is the raw material that cultures shape into evocative sequences of physical activity that we call dance. This phenomenon is universal. Courting and courtly dances; wedding dances and funeral dances; dances of healing and dances of instruction; dances to arouse, amuse, or uplift onlookers; dances to usher in the seasons and dances that appeal directly to the gods; dances that tell stories and dances that seek to create a formal beauty that cannot be put into words:

There is no end to the variety of purposes to which the dancing body can be put. But meaning as well as beauty is in the eye of the beholder; and one person's shudder of religious ecstasy may be another person's shimmy of sexual abandon. So intensely personal is dance, so closely linked to cultural identity, that when people disagree about the meaning and value of specific dances, the resulting confusion may breed contempt, anger, even violence. To question or belittle other people's dances is to challenge their right to be themselves. As the famous line of W. B. Yeats reminds us (and no book about dance would be complete without quoting it): "How can we know the dancer from the dance?"

The classical court dance of Cambodia has embodied the essence of that country's national identity for over a thousand years. From the ninth through the middle of the fifteenth cen-

tury, the great Khmer empire ruled much of Southeast Asia from its capital at Angkor, in what is now northwestern Cambodia. Hundreds of carved reliefs on the magnificent temples in and around Angkor depict ranks of bejeweled dancers in elaborate headdresses and diaphanous skirts emerging foamlike from the sea to shower blessings and prosperity on the land. These were no figments of the artists' imaginations. The royal treasury supported thousands of court dancers who played a central role in the fertility rites and ancestor worship through which the empire maintained itself. During the twelfth century, King Jayavarman VII paid honor to the spirits of his mother and father by adding over three thousand dancers to those already in service in temples throughout his realm. According to historian Paul Cravath, "The extent to which dance and dancers were integral to the social and religious fabric of Cambodia is perhaps unequaled in world civilization."

When Angkor was sacked by Siamese armies in the mid-fifteenth century, among the treasures the invaders carried away with them were court dancers and musicians. But even though Angkor was abandoned for a time, the dance tradition survived; royal dancers, wearing gilded headdresses resembling those on the temple reliefs, took part in the funeral processions of Cambodian kings well into the twentieth century. Until 1970, an all-female troupe known as "the king's dancers" lived in the king's palace in the contemporary capital of Phnom Penh, where they continued to perform the ancient ritual dances and dance dramas based on Cambodian myths and folk tales and on Sanskrit epics like the *Mahabharata* and the *Ramayana*. For years the star of the troupe was the daughter of Prince Sihanouk, the last reigning monarch.

The classical dances of Cambodia are marked by a slow, almost hypnotic pace and smooth, wavelike, synchronized movements; performers may stand in

one spot for long periods, with one leg raised and bent behind them at the knee, while their fingers, taut with controlled energy, curl back toward their wrists in the characteristic gestures that are said to form a dance within a dance; through special exercises and long practice, fingers and elbows become so supple they appear to be boneless. As we will see in Chapter 3, the highly refined court dance of Cambodia has much in common with dances that express the hierarchical structure and tradition-bound perspective of other royal courts, both past and present, around the world.

The Khmer Rouge, who captured Phnom Penh in 1975, were determined to wipe out every vestige of Cambodia's "feudal past." As potent symbols of that past, the royal dancers were hunted down, imprisoned, put to death. Yet subsequent events have confirmed the power of the dance to serve as a rallying point for national consciousness. After the Khmer Rouge were overthrown in

One of the largest religious complexes in the world, Angkor Wat was built by the Cambodian king Suryavarman II (c. A.D. 1112–1153). Nominally a Hindu temple devoted to Vishnu, Angkor Wat embodies two linked ideas which are also to be found at the Buddhist temple of Borobudur in Java: the cult of the devaraja, or god-king, in whose being is centered both religious and secular power, and the World Mountain, which is the axis of the universe and the underlying structural principle of religious architecture. In this view, the central section of the monument rises above one of the two water tanks that border the great roadway leading from the monumental gate to the temple itself.

Opposite: Students and teachers at the National Khmer Dance School, Phnom Penh, Cambodia, 1991.

The celestial females found on the great temples of Cambodia evoke the style of life at the Khmer court in its heyday. The two celestial dancers (above) decorate a pillar in the Banyon at Angkor Thom, an enormous monument syncretizing aspects of Buddhism and Hinduism—but largely celebrating the god-king himself—built by King Jayavarman VII (c. A.D. 1181–early thirteenth century). Details of the pose of these figures are echoed by the two children (right) dancing at Angkor Wat in 1923.

Among the many issues that dance anthropologists address is how children acquire the dance "language" of their own culture. This photograph, of a young girl in Pokhara, Nepal, practicing a dance step while her friends clap in rhythm, captures a scene that is acted out in most societies.

1979 by Vietnamese-backed forces, the new communist government made it a priority to restore the dance (with the aid of a few surviving dancers and teachers) as a way of establishing its legitimacy in the eyes of the Cambodians. Meanwhile, thirty-five royal dancers who had escaped from the killing fields of the Khmer Rouge came together in the United States to form the Khmer Classical Dance Troupe, whose performances have heartened the thousands of Cambodians now living outside their homeland while introducing the glories of Cambodian dance to new audiences. Each troupe claims to be the true embodiment of the ancient tradition; in keeping with this tradition, the dancers are literally sewn into their costumes of sequined and hand-embroidered silk and velvet before each performance.

All dance is charged with power. To explore the idioms and sources of this power, a relatively new field of scholarship called dance anthropology views dance in its social and cultural context. Encoded in the form, technique, and structure of every dance are meanings and values of importance to the dancers and to those who share their view of the world. This is as true of the participatory dances that everyone does at social functions like weddings as it is of the dances performed by trained specialists for spectators drawn from the community as a whole or from various self-selected elites.

Wedding dances are found in a great many societies. In those that trace their roots back to the Judeo-Christian tradition, the dancing is usually kept separate from the wedding ceremony itself. This ceremony takes the form of a sacred ritual involving a formal procession and other symbolically structured acts, such as an exchange of vows and rings, ritual kissing and wine drinking, the breaking of a glass, and so on. Significantly, none of these acts is thought of as dance. Only when the ceremony ends does the dancing begin—traditionally with a waltz performed by the just-married couple before the assembled guests. This dance, which inaugurates the secular (that is, nonsacred) part of the celebration, follows a strict protocol of its own. As if to demonstrate that weddings unite not just two people but two families, the bride and groom separate after a few turns and begin inviting their relatives and in-laws to dance until the floor is filled with dancing couples from both families. At a Jewish wedding, a group of men may lift the bride and groom up on chairs and dance around the hall with them, or the dancing may take the form of a hora, an all-inclusive circle associated with both Eastern European Jewry and the modern state of Israel.

As we will see in Chapter 2, it is no accident that wedding dances in most Western societies are relegated to the secular part of the celebration; the Judeo-Christian tradition has always been uneasy about the role of the dancing body in sacred settings. This ambivalence can take many forms; among Hasidic Jews—who not only dance joyfully at weddings but, unlike their coreligionists, dance during divine worship as well—all dancing is strictly segregated by gender.

The distinction between sacred and secular, which looms so large in the Judeo-Christian tradition, has little meaning in most non-Western cultures. In the communal religious ceremonies of such cultures, dance often plays an indispensable role. Precisely because their underlying assumptions about dance and the body are so different, Europeans and non-Europeans have often clashed over such issues as what the proper function of dance should be, and what kinds of dance movements are appropriate in a healthy society.

The women came down [to the beach] and stripped themselves naked and made all the alluring gestures they could to entice [the sailors] onshore again. . . . " The year is 1767; the writer is Samuel Wallis, captain of HMS *Dolphin*, the first European vessel to make landfall on the Polynesian island now known as Tahiti. Wallis had no doubts about the intentions of the native women; when he ordered his men to stay onboard, the women pelted the ship with fruit and shouted what sounded like jeers in their native language.

This moment of first contact—like some bizarre science-fiction scenario—was repeated again and again during the European "discovery" of the South Pacific. In most cases the Europeans were struck by the initial friendliness of the natives, by their uninhibited (to European eyes) sexuality, and by their propensity to express themselves through dance. Speaking of the Tahitians, a French sailor reported that "their existence was in never-ending merrymaking." Captain James Cook, a keen observer who visited Tahiti a few years after Wallis, described their dances

John Webber, an artist who traveled with Captain James Cook on his third voyage (1776–79), sketched the head of a dancer in central Polynesia (top), showing a distorted facial expression of the sort that so disturbed the captain. Polynesian dances, like the Tongan "dance of the night" (above), performed only by men, published as an engraving in Cook's and James King's Voyage to the Pacific Ocean *(1784) after a sketch by Webber, quickly became the most powerful symbol of South Sea island life to Europeans.*

in more detail. To the accompaniment of a chanting man beating on a shark-skin drum, bare-breasted women wrapped in ankle-length bark-cloth skirts moved their hands and arms in elegant gestures, while shaking their hips in rotatory motions "with a velocity that excited our astonishment." Cook found the dances of the youngest girls (eight to ten years old) "indecent." He was also offended by the "demonic" expressions the dancers made by distorting their lips—a feature of the dance that seemed to give great pleasure to the natives themselves. One oddity the early explorers noted: Although the natives rubbed

noses to express affection, kissing was unknown, as was Western-style couple dancing in which a man and a woman face each other and place their hands on each other's bodies in public.

The European missionaries who followed the first explorers to Polynesia learned more, and liked less, about the native dances. On Tahiti and its neighboring islands, where food was usually plentiful, men and women seemed to dance at every opportunity, day or night—to please their gods, to celebrate the completion of communal work projects, to praise their chiefs, and, apparently, for the sheer fun of it. They

Contemporary Tahitian dance combines features of traditional dance forms, such as alternating ranks of men and women who perform gender-specific steps, with elements borrowed from the West or from other island groups.

also had an elaborate dance theater. A fleet of up to seventy canoes made a circuit from island to island carrying a troupe of actor-dancers called arioi, who had renounced ordinary life to devote themselves to the cult of Oro, god of rain and fertility. Some of their canoes were rigged with platforms for performances, so that the singing and dancing could begin even before the fleet reached land. Once on shore the performances continued through the night in houses specially built for this purpose.

Among the high points of the performances were mime shows featuring men with mock phalluses fashioned from distended animal bladders; their grossly exaggerated portrayals of sexual intercourse provoked the audience to waves of laughter, as did their satirical skits about the shortcomings (sexual and otherwise) of the most powerful chiefs. Under the rigidly hierarchical system that dominated life on these Polynesian islands, only the arioi were permitted to make fun of the ruling class in public— not unlike the court jesters of medieval Europe.

The first representatives of the newly formed London Missionary Society arrived in Tahiti in 1797 and began converting the principal chiefs and local priests. The arioi, who offended the new order both by their devotion to the old gods and by their open sexuality, were suppressed. Within a few years, no trace of their society could be found. By the 1820s dancing of the traditional kind was prohibited as immoral, and the prohibition was extended to all activities associated with dancing—even the making of bark cloth. But the islanders, despite their mass conversion to Chris-

tianity, continued to dance in private, away from the prying eyes of missionaries. When the somewhat more tolerant French ousted the English from control of Tahiti in 1842, the traditional dances began a slow comeback, although it was not until the end of the nineteenth century that dancing in public received official sanction. By this time, the Western custom of kissing was widespread.

Today, dance is again a significant part of Tahitian social life. Much of the music now uses Western scales and harmonies, the words of many traditional chants have been lost or are no longer understood, and few if any dances have been preserved intact from the pre-Christian era. But basic Tahitian attitudes toward the body have remained unchanged. In a society whose primary unit is still the extended (as opposed to the nuclear) family, troupes of dancers in alternating ranks of men and women still perform gender-specific steps that retain their age-old associations for the islanders. Similar steps are found in the tamure, the dance that Tahitians do in nightclubs and dance halls, which fuses Western-style couple dancing with traditional Tahitian body movements. In the characteristic male step, the men keep their heels together and their feet more or less flat on the ground while they open and shut their knees in a flap-

ping scissors movement; they are careful to keep their hips stationary, because a man who sways his hips from side to side looks effeminate to a Tahitian. Meanwhile, with bent knees and weight balanced on the balls of their feet, the women rotate their hips rapidly. Both sexes keep the pelvis thrust forward with the head erect and the arms posed and virtually motionless; the main action is below the waist.

According to the Tahitians themselves, the message of the dance can be paraphrased as follows: "I am young, healthy, and attractive. I know who and what I am, and I am happy with myself." The clear contrast between the movements of men and women illustrates one source of the power of dance: It serves as definer and reinforcer of gender distinctions perceived to be vital to the survival of society—especially an island society that could not easily recruit newcomers or encourage migration to neighboring communities and therefore had to rely on the control of reproduction to maintain an optimal population. As dance anthropologist Joann Keali'-inohomoku puts it, "When the shocked missionaries concluded that sex was central to Polynesian culture, they got it exactly right." What they failed to appreciate was the social and religious context of the dances they witnessed.

IA ORANA MARIA

Even the most spontaneous dancing occurs not in isolation but as part of some culturally shaped event; without an understanding of the activities that surround and sustain the dancing body, it is impossible to grasp the full import of the dance.

If the dances of Tahiti and Cambodia embody important aspects of those societies, the dances of the West must say something important about the societies that were nurtured in the Judeo-Christian tradition. As we will see in the next chapter, the couple dances that form so prominent a part of the European heritage probably go back to the late medieval period in southern France, where the ideal of courtly love caught the imagination of itinerant troubadours and their audiences. Later, the male-female couple dance found even more exalted expression in the duets of classical ballet.

Ballet, which is the quintessentially European form of dance drama, had its origins in the court entertainments of Renaissance Italy and France. The earliest ballets were participatory spectacles in which kings and queens and courtiers danced and listened to noble masqueraders declaiming poetry that praised the court in high-flown metaphor borrowed

Opposite: A benchmark date in the changing Western idea of Polynesia was the departure of the French painter Paul Gauguin for Tahiti on April 4, 1891, in search of an experience outside the conventions of European culture. Key among the works that he painted there was Ia Orana Maria (1891), an Adoration of the Virgin that combined Christian and Polynesian themes. Gauguin portrayed the worshipers as native girls, in traditional dress that would hardly have met the approval of the missionary. In a gesture that united East and West, he adapted the postures of the worshipers from photographs of celestial dancers on the reliefs at Borobudur in Indonesia that he had purchased at the 1889 Paris Universal Exposition.

At a wedding ball at the Louvre on September 24, 1581, the bride and groom share the first dance. The occasion is the marriage of the Duc de Joyeuse and Marguerite de Vaudémont, painted by an unknown Flemish master working at the French court.

from Greek and Roman myths. To be assigned a role in these spectacles was a mark of honor for a courtier. Only slightly less structured were the frequent balls around which the social life of the court revolved; the social station of each gentleman and lady was revealed by the order in which they danced, couple by couple, before the assembled nobility; those of highest rank danced first, a protocol echoed today in the custom of reserving the first dance at a wedding for the bride and groom (who are treated as royalty for a day).

Out of the court spectacles of Europe's grandest monarch—Louis XIV of France—evolved the wordless dance drama we know as ballet; during its evolution many ideals of courtly bearing and behavior were refined into aesthetic principles. As we will see in Chapter 5, the emphasis on an erect, uplifted body with an unbending torso and shoulders pulled up and back can be traced to ballet's origins at court. By the beginning of the eighteenth century, ballet had been recast into a theatrical spectacle performed by professional dancers for paying audiences. To ensure a supply of trained dancers, schools were established; instruction was based on a repertoire of positions, exercises, steps, and movements which European ballet masters codified under a technical vocabulary of mostly French terms (pirouette, entrechat, etc.) that are still in use.

For the largely upper-class audience, going to the ballet was a social event of great importance; being seen at the theater by the right people was as important to some spectators as the stage spectacles they went to see. But the core of the experience remained the dancing of skilled professionals who were applauded for their feats of expressive and athletic grace; as time went on, more and more attention was directed to the dancers' appearance of lightness and the seeming effortlessness with which they launched themselves through the air, as if gravity were nothing but a minor inconvenience to the dancing body. During the nineteenth century, audiences took delight in the illusion of weightlessness projected by ballerinas in toe shoes. In its resolve to prevail over, rather than accommodate, the forces of nature, ballet gives expression to one of the characteristic aspirations of Western societies.

Although much has changed on and off the stage, the ballet schools of today are lineal descendants of the ballet schools of the Baroque era. Would-be ballet dancers begin training their bodies at the age of nine or ten. As long as they continue to perform, no matter how exalted their position in the ballet company, dancers attend class daily because they cannot afford even the slightest diminution of control. What

they do to achieve and maintain this control has been lovingly described by Lincoln Kirstein, the impresario who brought George Balanchine to New York in the 1930s and who helped him found both the School of American Ballet and the New York City Ballet:

"The daily lesson, lasting an hour and a half, is not a rehearsal but a training session, identical in progression for both beginners and accomplished professionals. It commences slowly with the body supported by a barre, permitting canonical correctness impossible without this aid. Later, students are released into the hall for center practice. Slow movements are followed by faster (*adagio* to *allegro*). The lesson ends with practice in toe shoes for girls and aerial action for boys.

"At the start . . . the pupil grasps the barre. Before moving, one must stand well. Pelvis is centered, neither tipped back nor forward. Abdomen is drawn in, diaphragm raised. Shoulders drop naturally; head is straight, eyes front. Arms are carried downward, rounded from shoulders to fingertips. The desired "turn-out," in which, with heels together, the feet are spread to form an angle of 180 degrees, supporting the erect upper body, is only slowly gained. Muscles eventually accommodate it without strain, but this is neither a swift nor easy process. However, the turn-out offers maximum base and support for any movement; it is the bedrock of ballet style and practice."

As a form of dance drama, ballet has drawn its plots from a variety of sources over the years. After the use of Greek and Roman mythology waned at the beginning of the nineteenth century, librettists experimented with European

folk tales (especially those with supernatural elements), legends set in exotic locales (especially those involving foreign royalty), and stories about star-crossed lovers from the upper and lower classes. This century has seen the emergence of the "plotless" ballet, which probably makes even greater demands on the bodies of dancers since, in the absence of a plot, it is the dancing itself that forms the subject of the ballet. Balanchine always insisted there was nothing "abstract" about such a ballet: "Two dancers on the stage are enough material for a story; for me, they are already a story in themselves. . . . Much can be said in movement that cannot be expressed by words. Movement must be self-explanatory. If it isn't, it has failed."

The illusion of weightlessness projected by a ballerina in toe shoes is captured in the delicate draftsmanship of Valentin Serov's 1909 poster design of Anna Pavlova in Les Sylphides (left). Pavlova (1881–1931) trained at the St. Petersburg Imperial Ballet Academy, today—after numerous name changes—the Vaganova School, which has probably trained more great ballet dancers than any other school in the world. In a rehearsal studio, students at the school (below) adopt the universal posture of ballerinas at rest: back straight, feet with slight turnout. The school was renamed in 1957 in honor of Agrippina Jacovlevna Vaganova (1879–1951), a dancer, teacher, and choreographer whose teaching system forms the basis of ballet education in many schools around the world.

When a dance performance succeeds, it can transform passive spectators into active collaborators who may actually feel their bodies moving in sympathy with the dancers onstage; at such moments, energy flows back and forth between performers and audience, and exciting, unpredictable things can happen. This transforming experience is not restricted to the theater. No stage, costumes, makeup, or music are required for what might be called the impromptu dance performances of everyday life.

Mark Twain describes such a moment among the rough-and-tumble raftsmen whose drunken quarrel Huck Finn observed one foggy summer night on the Mississippi. There were thirteen men in all, and when one of them started singing a very long, very loud, and very boring song, the others told him to leave off in no uncertain terms. Taking offense, the singer "jumped up, and began to cuss the crowd" and challenged the whole lot of them to a fight. In response, the biggest man of the thirteen got to his feet and announced to the others:

"'Set whar you are, gentlemen. Leave him to me; he's my meat.' Then he jumped up in the air three times, and cracked his heels together every time [and started boasting], 'Look at me! I'm the man they call Sudden Death and General Desolation! . . . Stand back and give me room according to my strength! Blood's my natural drink, and the wails of the dying is music to my ear!' . . . All the time he was getting this off, he was shaking his head and looking fierce and kind of swelling around in a little circle, tucking up his wristbands, and now and then straightening up and

The dances you find yourself doing without remembering how you learned them have always been with us. The American painter George Caleb Bingham's The Jolly Flatboatmen *(1846) shows a scene that was becoming increasingly rare by the 1840s, when steamboats had all but replaced flatboats on the Mississippi River. The raised platform on which the dancer stamps his feet amplifies the sound; in jigging contests in Ireland today judges often sit underneath the stage to better evaluate the speed and precision of the dancers' percussive steps.*

beating his breast with his fist, saying 'Look at me, gentlemen!' When he got through, he jumped up and cracked his heels together three time, and let off a roaring 'Whoo-oop! I'm the bloodiest son of a wildcat that lives!'

"Then the man that had started the row tilted his old slouch hat down over his right eye; then he bent stooping forward, with his back sagged and his south end sticking out far, and his fists a-shoving out and drawing in in front of him, and so went around in a little circle about three times, swelling himself up and breathing hard. Then he straightened, and jumped up and cracked his heels together three times before he lit again (that made them cheer). . . ."

T he potent relationship between dancer and audience is at the heart of one of the world's oldest uses of dance—the dance performed for an invisible audience of spirits, ancestors, deities, and other entities whose goodwill is considered necessary to the well-being of the community. This kind of dance was central to the lives of the people who inhabited the North American continent before the Europeans arrived.

Only in a few cases, such as the Hopi of the arid Southwest, have Native American societies managed to keep their traditional dances intact in the face of efforts by outsiders (from conquistadors in the sixteenth century to missionaries and federal agents in the nineteenth and twentieth centuries) to suppress or modify them. For at least a thousand years the Hopi calendar has revolved around a cycle of danced cere-

monies that are performed in every Hopi community. Although not everyone dances every dance, all those who attend are thought of as nondancing participants since their faith in the efficacy of the ceremony helps make it spiritually powerful.

Through dance, the Hopi get in touch, quite literally, with the forces of nature that govern the world. The ultimate purpose is to bring rain to the patient crops in the fields. One of these rain dances, the Snake Dance, is held in late summer after months of preparation which includes the gathering of live snakes by the initiated men of the community. According to Hopi belief, snakes come from "another world" under the earth and are brothers to the spirits who control the clouds and rain. During the dance, live snakes (including rattlesnakes) are carried reverently in the hands and mouths of the dancers, who chant prayers to them about the people's need for moisture. Everything contributes to the act of invocation: the fringed sashes worn by the dancers symbolize falling rain, the sound of the gourds they shake recalls the sound of falling rain. At the end of the dance, the snakes are released in the hope that they will return to their underground homes, tell their brother-spirits how well they were treated on the surface, and urge these spirits to answer the people's prayers for rain. The Hopi believe that their sacred dances are instrumental in providing life-giving moisture not just for themselves but for the entire world.

On the more fertile plains to the north, conflicting cultural expectations about dance led to tragic consequences

in what has been described as "the last Indian war." During the nineteenth century the westward pressure of white settlers, backed by the U.S. Army, swept aside the armed resistance of various Plains tribes and decimated the herds of buffalo on which the tribes depended for many of the necessities of life. A decade after the Civil War most Plains Indians were confined to reservations. Unable to feed themselves, groups like the Sioux and the Cheyenne became dependent on handouts from U.S. government agents. When the promised quantities of food failed to arrive, tempers shortened. The authorities, mindful of the power of dance to focus discontent among the Plains tribes, banned all danced ceremonies.

As if in response, a ceremony known as the Ghost Dance appeared in the late 1880s. The Ghost Dance was linked to a messianic prophecy by a Western Paiute leader named Wovoka (c. 1856–1932). Wovoka prophesied the coming of a great earthquake; this natural convulsion would bring back the prairie grasses and the herds of buffalo that had thrived on them. All nonbelievers would be swallowed up in the transformation, but those people who hastened the change by zealously devoting themselves to the Ghost Dance would rejoin their resurrected ancestors on a new-made earth of peace and plenty.

Like the Hopi, the Plains Indians believed in the transforming power of dance. Dance was good for the body and good for the spirit and essential to integrating the two. The natural world pulsed with powers; since the same powers animated the human body, the body could serve as a kind of lever to bring

Hopi snake dancers, Walpi, Arizona, 1903. No photographs of this sacred ceremony have been permitted since the early decades of the century.

about changes in the world. Some kinds of dance led to states of altered consciousness; through trance it was possible to make contact with the ancestors who lived on in another realm and who provided wise counsel in times of need. Threatened with starvation and the destruction of their way of life, thousands of Plains Indians gathered at remote camps throughout the West where they danced for days at a time until they fell to the ground in a trance. Many of the dancers experienced visions in which revered ancestors confirmed to them the prophecy of Wovoka. Among many Sioux warriors the belief spread that anyone who wore white "ghost shirts" would not be harmed by the white man's bullets.

The Ghost Dance brought together, in a common cause, members of tribes that had long been enemies. The dancers (mostly but not exclusively men) formed a large circle and moved slowly in a clockwise direction, advancing with the left foot and following with the right in a dragging step, while singing and chanting in unison. One of their songs proclaimed: "I bring the whirlwind that you may see each other/ We shall live again!" A non-Indian eyewitness recorded this description of the Ghost Dance: "Sometimes before falling the hypnotized subject runs wildly around the circle or out over the prairie. . . . In many instances the hypnotized person spins around for minutes at a time like a dervish, or whirls the arms with apparently impossible speed, or assumes and retains until the final fall most uncomfortable positions which it would be impossible to keep for any length of time under normal conditions."

Alarmed by the numbers of Indians who rallied to the Ghost Dance, government authorities acted to contain what they saw as the imminent threat of armed resistance, although Wovoka had explicitly preached against war. There followed a series of violent confrontations in which Indians wearing "ghost shirts" as protection against bullets were gunned down by rifle and Gatling-gun fire. At Wounded Knee, South Dakota, the U.S. Seventh Cavalry massacred an entire Sioux encampment including hundreds of women and children.

To ensure that the Plains Indians did not rekindle their resistance, government authorities continued to discourage all ceremonial dances until the 1930s, by which time many of the dances existed only in the memories of a few tribal elders. In an effort to save what was left, the informal intertribal gatherings known as powwows were recast into formal dance competitions. At these new-style powwows, traditional dances were passed from the older gen-

eration to younger Indians who had previously had no chance to learn this part of their heritage. Today, powwows have become major events, drawing thousands of participants and spectators from many different tribes to long weekends of dancing and socializing. Tourists may attend, but the performances are basically by Indians for Indians.

In traditional North American Indian dances, the dancer's knees are usually bent and the body tilted forward toward the ground. Head movements can be elaborate, especially when miming animals; the arms are generally kept close to the body except for gestures that imitate birds. Chants, drums, rattles, and bells attached to the dancer's legs provide the typical accompaniment. But the highlight of most powwows is the "fancy dance" competition in which young men decked out in ornately beaded and feathered outfits display the fastest, most difficult footwork. The purpose is not to reconstruct with scholarly accuracy the dances of the past but to

The American painter Gilbert Gaul was employed by the federal government in the 1880s to make pictures to illustrate the census of 1890. Gaul made sketches and photographs to assemble material for paintings that he executed in his studio, and it seems clear that he either witnessed the Ghost Dance or interviewed participants for this painting of c.1890. The dancer on the right is wearing a Ghost Dance shirt.

Opposite: Today, powwows are held throughout the West. The highlight of these events is the fancy dance competition. Here, men compete in fancy dancing at a powwow in Denver, Colorado, in 1991 (above left), and a young woman fancy dancer does an athletic dance called magic moccasins at a powwow in Gallup, New Mexico, in 1988 (above right). The fringes on the woman's shawl crack like whips as she spins. Powwows open with a grand entry of the dancers, like the one below at the Windriver Reservation in Ethete, Wyoming, in 1978. The dancers— Arapaho and Shoshone—are wearing traditional ceremonial costumes of the northern plains.

inspire pride in a common heritage. And no matter how fancy the jumping and twirling gets, the powwow dances always dramatize a closeness to the earth that Native Americans share with other dance-centered cultures—a closeness manifested by an insistent stamping of the feet with knees bent, as if the entire body were acknowledging the pull of that nurturing presence so many of the powwow cultures call "the mother."

As in the Ghost Dance ceremony, the power of dance is often associated with the experience of trance. Trance is found in some Native American ceremonies today but not in powwow. In modern industrial societies that trace their development through Western Europe, episodes of trance are usually treated as extraordinary events, peripheral to the concerns of daily life; trance may be equated with such out-of-control behavior as drunkenness, sleepwalking, or being hypnotized. Hypnosis, the most studied trancelike experience in the West, remains a scientific question mark; skeptical researchers have so far failed to find reliable physical signs to distinguish a hypnotized from an unhypnotized person.

Dominant Western attitudes toward trance are greatly at odds with the experience of the majority of the world's population. A team of scholars who surveyed 488 societies on every continent reported that at least 437 had "one or more institutionalized, culturally patterned forms of altered states of consciousness." Whether described as trance or altered consciousness or ecstasy or a dissociative state, the experi-ence is obviously too common to be called abnormal. People undergoing trance may report being "possessed" by a supernatural force or being. Not surprisingly, experiences of possession tend to be approached with that mixture of fear and exhilaration known as awe. Because these experiences are considered both dangerous and desirable, they are embedded in rituals that allow the community to support, guide, and protect the individuals who go into trance. In some, but by no means all, cases, special foods, drinks, smoking materials, or regimens of exercise and diet—all of which can affect the human nervous system—play a part. But rituals in which trance is induced solely by drugs or fasting or meditation are the exceptions. More typically, the rituals are communal events structured around rhythmic movements of the body that fit most definitions of dance. Indeed, the entire event involves a kind of choreography; everyone present has a well-defined role in helping the initiate attain a state of trance, perform certain functions while in trance, and return to a normal state.

Through dances of different types, Korean shamans and African fetish-priests and evangelical Christians and Indian outcastes and Javanese Muslims open channels of communication with the powers-that-be. According to the people who participate in them, these danced rituals reliably produce tangible benefits for both the individual and the society at large—including such benefits as knowledge of things past and to come, good health and good fortune, and a reassuring sense of belonging to a supportive community in a daunting but ultimately comprehensible world.

Where such views predominate, the power ascribed to the dancing body is quite literally awesome.

One such place is the state of Kerala in southwestern India. This narrow strip of palm trees, rice fields, and white-sand beaches extends for some two hundred miles between the mountain range known as the Western Ghats and the Arabian Sea. Over the centuries, Kerala has absorbed cultural influences from the north, from the Muslim world, from Europe, and from the East without losing its own identity. The caste system, which came to India with the Aryan tribes that conquered the north sometime after 1500 B.C. is firmly established in Kerala; but so is a reputation for independent thinking and a tolerance for new ideas. For years, the state of Kerala had the only freely elected communist government in the world. In the temples of Kerala, the gods of the Hindu pantheon, especially Shiva, Lord of the Dance, are fervently worshiped; but many Keralans continue to honor the older gods who were in place before the religion of the north arrived. Among these are the serpent gods and goddesses who inhabit carefully tended groves behind certain higher-caste houses. They are powerful but capricious deities whose enmity can bring bad luck in the form of disease (especially skin disease) and infertility. To guard against such ill fortune, the serpent deities must be propitiated from time to time in a danced ritual of possession that has the power to make the invisible visible, and to bond the individual to the community and the community to the cosmos.

The people who perform this ritual belong to an outcaste group known as

Pullavas. As outcastes they are not allowed to enter traditional Hindu temples; even their presence in higher-caste homes is thought to be polluting. Yet when a higher-caste family feels the need to get in touch with the deities of their own serpent grove, they call on the Pullavas. The correct performance of the ritual in all details is crucial to its efficacy; throughout India, as in many other societies, such rituals are entrusted to specially trained groups or lineages who pass down the requisite knowledge from generation to generation.

Depending on how long it has been since the serpent deities were last invoked and how much ill fortune the higher-caste family has suffered, the serpent ritual may be performed for as many as twelve consecutive nights. At the agreed-upon hour, a family of Pullavas arrives at the higher-caste compound to construct, in the well-swept courtyard before the main house, a ritual space. This consists of four stripped banana-tree trunks, about four feet high, set in the ground ten feet apart, and hung with palm fronds, flowers, and little "birds" woven and folded like origami out of palm leaves.

When the space is properly consecrated, the Pullavas begin to create an elaborate floor painting of a mandala, a ritual diagram that shows eight cobra-hooded snakes intertwined within an abstract representation of the original forest home of the serpent deities. Using dried half-shells of coconuts in which two small holes have been punched, the Pullavas drizzle lines of variously colored powders made from ground rice, charred rice husks, spices such as turmeric, powdered leaves, and lime. They work in

silence, four, five, six at a time, without getting in each other's way, squatting over the developing mandala and adding white, red, green, yellow, gray, and black powders according to a time-honored pattern. The addition of powdered silver highlights is a recent innovation.

The making of the mandala is itself a dance of creation, a performance witnessed not only by the family sponsoring the ceremony but by their neighbors in the village who come to be entertained as well as uplifted. When the mandala is complete, mounds of rice, coconut, spices, plantain, flower petals, sprays of incense, and other offerings are laid on banana leaves around the perimeter. By now the sun has set and the scene is illuminated by oil-fed wick lamps and a few dim electric bulbs. In the flickering light, the mandala is revealed as an exquisitely prepared table, a feast literally set for the gods.

Now it is time for a higher-caste priest to bless the offering and remove the stigma of its creation by the family of outcastes. This blessing takes the form of a dance in which the priest, barefoot and bare-chested, wearing only a white dhoti wrapped around his waist, circles the mandala in a clockwise direction, carrying first a basket of flowers, then a flaming wick, while four Pullava men and women pound out repetitive, percussive music on traditional instru-

Entranced dancers (top), under the power of the evil witch Rangda, press daggers against their own flesh during a Barong ceremony in Bali, Indonesia; they are kept from harm by the influence of the Barong, a lion-figure that embodies the forces of good. When illness or some other calamity menaces a community, this ceremony restores the balance between good and evil. The entranced vodun worshiper in Haiti (above), enacting a ritual with roots in west and central Africa, dances through the hot ashes of a fire before the eyes of the religious community.

The mandala created as a temporary abode of the serpent deities during a possession ritual known as Sarpam Thullal, in Vellarthanjur, India, 1991.

ments. At no time does the priest step inside the sacred space defined by the painting.

When the priest is finished, a young Pullava man performs what is known as a "fire massage" around the rim of the mandala. Like the mandala itself and the mounds of food and incense, this dance—in which the young man does somersaults, twists his body into serpentine postures, bounces up and down on his belly, rubs lit torches over his bare skin, and puts out the flames in his mouth—is an offering, an act of devotion. At the same time, it is a performance (a "circus" in the idiom of the Pullavas) designed to hold the interest of the audience during the hours-long ritual. Some of the movements are borrowed from the drills and exercises of a local form of martial arts.

The climax of the ceremony is the appearance of two young girls who earlier led a procession to the serpent grove behind the house where they invited the deities to come join them in the mandala. The young girls, clutching palm-leaf brooms, sit cross-legged in the middle of the painting; the food offerings are removed (these become the property of the Pullavas), and under the influence of the repetitive, percussive music, the girls begin to toss their heads from side to side; within minutes they have been possessed by the serpent deities who, when questioned by the headman of the Pullavas, give their names in the local language and confirm their acceptance of the night's offerings. During this stage of the ceremony, members of the sponsoring family (especially widows and divorced women) may go into trance and express grievances

Contemporary Indian dance, which intertwines religion and aesthetics, can trace its roots back some two thousand years in a culture that defines dancing as a primary activity of one of the most powerful Hindu deities, Shiva. At the great religious monument of Ellora in central India there are some thirty-three caves that contain Buddhist, Jain, and Hindu shrines. Ramesvara (cave 21) contains one of the earliest representations of the dancing Shiva, dating from c. A.D. 640–75.

against other family members; the deities, speaking through the girls' mouths, may suggest specific remedies to restore family harmony.

Finally, the two girls, still possessed, begin to slide around the mandala on their haunches, erasing in a few minutes, with convulsive body movements, sweeps of their long hair, and jerky motions of their brooms, the design that the Pullavas took so long to create. Only when the mandala is obliterated can the gods return to their grove behind the house and the girls, after slumping into a comalike sleep, regain their senses.

Caste in India, though inherited, is thought of as occupational; the Pullavas are considered outcastes because, like the castes that dispose of the carcasses of dead animals, their job is to cleanse the community of "pollution" and in so doing they inevitably become polluted themselves. While discrimination based on caste is now against the law, and education and political reform have opened up new opportunities for those at the bottom of the social pyramid, the traditional ceremonies (and with them the traditional occupations and the traditional arts) retain much of their power. There is nothing theoretical or speculative about this power: To those who perform and witness it, the serpent ritual not only works, it is *seen* to work—in the bodies of the fire-dancer and of the possessed girls, in the sense of community that the spellbound spectators share, in the reaffirmation of an order that (according to the most revered traditions of Hindu thought) sustains and justifies all creation. Such is the power of dance in a dance-centered culture.

It should be clear by now that any attempt to define dance must take into account the great variety of dancelike behavior found in cultures around the world. For this purpose, the analytical categories of classical Western thought are far too parochial. As we will see in the next chapter, Plato and Aristotle lumped dance together with the other mimetic (representational) arts. Aristotle distinguished it from music by stressing what it lacked: "Rhythm alone, without harmony, is the means of the dancer's imitations, for even he, by the rhythms of his attitudes, may represent men's characters as well as what they do and suffer." The idea that dance should "imitate" nature has stayed current in the West, if only as a foil for competing viewpoints. Aestheticians, usually with their eyes fixed on ballet, have argued that the first duty of dance is the creation of beauty. Nineteenth-century poet Théophile Gautier, who wrote the libretto for *Giselle*, declared, "The dance is nothing more than the art of displaying beautiful shapes in graceful positions and the development from them of lines agreeable to the eye."

One problem with defining dance in strictly Western terms is that few people outside the European tradition think of dance in isolation from the other arts, from religion, indeed from the daily activities of life. Throughout sub-Saharan Africa, dance is so much a part of everyday experience that defining dance is akin to defining life itself. According to a nineteenth-century observer, a common greeting exchanged when two Bantu met was, "What do you dance?" A contemporary African scholar, when asked why dance was so important to

the Asante, put it this way: "Why do we dance? We say we dance because we are alive and not stones. Have you ever seen a stone dance?" In India, which has a tradition of aesthetic analysis going back two thousand years, dance has always been considered part of a larger dance drama with transcendental ambitions. While the Indian tradition distinguishes between pure dance and interpretive or imitative movement, the goal is a single artistic experience so powerful that it can trigger spiritual enlightenment.

In an attempt to do justice to all possible traditions as well as all possible experiments by contemporary dancemakers, scholar Roger Copeland half-seriously suggested that dance be defined as "any movement designed to be looked at." This would presumably include everything from professional wrestling to professional sleight-of-hand to the impassioned hand gestures of a litigating attorney—not to mention the strictly automatic reflex movements induced by a physician's rubber mallet.

When social or political forces threaten dance traditions, their fate is often determined by dancers and musicians who work to preserve the legacy of the past. The exquisite legong in Bali was once performed by young women who were trained in the island's royal courts. With the destruction of the courts by the Dutch in the early twentieth century, the dancers returned to their villages, where they kept the dance alive. Today, legong is thriving and the values it embodies are widely admired, but the political system that nurtured it is long gone.

After careful consideration, anthropologist Joann Keali'inohomoku has proposed a somewhat more elaborate definition: "Dance is a transient mode of expression, performed in a given form and style by the human body moving through space. Dance occurs through purposefully selected and controlled rhythmic movements; the resulting phenomenon is recognized as dance both by the performer and the observing members of a given group." For all its scholarly breadth and depth, the most admirable thing about this formulation is that it leaves the final decision about what is and what is not dance to the people with the most at stake: the dancers and their audiences.

Even in the most traditional settings, the forms and meanings of dance change when dancers feel the need to come up with something new, or to alter or adapt something old, to fit new circumstances. Perhaps nowhere is the adaptability of dance in a dance-centered society so vividly illustrated as in the history of the Zezuru, a branch of the Shona-speaking people of southern Africa who are noted for their artistic metalworking. During the intertribal wars of the nineteenth century the Zezuru developed a unique form of military strategy based on dance. The moment that enemy marauders were spotted approaching a Zezuru village, a troupe of young women rushed out of the village compound and formed a kind of chorus line. While the old men of the village beat a polyrhythmic accompaniment on wooden blocks, drums, and gourds, and the young women shook their shoulders and undulated their hips enticingly, the village's own warriors assembled out of sight.

At a signal, the chorus line parted and the warriors burst forth to do battle with the distracted invaders. With characteristic wit, the Zezuru called this dance mbende, which means "mouse that runs fast."

The advent of Europeans in Shona territory ended the native wars, and the missionaries who arrived in the first decade of the twentieth century outlawed mbende as "licentious, lustful, and indecent." Anxious to have the prohibition reversed, the Zezuru Council of Elders sent a chief to a leading missionary to recount a prophetic dream he had had. In his dream, the chief said, he had seen his people journey in spirit to the holy city of Jerusalem, where they danced in praise of the infant Jesus, who was greatly pleased. Unwilling to condemn such devotion, the missionaries rescinded the ban on the mbende, which was now renamed the Jerusarema.

Over the next two decades, changes in the economy of colonial Rhodesia drastically altered the lives of the Zezuru. To hold down jobs as servants, clerks, and laborers in the white man's homes, offices, and factories, Zezuru men left their villages and settled in newly built townships. The social center of each township was a beer hall. Old village customs lost their hold; getting drunk and dancing the Jerusarema became the principal leisure-time activities. The dance became wilder and lustier; its sole purpose seemed to be sexual arousal—the very snare that the Zezuru had originally devised for their enemies.

Just when its reputation among both whites and traditional Zezuru could sink no lower, the Jerusarema was resurrected as a theatrical dance. This was accomplished by families of drummers and dancers who worked with tribal elders to restore pride in what had once been a unique Zezuru tradition. Festivals were organized, prizes were awarded for the correct performance of the Jerusarema, feats of acrobatic skill were added to the basic vocabulary of steps—fully upright hip-shaking for women, darting leg extensions for men in a squatting position. Although the basic movements look simple enough when performed in isolation, it takes long practice to learn to combine them in improvised sequences at ever-increasing speed and with mounting intensity. The best dancers become known throughout the country and are held up as exemplars of Shona culture and history.

Today, the Jerusarema is featured in performances of the National Dance Company of Zimbabwe. It has become the dance of choice at funerals, where both men and women dance bare-chested and wear traditional grass skirts with ankle rattles. At Jerusarema clubs in the cities, men and women dance close to each another but they never touch; the Zezuru, like other Shona-speaking peoples, are offended by European cheek-to-cheek dancing, which violates their idea of proper public behavior.

Chapter 2
Lord of the Dance

n India, the gods dance. Shiva, the great Hindu god of creation and destruction who is worshiped throughout India, is classically represented as Nataraja, Lord of the Dance. Bronze icons found in south Indian temples and domestic shrines show a four-armed deity, ringed by fire, in the midst of what has been called Shiva's cosmic dance. In one hand he holds a drum, which symbolizes the sound that kindles creation; another hand cradles a ball of flame, symbol of destruction and renewal; his right leg, bent at the knee, crushes to earth the demon of ignorance; while his raised left leg, swung across his body, signifies the release from worldly cares that is one of the blessings dance bestows on its devotees the world over.

Shiva is by no means the only dancing god in the Hindu pantheon. Vishnu, the other great deity that Hindus worship, periodically takes on human form to rescue the world when it is threatened. He has long been worshiped in his incarnations as Rama and Krishna.

The latter, with his characteristic flute, is especially associated with dance; his legendary dalliances with village milkmaids inspired a tradition of sensual devotional dance that struck sympathetic chords far beyond the subcontinent. The *Ramayana* and the *Bhagavata Purana*, millennia-old Sanskrit epics celebrating the exploits of Rama and Krishna respectively, are held in reverence wherever Indian culture has left its mark; dance dramas based on these works, and on the epic known as the *Mahabharata*, are presented in ritual settings throughout southeast Asia. When the gods dance, it is not surprising that dance itself should be considered an offering to them.

Another important tradition of religious dance is found in Africa south of the Sahara and throughout the Western Hemisphere where enslaved Africans preserved and extended the religious practices of their ancestors, especially the Yoruba-speaking peoples of west Africa. From the Sango and egungun

ceremonies of Yorubaland in southwestern Nigeria to the candomblé of northeastern Brazil, the vodun of Haiti, and the santería of Cuba (and New York and Miami), dance opens direct channels of communication to the world of the gods and the ancestors. In some of these ceremonies, the goal is to "make a god within one's body." The initiate (who has undergone a long period of instruction and training) dances to invite a particular god to visit the world of the living. When the invitation is accepted, the god takes possession of the initiate's body and begins dancing with characteristic movements and energy that other members of the religious community recognize as signaling the presence of that deity. During this time, the initiate remains in a state of suspended consciousness sometimes called trance. The Yoruba themselves speak of being "mounted" by a god. To be mounted is a transcendent experience that brings spiritual and material benefits to the individual and the entire community.

Day after day, night after night, under widely varying circumstances but with the same fierce conviction, dancing worshipers call upon the gods, and the gods come.

The basic vehicle of dance is the human body. When and how people dance is determined by their attitudes toward the body; such attitudes are powerfully shaped by religious beliefs. In both India and west Africa we find cultures where dance plays a central role in worship; the attitudes toward the dancing body that emerged from these cultures have strongly influenced other cultures around the world. The influence of Indian dance has been felt not just in Southeast Asia but as far away as China, Japan, and even, some scholars believe, the islands of the South Pacific. The enforced diaspora of large numbers of Yoruba from west Africa not only implanted a vigorous tradition of religious dance in the Caribbean and the Americas but also (as we will see when we trace its influence on social dancing

in the twentieth century) changed the way the rest of the world dances.

In contrast to the Hindu and Yoruba traditions, the Judeo-Christian world view has always been ambivalent about the religious uses of dance, an attitude that reflects a deeper ambivalence about the body that dances. The ancient Hebrews were surrounded by people for whom, in the words of historian E. Louis Backman, "dance was a means of influencing the invisible powers and of establishing contact with them." The Hebrews shared this view of dance, but at the same time sought to distance themselves from the practices of their neighbors. Their ambivalence was passed along to the early Christians who combined it with another tradition of ambivalence about the dancing body that ran through Greek and Roman thought. The result was an internal debate between the proponents and opponents of Christian liturgical dance in which the opponents usually had the upper hand. Ultimately, removed from

consecrated ground, dance in the West flourished as a secular arena for social interaction and as the basis of a vigorous secular theater. Indeed, the split in the Christian world view between the sacred and the secular—a distinction that is profoundly alien to the Hindu and Yoruba traditions—may be related to Christianity's denial of the body as something holy in and of itself.

Judaism's ambivalence toward the dancing body is recorded in its earliest scriptures. From the beginning there was a right kind of dance and a wrong kind. After the Lord closed the Red Sea on the pursuing Egyptians, Miriam, sister of Moses, led the surviving Hebrews in a dance of thanksgiving (Exodus 15:20). King David, harpist, psalmist, warrior, and lover, once danced "with all his might" before the Ark of the Covenant (II Samuel 6:14–16); when his wife mocked him for it, she was punished with barrenness. Psalm 149 exhorts, "Let them praise His name in the dance"; some scholars maintain that all the psalms were originally meant to be

danced, by groups of worshipers, as well as sung. A close examination of these texts suggests that the dances of praise included processions and circle dances, with hopping, whirling, and stamping steps. Yet when Moses came down from Mount Sinai with the tablets of the law and found his people worshiping a golden calf in the Lord's place, the fact that they were singing and dancing is especially noted, as if to sum up the horror of their idolatry (Exodus 32:19). This was, definitively, the wrong kind of dance.

As Ecclesiastes reminds us, there is a time to dance (3:4). The Talmud (500 B.C.) says that the angels dance in heaven; and according to rabbinic laws, dancing at a wedding is a mitzvah, a commandment of Jewish life; Jews *must* dance at weddings. It is possible that this injunction gave rise to the profession of dancing instructor; history tells us that Jewish dancing instructors played an important role in the spread of social dancing in early Renaissance Europe. But devotional dance, dance as an integral part of the worship of God, was something else again. The religious

rituals of the ancient Hebrews were clearly influenced by their encounters with the pagans who lived in lands that the descendants of Abraham claimed by divine right. These pagans regarded dance as an essential element of their religious practices. Scholars may argue over which dances the ancient Hebrews performed at which festivals, but the emphasis throughout the Hebrew scriptures is on approaching the divine through words rather than movement. As a transcendent deity, the Lord of the Hebrews could not be envisioned in any graven image, much less one that danced. The contrast to Hindu and west African (as well as Greek and Roman) iconography is telling. The Israelites made room for dance in their daily life and in their seasonal festivals. But compared to the detailed injunctions about how to conduct sacrifices and wars and business and domestic affairs, the references to dance in the Hebrew scriptures seem both modest and restrained. It is hard to escape the conclusion that the priests, prophets, and lawgivers were taking care to discourage the fervent, not to say frenzied, dancing associated

Opposite: Christian iconography provided Renaissance painters few opportunities to portray dance. One was the Biblical story of the worship of the golden calf, which has various possible origins in antiquity. Filippino Lippi's Worship of the Egyptian Bull-God, Apis, c.1500, a reconstruction of a pre-Christian Egyptian cult centered in Memphis, shows pagan religious dancing. The cult of the sacred bull Apis was so widespread that it was given official recognition under the Ptolemaic and Roman rulers of Egypt, and its feast days were celebrated throughout the country.

Among the Greeks, dance was frequently associated with Dionysian revels. Inspired by Dionysus to ecstatic frenzies of singing and dancing, Maenads (top) existed beyond all human conventions. Sileni (left) were woodland creatures who also were drawn into the circle of Dionysus. Not all orgiastic dancers were followers of Dionysus, however. The dancers above are thought to be worshiping the god Apollo Karneios, a deity presumed to be a synthesis of the Greek Apollo with a still-older god called Karneios. These examples are drawn from vase paintings of c.540–415 B.C.

with religious worship among their neighbors—especially those forms of dance that brought men and women together in ways that could excite lascivious thoughts.

The ambivalence toward the dancing body found in Greek and Roman thought sprang from different roots. Like the Mycenaeans, the Minoans, and the Egyptians before them, the Greeks danced at religious ceremonies; they danced to insure fertile fields and fertile women; they danced to prepare for war and to celebrate victories; they danced at weddings and funerals; they danced to overcome depression and to cure physical illness. Yet they were also aware that the energies released in the wilder forms of dance could threaten the established order—as exemplified in myth by the dance-intoxicated devotees of Dionysus who did violence to members of their own families. There was obviously a need to channel such energies into constructive channels under the control of the community. An example of how the Greeks dealt with this problem can be seen in the evolution of the danced revels of Dionysus into the classical theater of Athens, where the old myths were acted out in the plays of Aeschylus (525–456 B.C.), Sophocles (495–406 B.C.), and Euripides (480–406 B.C.).

According to the Greeks, Dionysus, a nature god identified with the vine, came from "the East." In adopting the rites of Dionysus with such ardor, the Greeks were only reaffirming the importance of dance in their own mythical past. In Greek cosmology, Zeus, first among the Olympian gods, owed his very survival to dance. Hidden away from his father who was trying to kill him, the infant Zeus began to cry; before his hiding place could be discovered, his cries were drowned out by the clashing swords and shields of the loyal Curetes—semidivine beings later associated with the wildly dancing devotees of Dionysian cults. Dancing figures adorn the earliest Greek pottery. The Greeks had a single word—*musike*—for song, dance, and instrumental music; the evidence suggests that they never sang or chanted without moving their bodies.

Processions of dancers led by the priests of Dionysus figured prominently in the great spring festival at Athens. During the sixth century B.C. these processions were gradually transformed into choral competitions, which in turn developed into dramatic competitions. Each type of presentation—tragedy, comedy, the satyr play—had its characteristic dances, some staid and solemn, some featuring lewd miming with phallic props. But the precise mix of words and body movements remains a mystery; no one today knows what the plays of the Athenian dramatists looked and sounded like in production. In place of precise descriptions, we have the analytical writings of philosophers like Plato (427–347 B.C.) and Aristotle (384–322 B.C.), who left an elaborate literature of dance theory and criticism. Unanimous in recognizing the power of dance (both constructive and disruptive) in their society, they disagreed on how such power could be wielded safely under the overall control of reason. Their ambivalence has colored Western attitudes toward dance ever since.

Plato agreed with his mentor Socrates that every educated man should know how to dance gracefully—by which he meant the manly exercises that kept a body strong and supple and ready to do its duty on the battlefield should war threaten the city-state. The pyrrhic, or weapon, dance (a form of mock combat borrowed from Crete and perfected in Sparta) was the ideal, although choral dances with modest, beautiful movements were also acceptable to Plato because they made manifest to the dancer the order that rules the cosmos. The true purpose of art (as of philosophy) was to reveal the Good, the Beautiful. He deplored the "dirty dancing" of his day. In general, steps that stayed close to the ground were preferable to leaping and jumping, and group dancing was safer than solo performances. Plato knew that the wilder forms of dance could induce trance and possession, with unpredictable results, and rouse the sexual passions, with all too predictable results. To be on the safe side, he banished professional actor-dancers from his ideal republic.

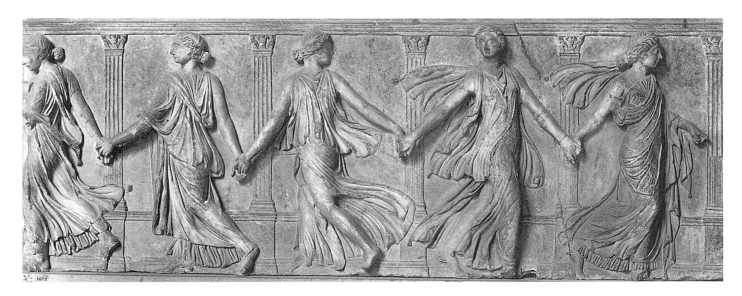

Plato's philosophical quarrel with dance drama was that, like all representational art, it showed events contrary to fact; the performers were not actually feeling what they pretended to feel. In banning professionals from the stage, Plato was willing to forgo the benefits that only trained performers can bring to dance: the ability to focus every resource of the body—every limb, joint, sense, and sinew—on a specific task of expression or communication. For Aristotle, the benefits of professionalism outweighed the drawbacks. By dance Aristotle understood the representation of the actions and passions of men through rhythmic movements. He argued that all Greek citizens had an obligation to attend well-executed dance performances, since dance, like poetry, could teach important lessons through imitation of real-life events, and especially through the "purging" of the emotions of pity and terror. Yet Aristotle also feared the corrupting influence of a life devoted exclusively to dance. In order to spare his fellow Greeks this risk, he urged that the profession of dancer be reserved for slaves, ex-slaves, and foreigners.

The picture of classical Greece that historians paint for us is full of anomalies. The most literate culture of the Mediterranean world was also dance-mad; the power of dance was both venerated and feared; the status of dancers rose and fell depending on who danced and who watched; and the debate over the proper relationship between the word and the body was never-ending. As with so many other things Greek, the Romans took over both sides of this debate.

Except for choral processions and martial exercises, the early Romans were apparently not partial to dancing. Later, under Greek influence, Roman patricians sent their sons and daughters to dancing schools to learn graceful movements. Around 150 B.C. the guardians of public morality ordered these schools closed before their influence could weaken the fiber of Roman youth, but the ban (like so many others before and since) was unsuccessful. Dance (by non-Roman slaves) was also a feature of the public games that became an obsession wherever Rome ruled. The stern republican Cicero (106–43 B.C.) held that real men do not dance—unless they are drunk or insane.

Shortly after Cicero's death a form of theatrical dance known as pantomime became wildly popular in Rome. Contemporary writers praised the ability of the pantomimists to convey the most complex narratives through gestures alone. Exactly how the pantomimists achieved their effects has been lost to history, but as the performances grew bawdier, they were roundly condemned by moralists—which of course did nothing to diminish their popularity. As for other uses of body language in imperial Rome, we have the testimony of Lucian (A.D. 120–180), who reminded his readers that dancing is as old as love. Throughout the Roman era the association of dance with love, with lust (both personal and professional) and with violence (the public games) was proverbial, as the New Testament story of Salome and John the Baptist makes clear (Matthew 14:6–8). So too was the link between dance and the mystery religions that flourished throughout the empire; according to Lucian, there was not a single mystery religion that did not include some kind of dance in its initiation ceremonies.

Early Christianity offered itself as a fulfillment of the Word that had been revealed to the Hebrews and as a cleansing of the moral filth that had polluted Roman society. Given this mission, and the desire to distinguish itself from other mystery religions, it was not easy for early Christians to accommodate the dancing body in their worship. Indeed, despite the fact that incarnation was the medium of Christ's message, Christianity from the start manifested a love-hate relationship to the body.

The earliest followers of Christ, looking toward an imminent Second Coming, were concerned with living a pure life that required the denial of bodily desires. Their goal was not to sanctify the body but to transcend it. Celibacy was the ideal held out to them by Paul—who nevertheless conceded that for

those who could not abstain from sex, "let them marry: for it is better to marry than to burn" (I Corinthians 7:9). The debate among early Christians about the place of the dancing body in worship was fueled by references to the Scriptures and to the writings of the Neo-Platonists, a school of philosophers who held that the world of time, space, and flesh was inferior to the transcendent realms of intellect and spirit. The early church fathers, believing that the body was inferior to the spirit, were drawn to the Neo-Platonic concept of an "ideal" body free of unseemly lusts. This was the kind of body that, properly purified and controlled, could perform sacred dances to the greater glory of God.

Like the ancient Hebrews, the Christians of the first three centuries after Christ were surrounded by examples of pagan dance that they abhorred; and they could cite any number of scriptural verses disapproving of dances—from the Golden Calf to Salome—performed in

the wrong way, at the wrong time, and for the wrong purpose. But they could not ignore the dances of David and Miriam or the approving references to dance in the Psalms and the Book of Ezekiel (6:11). In their own scriptures, Paul admonished them to "glorify God in your body" which is "the temple of the Holy Spirit" (I Corinthians 6:19–20); and both Matthew (11:17) and Luke (7:32) quoted Jesus as saying, "We have piped unto you, and ye have not danced." At the same time, there were more and more converts to Christianity from sects where dancing was central to worship; rather than expect these converts to stop dancing the moment they were baptized, the church fathers found ways to "baptize" dance by refining and spiritualizing it, just as they had found ways to give a Christian interpretation to pre-Christian myths and symbols.

The dances that won the approval of the church fathers were group dances, typically processions or circles in which

Etruscan painting portrayed dance in a freer and livelier manner than any surviving images from Greek or Roman art. These dancers and musicians from the Tomb of the Triclinium in the necropolis of the Monterozzi, Tarquinia, Italy, 480–470 B.C., are part of a larger scene of a banquet. Whether the feasting and revelry refer to the life of the deceased or the life he could expect after death is not known.

The story of Salome, with its overtones
of sadism and depravity, was especially
spellbinding to audiences of the fin de
siècle. In art, the symbol of the sexually
demonic woman began to appear about
thirty years before the end of the century,
as in French painter Gustave Moreau's
Salome Dancing Before Herod
(1874–86; above right). Interest in the
story gathered momentum with Oscar
Wilde's play Salome, which was banned
in England, but produced in Paris by
Sarah Bernhardt in 1894. English artist
Aubrey Beardsley produced a well-
known series of illustrations based on the
play, and Richard Strauss his startling
opera of 1905. Salome was soon
embraced as a popular subject by movie
makers and modern dancers. Maud
Allen (above left), an American dancer
of the turn of the century, was among
the latter. Silent film star Theda Bara
made a Salome in 1918, but more
amusing by far was the Salomé of 1923,
based on Beardsley's drawings as adapted by Rudolf Valentino's wife, Natacha
Rambova. Nazimova (right) played the
title role.

men, separated from women, performed solemn, decorous movements in "the fear of God." While shunning the ecstatic, lascivious dances of the pagans, Christians could dance as a congregation during ritual prayer; dance could also abet mystical practice, further spiritual healing and cleansing, and explicate scripture and doctrine through symbolic enactments such as the "dance of the blessed" and "the dance of the angels." The circle, or ring, dance in particular was seen as an earthly counterpart of the heavenly dance of the angels, which was itself a celebration of the Resurrection. The dancers sang hymns and psalms, clapped their hands rhythmically, hopped and stamped their feet. Participation by women in sacred dance was always suspect because of the temptation it posed to men. Basileios the Great (344–407), bishop of Caesarea, wrote: "Could there be anything more blessed than to imitate on earth the ring dance of the angels?" But in a sermon condemning a drunken Easter celebration, he railed against women who "dance with lustful eyes and loud laughter; as if seized by a kind of frenzy [to] excite the lust of the youths. . . .You [women] move your feet and hop about madly and you dance the ring dance, which you should not do, for you should more properly bend the knees in prayer."

The tendency of dancers to go beyond the bounds of propriety, even on consecrated ground, led some authorities to harden their opinion against dance itself. One of the most influential of these authorities was Augustine (354–430). As a self-proclaimed expert on temptation (he confessed to having taken pleasure in the Roman games as a young man), Augustine denounced all wild, abandoned dancing, even when accompanied by psalm-singing. Unable to condemn all dance (since it was clearly sanctioned by scripture), he damned it with the faintest possible endorsement: "Let him who dances, dance." Augustine went on to suggest that the dance of Christians may be purified of all fleshly taint by following the example of St. Cyprian the Martyr: "He heard the song, he revealed himself dancing, not in the body, but in the spirit." Augustine would no doubt have approved of the discreet dancing depicted in Byzantine church mosaics from the fifth through the eighth centuries. Angels float in the sky, holding hands and apparently moving in a circle to heavenly music; their long robes cover their legs so that their feet are invisible. (This motif remained popular through the Middle Ages into the Renaissance, as can be seen in Botticelli's *Mystical Nativity* of c. 1500. When the feet of the angels and the blessed entering heaven are visible, they are shown dangling down without support, as if to emphasize the ethereal, incorporeal nature of this dance.)

Condemnation of the wrong kinds of dancing became a function of the church councils that met periodically to instruct the faithful in doctrine and practice. It was not dance alone that worried the hierarchy; from the sixth century on, proclamations against shameless dancing in churches, churchyards, and at sacred festivals were accompanied by denunciations of unseemly art and excessively embellished music. But the status of dance in the churches of Western Europe was always less secure than that of art and music. The issue was control. Christian worship was a communal function whose goal was salvation. The hierarchy wanted to be sure that nothing heard or seen on consecrated ground would distract the congregation; and art and music were inherently more controllable than dance. Commissioned paintings, statues, mosaics, and windows could be rejected if deemed unsuitable; once installed, they could be removed or covered over if the hierarchy changed its mind. Singers in a choir had to follow a score, whether written or not. But the dancing body was unpredictable, suspect in its individuality, notoriously prey to temptation and corruption; wild dancing, seen as a vestige of "pagan customs," was explicitly associated with the Devil as early as the fourth century.

The fact that church councils kept condemning the wrong kind of dancing for more than a thousand years indicates how prevalent the prohibited practices were. Bans on dancing were most frequent between 1200 and 1500—a period in which Western Christian churches were by no means inhospitable to carefully controlled liturgical dance. On church floors in France, Italy, England, and Germany large labyrinths were laid out in multicolored stones; the one in Chartres Cathedral measures forty feet in diameter. The precise nature of the dances or dancelike processions performed on these labyrinths is a matter of conjecture; congregants probably followed a leader in tracing out a winding path that symbolized a mystical journey through Satan's realm and, at the conclusion of the ceremony, the

triumphant arrival in Jerusalem or heaven. One variant, the pelota, or ball dance, is well-known from church records dating back to the fourteenth century; the pelota was performed in the cathedral of Auxerre, a city in central France, as late as 1538. On Easter Sunday the dean of the cathedral led his canons, linked hand to hand, in a dance around the labyrinth in the nave while all sang the Easter hymn; under one arm the dean held a large ball which he threw back and forth to one or more of the dancers. In some variations, the dance itself was a hopping three-step— three steps forward, one step back.

Besides these labyrinth dances, other kinds of liturgical dancing familiar to Christian congregations during the later Middle Ages included the prescribed movements of the priest around the altar, the mystery and morality plays staged on the porches of cathedrals, and the carefully choreographed processions of choristers. In fifteenth-century Seville, six young boys dressed as angels with gilded wings danced before the high altar while accompanying themselves on castanets. Despite opposition from those who questioned its propriety, this "children's dance" received the approval of two popes. It can still be seen today; the choristers, who now number ten, dance in the costumes of Renaissance pages.

The unrelenting efforts of medieval church officials to distinguish between acceptable and unacceptable dance had important consequences for European society at large. Put simply, if unacceptable dance—the wilder "Dionysian" dance that offers release from the constraints of daily life and that is often

The labyrinth in Chartres Cathedral, located in the center of the nave, is made up of 365 black and white stones. It can just barely be seen as a polished area in the floor of the nave in the unobstructed photograph (below) of the interior of the cathedral. If you trace the route through the maze (left), you will see that the clever design would have taken the line of dancers down every possible avenue before delivering them to Jerusalem, in the center.

The many great public squares in European cities, like the Piazza San Marco in Venice (below), were well suited to carefully choreographed religious pageantry. In Gentile Bellini's Procession of the Reliquary of the True Cross in the Piazza San Marco (1496), the procession is emerging from between the church of San Marco and the Doge's Palace in the upper right. It curves around to the front of the picture, where we can see the reliquary being carried under a canopy. To the upper left, people from the head of the procession are beginning to take their places for a formal ceremony.

Opposite: Sandro Botticelli's Mystical Nativity (c. 1500), a painting of richly symbolic if obscure imagery, depicts a circle of angels dancing above the Holy Family in the manger.

associated with trance and possession—was excluded from the church, where was it supposed to go? The medieval church claimed jurisdiction over virtually everything a person did, from waking to sleeping, from work to play, from birth to death. Nevertheless, there were areas where vigilance was sporadic and largely ineffectual. This came about because Christians tended to separate human activity into two realms—the sacred and the secular. This sharp dichotomy, which goes back to Christianity's origin in a world dominated by a hostile imperial power, is inherent in such statements as "Render therefore unto Caesar the things which are Caesar's; and unto God the things that are God's" (Matthew 22:21). In terms of doctrine, a clear line was drawn between the life of the spirit to which men should aspire and the material world (including the body) from which men should try to free themselves. As a practical matter, this split opened the way for secular forms of dance that would not have been allowed in the sacred precincts of the church.

Many of the traditional dances of the European countryside were originally associated with pre-Christian festivals that marked the changing seasons or the worship of local deities. These dances were often energetic, involving lots of whirling and stamping; men and women danced in sight of each other and even with each other. Rather than forbid them outright, church officials baptized the old festivals with new names honoring events in the Christian calendar.

Under this dispensation the traditional dances not only retained much of their pre-Christian flavor but were relatively free to evolve in new directions beyond the purview of the hierarchy. In time, this contributed to the creation of a purely secular dance tradition in Western Europe.

Another kind of dancing that tested the limits of church control was dancing during Carnival—the days of public merrymaking just before the penitential season of Lent. Some scholars trace the origin of Carnival to the ancient Roman New Year festival of Saturnalia, when masters and slaves briefly swapped roles and disorder reigned in the streets; or even further back to the Greek revels of Dionysus that celebrated the earth's fertility. Whatever its roots, dancing at

Carnival was wild and abandoned. Church officials condemned it as early as the seventh century. Isidore, bishop of Seville, who lived from 560 to 636, recorded this description: "[The revelers] assumed monstrous forms and transformed themselves into wild shapes; others womanized their masculine faces and made female gestures—all romping and stamping in their dances and clapping their hands and, what is still more shameful, both sexes danced together in the ring dance. . . . " Authorities in Spain were issuing proclamations against such behavior well into the sixteenth century. Similar customs, including blasphemous parodies of the divine service within the church itself, persisted throughout Europe, despite repeated bans.

Clearly, the approval of certain forms of dance, both in and out of the church, did not mean that medieval Christianity had resolved its ambivalence toward the body. Denial of the body through mortification (such as hair shirts and penitential whipping) was enthusiastically sanctioned; sensuality was denounced. But the impulse to dance can take many forms. In the wake of the Black Death that ravaged Europe between 1348 and 1351, killing more than a third of the population, processions of flagellants appeared on the Continent and in England; barefoot and dressed as pilgrims, they publicly lashed themselves with leather and rope scourges in an effort to prevail upon Christ and Mary to end the plague. The penitential whipping was carried out as they moved in a circle dance, singing hymns. Both civil and church authorities acted swift-

Pieter Brueghel's Battle Between Carnival and Lent *(1559) is an allegory of the abrupt change in mood from the exuberant Carnival to the austere Lent. The overindulgent fools of Carnival are championed by a fat man riding a wine barrel and wielding a spit with a roasting boar on it. His rival leading a Lenten army of the well-intentioned is an old hag whose weapon is a shovel bearing two modest herrings. In the far distance, on the Carnival side of the painting, is a circle of dancing figures.*

ly to suppress the flagellants, whose fervor was seen as threatening to the public order.

History assures us that, no matter what the circumstances, people *will* dance. During the period when mortification of the body was most widely practiced in Europe, outbreaks of what was called "dance mania" reached epidemic proportions. In the late summer and fall of 1374, unruly crowds of men and women, from all classes of society, appeared in Aachen, Cologne, and other cities along the Rhine; holding hands and "dancing" in a crazed manner, they leaped high in the air and jerked their bodies about in terrible spasms, at times shouting incomprehensible syllables and foaming at the mouth. From their behavior it was clear to bystanders that these half-naked "choreomaniacs," as they were called, were possessed by demons, whose names they sometimes cried out in their agony. Often they "danced" before the relics of saints that were known for their ability to exorcise demons that caused physical pain.

Medical historians, sifting through accounts in contemporary chronicles, believe that many of the choreomaniacs were suffering from convulsive ergotism, a condition they could have contracted by eating bread made from rye flour contaminated by the ergot fungus. Ergot is a potent poison that can produce violent and painful cramps; among the symptoms of ergot poisoning are severe muscle spasms and twitching. By the beginning of the seventeenth century such symptoms were widely recognized as having natural causes. But in the late Middle Ages both sufferers and onlookers immediately associated the malady

In the wake of the Black Death that ravaged Europe between 1348 and 1351, killing more than a third of the population, processions of penitential flagellants, such as these from an illumination in the Belles Heures of Jean, duke of Berry, painted by Pol, Jean, and Herman de Limbourg in c. 1410–1413, appeared on the Continent and in England.

A Jewish congregation celebrates Simhat Torah (right), which marks the completion of the annual cycle of Torah reading, with joyful dancing outside a synagogue in the village of Dubrovna, Belorussia, before World War I.

The Shakers (below), a religious group that settled in the United States in the eighteenth century, lived as celibates in strictly segregated men's and women's dormitories, but danced together in intricate formations as a form of worship, as seen in this vigorous circle dance in a Shaker meetinghouse, New Lebanon, New York, 1873.

with dancing and possession by malign spirits. This confirms, if further proof were needed, that medieval Europe knew, and feared, the role that the dancing body could play in making contact with a supernatural realm.

The long-standing debate about the propriety of dance in Christian worship was resolved by the Reformation and the ensuing Counter Reformation. Protestant reformers, in their zeal to rid the church of everything that distracted worshipers from concentration on the Word of God, banished all displays of wealth and pomp; poetry and music were permitted, beautiful images and liturgical dance were not. The Roman Catholic hierarchy, with some reluctance and with some notable exceptions (as in Seville), responded in kind. Carnival excesses were brought under firmer control, and most dances inside churches were halted. The labyrinth in Auxerre Cathedral was torn up in 1690.

In his 1685 tract against *Mixt or Promiscuous Dancing*, the New England Puritan divine Increase Mather admitted that "sober and grave Dancing of Men with Men, or of Women with Women" was permissible "in due season, and with moderation." But as for wanton dancing of any kind, and especially "Gynecandrical Dancing," Mather had no doubt that this was literally the invention of the Devil.

In Europe, the almost complete excising of dance from Christian worship only reinforced the growing importance of dance in secular life. This was true among all social classes. The dances of the countryside had their counterparts in the dances of the nobility, which, under the influence of Renaissance humanism, evolved into increasingly elaborate court entertainments and courtship rituals. While court and country dances differed in style, there was a constant interchange between them; and both developed along lines that would have been impossible within the church proper—men and women were not only dancing in each other's presence but together, physically linked, as couples.

No one thought to record the exact date and place, but it may have been in twelfth-century Provence—home of the troubadours and the birthplace of courtly love—that Western-style couple dancing began. At its origin the new style of dancing probably looked nothing like the intimacy seen on later dance floors. A man and a woman might break from the formation of a line or circle dance or from the stately procession of a court entertainment, and execute a few steps in unison with perhaps a brief touching of the hands to help coordinate their movements, before rejoining the formation, to be followed by another couple and then another. This public dancing in couples was not only unprecedented in the Judeo-Christian tradition, it was something that would have been frowned on in many parts of the world as a violation of public decorum; inevitably, there were unsuccessful attempts throughout Western Europe to ban couple dancing.

Here and there, Protestant visionaries like the Shakers (who originated in England and migrated to the United States in the eighteenth century) placed dance at the center of their worship. Independently, the Hasidic movement that arose in Eastern European Judaism in the eighteenth century sought a more personal form of worship through ecstatic dancing in the synagogue, either in groups or in solo improvisations (with men and women always strictly segregated). But these were exceptions. From the Renaissance on, dance in Judeo-Christian societies typically expressed secular rather than religious concerns. Which is not to say that the West's long history of ambivalence about the dancing body left no mark on the aesthetics of Western dance. As we will see in later chapters, the ballerinas of the nineteenth century who danced on their toes were seen as ethereal creatures, symbols of a longing to rise above the earth, to aspire toward a purer realm, to seek an ideal beauty that transcends the flesh. In popular lithographs of the period, barefoot ballerinas are depicted hovering in the air, dressed in gauzy white—secular angels beckoning the onlooker not to the glories of Heaven but to the ineffable pleasures of Art.

A mong the Yoruba of west Africa, dance is typically grounded, with movement directed not upward but down toward the life-sustaining earth. This does not mean that Yoruba dance is in any way separated from the realm of the spirits. Indeed, nothing resembling the Western split between sacred and secular exists in Yorubaland. Yoruba cosmology recognizes two closely related realms of existence: the tangible world of the living and the invisible realm of gods, ancestors, and other spirit-beings. Despite their differences, these two realms are closely linked be-

cause both partake of the life force that runs through the universe. The ultimate source of life is the divine creator, an indefinable figure neither male nor female, who mostly stands aloof from the created universe. Human interaction is with the potent (but far from omnipotent) gods and ancestors; the dancing body is the place where the two realms meet.

In Yorubaland worshipers communicate with gods and ancestors through both words and dance. Some ceremonies are designed to induce possession. These are communal gatherings that involve drumming, dancing, and the chanting of praise songs, called oríki, which are addressed to specific deities. When properly invoked, the gods enter the human community by possessing certain priests and priestesses who have been initiated into their service. The moment of possession may be signified by a sudden change in the movements of the initiate or by a loud guttural cry.

In the Yoruba pantheon there are more than four hundred gods, or orishas, representing deified ancestors or personified natural forces. Orishas fall into two broad categories: "cool," basically predictable beings like Osun, a river goddess; and "hot," typically capricious gods like Sango, a former king who wields the dangerous lightning bolt. According to Chief Bayo Ogundijo of the Institute of Cultural Studies at Ile Ife in Nigeria, all the orishas were "people who lived on the earth once" and made a strong impression on their contemporaries; after they "disappeared," the people "proclaimed them deities." A devotee may follow a particular deity or several deities. At shrines where their images

are kept, orishas are praised with oríki and fed with bits of food and water; worshipers will also offer sacrifices on the advice of specialists in divination, and dance for, and with, the orishas at the large seasonal festivals held in their honor.

A particular locality might have ten festivals a year, each lasting a week or more. The relationship between deity and devotee is thought of as reciprocal; in return for devotion, an orisha will protect the devotee, drive away disease, ensure healthy children, and the like. Deities that are not regularly fed and honored by devotees are said to "die." In the words of a Yoruba proverb: "Without human beings there would be no gods."

Like other orishas, the thunder god Sango loves dancing. His worship was originally associated with the Oyo Empire which dominated what is now southwestern Nigeria in the seventeenth and eighteenth centuries. Today he is widely venerated throughout Yorubaland and in the Americas where the descendants of west Africans practice variants of their ancestral religion. Sango's enduring popularity may have something to do with his tragic and all-too-human entanglement with the levers of ambition during his time on earth. As a king of Oyo he was a great warrior but so headstrong that his own people dethroned him. According to one legend, he dabbled in magic that he did not fully understand, triggering bolts of lightning that killed all his children and all his wives but one. In remorse he hung himself, but his followers had him deified, as a thunder god, in an attempt to placate the awesome power of nature that he had become identified with.

A Yoruban Sango priestess (top left) dances with her dance-wand, Ohori, Nigeria. As she chants an oríki, or praise song, she gesticulates with the dance-wand. The worship of Sango has spread beyond the Yoruba-speaking peoples of west Africa to other groups in the region: In a Sango temple in Benin City (above), worshiped by Edo-speaking peoples, a possession ceremony is in progress. The priestess on the left is in a trance. Behind the dancers, women are shaking calabashes strung with beads. Left, worshipers at a Sunday service at the Celestial Church of Christ, an aladura church in Gbongan, Nigeria, 1991.

An egungun dancer (below) in the market-place, Gbongan, Nigeria, 1991. When the dancer spins fast enough, the outer strips of cloth lift to reveal a different design, of a contrasting color, underneath; with some masks, the costume reverses entirely, pre-senting an entirely different appearance at the end of the dance. Right, Sango posses-sion priest Sangodele Ibuowo, Oyo, Nigeria, 1991.

Sango the family-destroyer is now worshiped as giver and protector of children, the scourge of adulterers. His followers chant poetic verses reminiscent of the Book of Job:

The dog stays in the house of its master
But does not know his intentions.
The sheep does not know the intentions
Of the man who feeds it.
We ourselves follow Sango
Although we do not know his intentions.
It is not easy to live in Sango's company.

The priests and priestesses of Sango carry beautifully carved wooden "dance-wands" that depict images not of the unknowable god but of his rapt followers. Dressed in robe, shirt, shorts, and baggy trousers, the Sango priest sings the god's praises and moves rhythmically to the "hot" drumming that Sango is known to like. As the moment of possession approaches, the priest dramatically strips off his outer garments

and bares his upper body to the deity; his steps become irregular; rising on the balls of his feet he slowly twists his torso from the waist up. When the god "mounts" him, the priest cries out and his movements change suddenly to reflect the nature of Sango himself: energetic, abrupt, angular. Omofolabo Ajaji, who teaches at the University of Kansas, has compared the dance of Sango to "an inferno, a whirlwind, dizzy and confused, virile, full of body contortions, restless gestures, diagonal leg flicks and jerky shoulder movements."

By contrast, the dance of Osun, a deity who cures the sick and blesses her followers with children, is sinuous and flowing, like the river she is associated with. Her priestesses wear white robes hung with colorfully beaded "dance panels" and carry on their heads brass bowls filled with medicinal waters and herbs; their shoulders are bared to the deity. They take short steps, close to the ground; their body movements are fluid;

their extended arms make graceful circular motions from the shoulders as their hands revolve at the wrist. Their dance does not change radically when they are possessed, but their bodies may shake briefly, and a moment of rigidity may interrupt the smooth flow of their dance.

In addition to possession ceremonies, Yoruba communities come together periodically to take part in a kind of dance drama called egungun. During egungun festivals, family ancestors are honored by maskers who don elaborate costumes that cover them from head to toe. Once concealed beneath these full-body masks, they are treated as if they were the ancestors come back to life. Accompanied by crowds chanting oríki, the egungun move through the community, animating their masks with distinctive steps and gestures that express the ancestors' personalities: fierce and aggressive for famous warriors, gentle and graceful for the matriarch of a lineage.

In addition to masks honoring ancestors, there are egungun animal masquerades — such as the one opposite at an egungun festival in Imasi, Nigeria, 1978 — and satirical masquerades, which depict human stereotypes. An example of the latter is the couple at right, in Ilogbo, Nigeria, 1982, who are poking fun at visiting tourists. She clutches a purse while he holds a ballpoint pen. Writing, not dancing, is the chosen form of expression of the white man.

Colorful and imposing in themselves, the egungun masks only reveal their full power when they are "danced."

In egungun festivals, as in Yoruba ceremonies of possession, the body serves as a conduit to the realm of the spirits. But the role it plays in each event is quite different. Where the initiate of an orisha openly offers his or her body to the god, the egungun masker conceals all evidence of his identity. Most egungun masks are huge, enveloping, sacklike, many-layered; the face is usually hidden behind tight mesh netting. The more elaborate costumes are topped by carved headpieces that combine animal and human features. The masks are the property of prominent families or secret societies; ownership of an egungun mask is a mark of status in the community. Each year new decorations and new layers are added; the outer layers typically consist of long strips of cloth attached only at the top so that they flutter with each step of the dancer and fly out in all directions when he suddenly changes direction or whirls around. Some costumes are designed to turn completely inside out when the masker goes into a sustained spin. The honored ancestors are mostly male; the maskers who animate the costumes are invariably male. Women are kept away from the sacred groves and cult houses where the masks are prepared. Yet it is principally women who chant the praise-songs that, along with the drums, rouse the egungun to action.

Egungun masquerades make tangible the presence of the past in the life of a community. Accordingly, they vary from locality to locality and from performance to performance. Even when the people of the community know who is under the mask (as they often do), they greet the mask as the ancestor incarnate, in a willing suspension of disbelief that is essential to the success of the masquerade. In the words of Chief Bayo Ogundijo: "What would happen if my father who died many years ago reappeared in our house exactly as I knew him before he died? I would not have the courage to meet with him, no matter how deeply I felt about him. That is why it is good to meet with one's old, old father covering himself with cloths. It is just as a disguise, so that people may not be gripped with fear." Occasionally, under the influence of the drumming and the chanted oríki and the dancing, a masker may become possessed by the spirit of the ancestor, but this is not necessary to the purpose of the masquerade.

In the western Yoruba town of Abeokuta, once an important military outpost, an egungun festival recalls the anarchic years following the fall of the Oyo Empire. When the powerful warrior masks take to the streets, they are accompanied by crowds of young men who enact a kind of mock battle that calls attention to the carnage and disruptions of past wars. People scatter to get out of the way of the more fearsome masks, who flail about in violent pantomime; later these same egungun will utter incantations and bless their followers in guttural, unearthly voices. Although such festivals can be thought of as dance drama, there are no "spectators" in the Western sense of "theatergoer." In egungun, as in the ceremonies where specific orishas are invited to possess the initiated, everyone present is a participant without whose collaboration the transforming potential of the event cannot be realized.

Worship that uses both words and body to communicate with the deity is a strong tradition among the Yoruba. This tradition can be seen at work among Nigerian Christians who practice a form of ecstatic worship in what are called aladura churches. (Aladura means "the ones who pray.") These churches, which are found not only in west Africa but throughout the Yoruba diaspora, represent a creative synthesis between the teachings of English Protestant missionaries, who were active in west Africa from the middle of the nineteenth century, and Yoruba religious practices. With the singing of hymns and dancing in the pews and the aisles and before the altar, white-robed worshipers invite possession by the Holy Spirit. Those possessed are specially trained members of the congregation. When the Spirit descends on them, they begin speaking "in tongues"—mysterious vocalizations that are not of this world but that can be decoded and put to use for the benefit of the worshipers. Prophetess Rachel Ajoke Ale of the Sacred Order of Cherubim and Seraphim Church, Proclaimer of Jesus Christ the Source of Peace, in Gbongan, Nigeria, describes the efficacy of the congregation's worship services: "Through me, God has performed many wonderful things since I became a Prophetess. Barren women come to us for God's blessing and when we pray for them, God answers. People who are sick when we pray for them, God delivers them from sickness; the lame walk through us; delayed pregnancies are delivered by God's power."

Shiva, the great Hindu deity of creation and destruction, is represented as Nataraja, Lord of the Dance, in this twelfth-century bronze icon from southern India.

In India as in sub-Saharan Africa, the dancing body occupies a place of honor in religious worship. While the Yoruba world view presupposes a steady traffic between the realm of the living and the realm of the deities, Hinduism suggests that the two realms are in essence one, and that one of the ways to affirm the underlying unity of creation is through dance.

"Hinduism" is actually an umbrella term for an ancient and enormously varied tradition of religious inquiry and experience. Unlike Judaism and Christianity, this tradition has no clearly defined beginning or identifiable founder. Instead of a single authoritative work of scripture, Hinduism finds expression in a vast body of written and iconographic material produced over a period of some two thousand years. So diverse are the religious experiences possible under the umbrella of Hinduism that some foreign observers have equated it with polytheism. More accurately, it is a tradition of multiculturalism that embraces many sects whose differing approaches to divinity vary in both the form and the object of their devotions.

What might appear in the West as a panoply of conflicting and even contradictory points of view is not seen that way in India. Indian philosophers and religious teachers have debated long and hard about the nature of the world and humanity's place in it; and different schools of thought have advanced different solutions to the problems of appearance and reality, good and evil, duty and desire, spirituality and sensuality. But all the competing formulations have at least two things in common: a belief in the underlying unity of existence and a determination to exclude no aspect of life in the search for the meaning of life. This insistence that *all* the pieces must ultimately fit together in a satisfying whole has shaped Hinduism's attitude toward the body. Far from being seen as an impediment to spiritual enlightenment, the body is treated as a tool for achieving greater insight and understanding. Is it any wonder that in India—where the gods dance—the dancing body can be both a source of pleasure and a vehicle of worship?

Dance in India takes a bewildering variety of forms. Of these, two in particular—bharata natyam and kathakali—exemplify the ways in which dance and religion intersect in Indian life. Both reached a high state of development at the southern tip of the subcontinent. Bharata natyam is a solo for a highly trained female dancer; it traces its origins to the devotional dances once performed within Hindu temples. Kathakali is a dance drama in which a troupe of highly trained performers enact stories about heroes, deities, and demons from the great epics of Hindu mythology. Both bharata natyam and kathakali have long histories, both have changed radically over the years, and both are now considered exemplars of classical Indian culture, although their survival was seriously in doubt only a few decades ago.

The basic strategy of Indian dance was laid down some two thousand years ago in the *Natya Shastra*, a treatise that describes and analyzes the techniques employed in the Sanskrit plays of that time. These plays were a form of dance drama, performed for an educated elite. In one sense, the *Natya Shastra* is a the-ater manual, spelling out in great detail all aspects of the performer's art, from an elaborate sign language of hand gestures, known as mudras, to specific conventions of makeup and costuming. Yet this eminently practical theater guide has long been revered as one of the hallowed texts of the Hindu tradi-tion. The cornerstones of that tradition are four works known as the Vedas (from the Sanskrit word for knowledge), parts of which date back to the second millennium B.C. The Vedas contain prayers, hymns, and ritual formulas for sacrifices to propitiate a pantheon of

The temple at Chidambaram in southern India is dedicated to the dancing Shiva, the favorite deity of the Chola kings (846–1173), who once maintained a palace close to this shrine. Among the many dance-related carvings in the temple are scenes illustrating all 108 karanas, units of movement that are discussed in the classic Indian treatise on dance, the two-thousand-year-old Natya Shastra. *Similar poses can be found in the dances of today's bharata natyam performers.*

deities identified with the forces of nature; to ensure their efficacy, the sacrifices had to be performed with the strictest attention to detail, down to the least spoken syllable and smallest ritual gesture. The *Natya Shastra* (which is known as "the fifth Veda") likens theatrical performances to Vedic sacrifices. It asserts that dance drama, properly performed, "emboldens the weak, energizes the heroic, enlightens the ignorant and imparts erudition to the scholars" by showing humanity and divinity as they really are.

This high purpose is accomplished by arousing certain emotional states in the audience—not ordinary, transitory emotions but emotions "universalized" to reveal what is common in everyone's experience. Such emotions are called rasas (after the Sanskrit word for flavor, or juice). The *Natya Shastra* identifies eight fundamental rasas; these can be rendered into English as love, humor, pathos, anger, heroism, terror, disgust, and wonder. (Later commentators added a ninth rasa, serenity, which is said to encompass all the others.)

A dramatic performance should aim at the arousal of rasa in the audience. The eight (or nine) rasas must be distinguished from the thirty-three "transitory" feelings, which include despondency, languor, envy, and elation; these feelings are personal in a way that the aesthetically refined rasas are not. Those in the audience who experience the rasa of love are not "in love" with the performer or the character portrayed, any more than those who experience the rasa of anger are led to begin fighting with the people sitting next to them. The *Natya Shastra* com-

pares rasa to the experience of eating an especially good meal. In South India, where spices are abundant and the cuisine is pungent and aromatic, a single dish may contain many different condiments. But rather than focus on the individual flavors, the gourmet derives pleasure from the overall impression produced by their blend. In the same way, the attention of the rasika, the knowledgeable spectator, is drawn to the underlying unity of the aesthetic experience, which at its peak resembles the bliss of the religious devotee contemplating the deity.

To realize this aspiration requires a joint effort by performer and audience. In classical forms like bharata natyam and kathakali, the performer is expected to bring the same single-minded dedication to a performance as the devotee brings to a prescribed ritual. The rasika must come prepared to appreciate the nuances of the performance and, by his vocal and physical responses, to enhance the performer's ability to evoke rasa, which in turn will heighten the rasika's responses. Instead of a separation between performer and spectator, the goal is a collaboration, a shared experience of rasa. Since physical control is essential to the performer's art, it is the performer's duty to bring his body under as complete control as possible. The techniques go far beyond anything taught in Western theater. For example, the *Natya Shastra* enumerates seven movements of the eyebrow and nine movements of the eyelid that must be mastered in order to evoke rasa properly.

The contemporary dance form known as bharata natyam is a direct descendant of the devotional dances

performed in the temples of south India from about the tenth century until the middle of this century. The focus of activity in a Hindu temple is an icon through which the presence of a god can be invoked by properly performed rites. These rites include "waking" the deity with prayers and bathing, clothing, feeding, and entertaining the consecrated image with offerings of various kinds. With the flowering of temple worship in the south, in what is now the state of Tamil Nadhu, there emerged a special class of temple servants called devadasis. These were women who were "married" to the god of the temple, somewhat as Roman Catholic nuns are wed to Christ; one of their tasks was to please the god with offerings of dance in which passages from Sanskrit texts were interpreted. Evidence for this practice can be found on the walls of many Indian temples which are decorated with reliefs of dancers in hundreds of graceful poses familiar to devotees of Indian dance today. The most famous of the temples dedicated to the dancing Shiva is at Chidambaram, 120 miles from Madras. Here, as in other temples throughout India, can be found variants of the basic position of all classical Indian dance: the dancer stands with knees bent, feet turned sideways, and arms either extended to both sides or placed firmly on the waist.

It is not possible to re-create the actual dance of the devadasis from the temple sculptures, but it is known that the principles of the *Natya Shastra* were adopted and passed down, in an oral tradition, by the dance instructors who taught the devadasis. Temple dance was supported by the royal patrons of the

One of the most famous Hindu temples, not least for its many erotic scenes, is the Surya Deul of c. 1240 at Konarak, in eastern India. Called the Black Pagoda by early European mariners, for whom it was a useful landmark on the route to Calcutta, it is dedicated to Surya, the sun god. Numerous dancers and musicians cover the temple, greeting the rising sun each day.

temples and by wealthy worshipers eager to earn religious merit. Some temples had as many as four hundred devadasis who took turns dancing in the sanctum of the temple, where only higher-caste Hindus could enter. But once a year, when the image of the god was paraded through the streets in a joyous celebration, the dancers of the temple displayed their devotional art to the entire population.

The devadasis had other skills as well. In later years, some functioned as court dancers, whose devotion was directed toward the king rather than the god. In order to fulfill their function as interpreters of Sanskrit texts, devadasis were often highly educated in music and literature as well as dance; and their companionship was sought after by princes, courtiers, and scholars. Historians argue about whether the eastern Mediterranean custom of "sacred prostitution" was ever widely practiced in India. In any case, the distinction between temple dancers and other dancers who entertained admirers for a fee was not always clearly drawn; and the moral reputation of the devadasis fluctuated from time to time and place to place. By the end of the nineteenth century the concerns of disapproving Indians were reinforced by the preconceptions of British moral reformers, and the standing of temple dancers fell to an all-time low. In 1927 Gandhi wrote: "There are, I am sorry to say, many temples in our midst in this country which are no better than brothels." After a campaign led by public-spirited citizens in the name of the exploited devadasis, temple dancing in India was banned.

But the dance itself refused to die.

A few dancers and teachers whose families had nurtured the art for generations continued to pass it down to a handful of disciples. In accord with the burgeoning movement for political independence, poets and writers who had championed the indigenous literatures of India took up the cause of India's traditional dances, alongside a vanguard of higher-caste women who braved criticism from their peers to study with the remaining devadasis. (It was unheard of at the time for women of the Brahmin caste to dance in public.) Foremost among these pioneers was the late Rukmini Devi, whose studies led her in 1934 to establish Kalashektra, a school in Madras that attracts musicians and dancers who want to combine religious devotion with the performing arts. Because the authorship of the *Natya Shastra* is traditionally credited to the sage Bharata, the newly invigorated

classical dance came to be known as bharata natyam. The social standing of this dance form, which is now seen exclusively in theatrical settings, has undergone a curious revolution; bharata natyam dancers today tend to be women of the middle and upper classes.

According to Dr. Kapila Vatsyayan, one of India's foremost dance scholars, the Indian dancer uses the body to suggest an abstract, universal form. Unlike classical Western dance, such as ballet, the conquest of gravity through impressive leaps has no part in bharata natyam technique: "The Indian dancer's preoccupation is not so much with space as with time, and the dancer is constantly trying to achieve the perfect pose which will convey a sense of timelessness." For this reason the dancer emphasizes not the muscles of her body but the skeleton, the joints and the underlying bone structure. The result is a "sculptur-

esque" quality in which all movement begins and ends in a moment of balance —visualized as a straight line dividing the body in half from head to foot.

The bharata natyam dancer appears on stage wrapped in a sari-like garment of brightly colored silk, highlighted in gold, over leggings of the same material; from her waist falls a fan-pleated apron that swings opens when she bends at the knees, her bare feet joined heel to heel beneath her in the characteristic pose seen in so many temple reliefs. The edges of her feet are outlined in bright red paint; around each ankle she wears a circlet of bells, and her hair, ears, neck, nose, and wrists are hung with jewelry. But the moment the dance begins any suggestion of pliant femininity in the dancer's appearance is belied by the sheer athleticism, the bodily control, the strength and power of her every movement. A bharata natyam performance

Malavika Sarrukai performing bharata natyam, a classical dance form that evolved from the dances of the temple servants called devadasis; bharata natyam is now performed in theatrical settings.

Opposite: These two paintings of c.1800 from Tanjore in the southern Indian state of Tamil Nadhu show a street entertainer and a temple dancer (devadasi), both with musicians.

The young Balasaraswati in Madras, India, 1934. Descended from a long line of dancers and musicians, Balasaraswati played an important role in the revival of classical Indian dance in the first half of the twentieth century.

blends two complementary styles of movement: abstract dance sequences that stress virtuosity and rhythmic improvisation, and expressive dance sequences that seek to interpret classical poetry through mime. The dancer, who is accompanied onstage by a drummer, two other instrumentalists, and a singer, is also the choreographer; she determines the basic rhythm cycles, the poetic text to be used, and the specific interpretation of the text.

In the abstract dance sequences, dancer and drummer play off each other as in a jazz ensemble, except that the goal is not to make a personal statement but to explore, with a kind of selfless joy, the endlessly intriguing possibilities of interlocking rhythms. As her feet beat out a complex tattoo on the

ground, the sound enhanced by the jingling of her ankle bells, the dancer becomes a percussion instrument who interweaves her cadences with the beat laid down by the drummer. Connoisseurs of the art claim they can judge the worth of a performer with their eyes closed.

In the expressive dance sequences, the singer establishes a mood by chanting a poetic verse, and the dancer elaborates on it in mime, using movements of her upper body, hand gestures, and facial expressions. The poetry is typically drawn from the allegorical genre of Indian literature that employs erotic language to evoke spiritual ecstacy—as in these lines from the *Gita Govinda (Song of Krishna as Cowherd)* by the twelfth-century poet Jayadeva:

Make a mark with liquid deer musk
    on my moonlit brow!
Make a moon shadow, Krishna!
    The sweat drops are dried. . . .
Fix flowers in shining hair loosened
    by loveplay, Krishna!
Make a flywhisk outshining peacock
    plumage to be the banner of
    Love. . . .
My beautiful loins are a deep cavern
    to take the thrusts of love—
Cover them with jeweled girdles,
    cloths, and ornaments, Krishna!

The dancer mimes the actions of each character in turn: Krishna the divine lover, Radha his beloved, and Radha's female friend and confidant. During these dramatic passages, knowledgeable spectators focus on the performer's arms, hands, and eyes; as she shifts back and forth between the three roles, she is judged by her interpretive skills and by the depth of the emotional response she elicits from the audience. While many of the hand gestures are standard—their codification goes back to the *Natya Shastra*—the dancer has a certain leeway in the way she approaches a scene. For example, in the legends of Krishna's childhood, the young god's mother catches him eating mud and orders him to open his mouth; when he does, she beholds the entire cosmos behind his jaws. Rather than attempt to mime "the cosmos," the dancer may choose to capture the essence of the scene by reproducing the look of wonder in the mother's eyes as she fathoms the true nature of the son she has raised.

To permit a bharata natyam dancer to delve more deeply into the layers of meaning in a particular line of poetry, the singer may chant the line over and over during a performance; on each repeat, the dancer can explore a different aspect of the text. The dancer Balasaraswati, who died in 1984 after a career that spanned more than forty years, was one of the key figures in the revival of bharata natyam. Heiress to a long family tradition of music and dance, she was especially acclaimed for the expressive quality of her mime. Her most famous interpretive piece was a poem beginning, "Krishna, come soon and show me your face; Krishna, come with bells on your feet and blue pendants in your ears. . . . O Lord, come dancing with me." Balasaraswati's admirers insist that she could "dance" the same line fifteen times in a row, each time differently.

Hindu devotional poetry traditionally expresses the longing of the devotee for union with the deity as the longing of the female for union with the male. But there is nothing in Indian tradition that warrants reducing physical union to a mere metaphor for the spiritual. Dr. Vatsyayan is emphatic on the point: "Let's make no mistake about spirituality in India being opposed to the body. I'm sorry, but this is not a life-denying culture. There is very early textual evidence, as early as one thousand B.C., of dance being used as a divine vehicle of temptation as well as salvation. The gods send the apsaras, heavenly nymphs, to distract meditating hermits from undue austerities. Of course, the ultimate purpose is to restore order to the universe. But the vehicle is carnal desire—seduction in the name of cosmic balance."

The preparation of a bharata natyam dancer is often compared to that of a ballet dancer. Instruction and physical training begin at an early age, typically six or seven. Like ballet dancers, bharata natyam performers must first master a vocabulary of basic steps, positions, and gestures, out of which the most complex dance sequences can be fashioned; and like ballet, bharata natyam requires enormous powers of concentration and bodily discipline. But to a performer like Malavika Sarrukai, who has traveled widely from her home base in Madras, there is a significant difference between the attitudes of the two traditions toward the dancing body:

"We don't have the same . . . what shall I say, aggression on our bodies? The things ballet dancers do with their bodies onstage, extending them to such great limits, so beautiful, but also painful and even dangerous. . . . We don't do it that way. We approach it in a different way. We put more emphasis on mind than on technique. For one thing, an Indian dancer can expect to keep performing into her forties and beyond, so we have more time to develop. Whenever I read a poem I ask myself: Does this have something in it that can be danced? Sometimes images come to me spontaneously: images, movements, symbols. If I like the feeling, then I take the poem to my scholar and ask him to give me a line-by-line, word-by-word interpretation of the text. Then I sit with the music and the poem and start constructing the dance.

"Really, dance is observation of life. As a dancer, you have to be open to everything happening around you—how does a flower blossom, how do people talk to each other, how do they stand, how do they sit, what are they expressing with their bodies?—and all this is stylized into the language of dance. I feel that there is a very close relationship between human emotions and nature. I would like, in the short time of the performance, for the audience to feel this."

Unlike bharata natyam, the all-male dance drama called kathakali (the word means "story play") did not begin as temple worship per se. But it traces part of its heritage to an ancient tradition of presenting Sanskrit plays as votive offerings in temples along the Malabar coast, in what is now the southwestern state of Kerala. This coastal region, which was conducting a vigorous spice trade with the Mediterranean world even before the rise of the Roman Empire, has always taken pride in its cultivation of

the dramatic arts. In the seventeenth century two neighboring kings composed devotional plays of their own and organized rival troupes to perform them. One of these plays, drawn from incidents in the life of Rama, brought together two innovations that led to the later development of kathakali. The poetic verses were written in Malayalam, the language of the region, instead of classical Sanskrit; and the burden of reciting the dialogue was left to two singers, who stood alongside two drummers at the back of the stage; this freed the performers to concentrate on communicating the sense of the poetry through mimetic body language. The performers, all male, were by no means lacking in physical resources, having been recruited from the local military caste.

During the eighteenth and nineteenth centuries kathakali underwent a remarkable evolution into a kind of "people's theater." Hundreds of plays, typically based on stories from the great Hindu epics, were written for troupes sponsored by rulers and rich landholders. At some point the kathakali troupes began performing in the public areas outside village temples. These areas, which serve as local meeting places and social centers, are open to people of any caste (which is not true of the temples themselves). A new audience for kathakali developed. Under the patronage of princes who regarded themselves as rasikas no conscious effort was made to cater to the taste of the uneducated; in fact, standards of performance were codified with an eye on the rules laid down in the *Natya Shastra*. Yet by the beginning of the twentieth century kathakali had evolved into a uniquely powerful form of dance drama, religious

Opposite: The Ramayana *and the* Bhagavata Purana, *millennia-old Sanskrit epics celebrating the exploits of Rama and Krishna respectively, are held in reverence wherever Indian culture has left its mark; dance dramas based on these works, and on the epic known as the* Mahabharata, *are presented in ritual settings throughout Southeast Asia. The traveling dance troupe (above) performed dance dramas in Indian villages in the 1920s. At the Kumari-jatra festival in Kathmandu, Nepal (below), a young boy is Krishna, the Dark Lord, with his characteristic flute and blue face.*

in content, classical in form, popular in appeal.

Then, during the same period that the devadasi tradition was coming under attack, kathakali went through a crisis. By the 1920s changing economic conditions had made it difficult for aristocratic patrons to continue their support of kathakali troupes. And influenced by British culture, some educated Indians had come to scorn kathakali as a kind of "primitive dumb-show." The art might have died out altogether if not for the efforts of the Malayali poet Vallathol Narayana Menon. In 1930 he established the Kerala Kala Mandalam, an academy of the dramatic arts, to ensure that future generations would be able to see kathakali performed according to the high standards established in the previous centuries.

Students enter the academy at the age of eleven or twelve for a minimum stay of six years. Many apply; those who gain admission are judged to have a strong physique, a strong sense of rhythm, and sufficient dedication to endure the more rigorous parts of the curriculum—including a daily "massage" in which a teacher walks over the student's oiled body. This is designed to render the joints supple and to facilitate the turnout from the hips that is required for the proper performance of kathakali. The walking massage, like other aspects of the regimen, was borrowed from the local schools of martial arts; these schools teach a method of physical discipline and body control that has a recorded history of more than a thousand years in Kerala.

In contemporary Western societies, physical discipline is typically thought

of in terms of athletics; the training regimen of a ballet dancer is compared to that of an Olympic runner, swimmer, or skater. But in India, as in ancient Greece, physical discipline is seen as a prerequisite to mental and spiritual discipline. In Kerala, young men (and recently young women as well) learn the arts of offense and defense through a carefully graded system of exercises embedded in a moral and religious context. Instruction takes place in a gymnasium called a kalari. Each time they enter the kalari—a windowless rectangular building with an immaculately swept earthen floor—trainees salute its guardian deity by reverently touching the floor with the right hand and then raising it to the forehead. During training they learn to center all their actions and reactions in the lumbar region, which is seen as the real source of breath, voice, and physical

Students at the Kerala Kala Mandalam, in the southern Indian state of Kerala. One young boy is receiving his daily "massage," in which a teacher walks over the student's oiled body to render the joints supple and to facilitate the turnout from the hips that is required for the proper performance of kathakali. Other boys are practicing the part of Krishna, the warrior Arjuna's divine charioteer, as he reins in a team of horses. This is a celebrated episode of the Bhagavad Gita, *a long devotional poem that forms part of the* Mahabharata.

movement. In mock combat advanced students perform spectacular leaps in which they turn in midair and land in a split ready to parry an opponent's thrust.

Kathakali performers must bring a similar physical prowess to their enactment of stories from the Hindu epics. No other Indian dance form makes such demands on the body. Although costumes are oversized and makeup is elaborate, the performer's feet are bare, as in the kalari. All movements on stage emanate from the basic kathakali stance, in which the performer bends his knees, arches his back slightly, and balances on the outer edges of his feet (which are kept apart); this stance produces a state of alert tension, as in a person on the verge of action. Dance sequences call for acrobatic leaps, spiral turns, vigorous leg extensions. The stamina of kathakali performers is legendary; many continue onstage well into their sixties.

The kathakali performer is physically transformed into a larger-than-life character through a process of costuming and makeup that can take up to three hours. This extended process of transformation resembles a religious investiture. First, thirty yards of starched white cloth are tightly wound around the performer's loins; over this go an elaborately embroidered, bell-shaped gown and several layers of bulky jackets and sashes, topped by an enormous halo-like headdress, which the performer salutes with a prayer before placing on his head. Makeup is designed to heighten facial expressions and to distinguish the different types of characters. Gods, kings, and heroes always have green faces bordered with thick ridges of white rice paste and

eyes outlined in black. Evil and vicious characters always have red beards, bristly white mustaches, and ugly white knobs protruding from nose and forehead. Characters that are generally nasty and arrogant but show some redeeming qualities have partly green faces with red mustaches and slightly smaller nose and forehead knobs. Most male characters display three-inch-long silver fingernails on the left hand. Female characters, also played by men, wear ordinary dresses with simpler makeup.

The basic purpose of kathakali costuming and makeup is to create an otherworldly atmosphere, to distance the action onstage from everyday life. The plays tell of legendary times, when gods and heroes and demons clashed in mighty battles of Good and Evil that shook heaven and earth and the netherworld. The atmosphere is charged with superhuman energies. In the words of Appukutan Nair, director of the Margi Academy of Dance in Kerala: "Different rules apply. If a man with a green face went walking on the sides of his feet down your street, you would laugh at him. If a kathakali performer walked like a normal person during a performance, *that* would be funny." To enhance the otherworldly atmosphere—and to make his expressive eye movements easier to see—the performer reddens the whites of his eyes with the juice of a crushed seed. Just before he goes onstage, he pauses to look in a mirror; this is said to be the moment when his own personality subsides and the character comes to the surface.

Except for demoniacal types who are unable to control their emotions and who emit rude grunts or growls, katha-

kali performers make no sounds whatever on stage. They must convey the rasa of a scene (as established by the chanted poetry and the mood-setting drumming) entirely through facial expressions and body movements. As in bharata natyam, a verse may be chanted two, three, four, five, six times in a row. This gives the performer an opportunity to mime more than one level of meaning, to improvise on the scene described in the poetry, and to squeeze every last bit of drama out of the situation. The different character types express their natures through distinct movement styles: A hot-tempered demon stomps about like an overgrown child to demonstrate his unwillingness to listen to reason; the Lord Krishna moves with a masculine grace, even when he goes down on his knees in an effort to avert an impending war. Among kathakali performers and rasikas there is little discussion of the psychological state of a particular character; instead, attention is focused on the proper execution of gestures and movements needed to evoke rasa, which is the goal of the performance.

The sign language of hand gestures (mudras) in kathakali is even more elaborate than in bharata natyam. During their years of training students memorize specific mudras and practice them endlessly in front of mirrors and with each other. There are twenty-four primary mudras which, through combinations and variations and intricately detailed hand-dances, can convey over eight hundred recognizable meanings. Some are descriptive, some are symbolic, all vary depending on context. For example, one of the twenty-four primary mudras is a closed fist, said to have originated with Vishnu who used it to fight the demon Madhu. In depicting the lotus flower, a traditional symbol of beauty, the performer begins with two closed fists, pointing downward, the right crossed over the left; as the fists are slowly relaxed, the hands pivot and turn upward, with palms facing and close together, to signify a tightly curled lotus bud; then, ever so slowly, the hands begin to open as if the bud were spreading its petals. Throughout this pantomime the performer's eyes respond with delight to each stage of the flower's growth; when its petals are fully open, the performer's nostrils quiver slightly at the first faint scent of the flower's perfume.

Some scenes in kathakali plays turn on an extended sequence of full-body pantomime, such as the "peacock dance" from the play *Narakasura Vadham*. Narakasura is in a garden (the typical setting for love scenes) with his wife. In a line or two of dialogue (chanted by the onstage singers), Narakasura directs his wife's attention to the peacocks roaming about the garden; by their graceful movements, the verse says, you can tell that they too take pleasure in the beauty of this setting. At these words the actor begins to mime the "dance" of the birds as they preen their feathers, stretch, and strut about; when the dance ends, the performer slips effortlessly back into his characterization of Narakasura.

Kathakali is often performed today in conventional theaters, under the sponsorship of local rasikas who band together into dues-paying kathakali clubs. However, this form of dance drama is best seen in something closer to

its original setting, on a raised stage of packed earth just outside a small village temple in Kerala. The performance begins shortly after the sun goes down; in traditional fashion it will end with the sunrise. In the gathering darkness the sound of drumming and clashing cymbals is heard. Spectators begin to take their places before the rectangular stage, women and children squatting cross-legged on the ground, men sitting on folding chairs along the sides. There is no admission fee; the performers who traveled to the village by bus earlier in the day will be paid by the temple's entertainment committee, which has organized the event to celebrate an important festival on the religious calendar. A large metal lamp with an oil-fed wick is set up at the front of the stage. Once this would have provided the only light for the performance; now its flickering flame is supplemented by a battery of electric bulbs. Small children dash about excitedly.

The play will depict selected episodes from the *Mahabharata*. Most people in the audience, even the children who may have seen only the popular comic-book version of the epic, are familiar with the characters and events; some of the rasikas have seen this particular play many times before. The audience is not expected to pay rapt attention at every moment; during the nine-hour performance people eat, talk, take a nap, get up to stretch their legs. But everyone settles down again when the major scenes begin. In one of those scenes, the green-faced hero Bhima confronts the red-bearded Dushasana who has humiliated Bhima's wife. The main rasa of this scene is anger. Bhima dances his hunger

for revenge; Dushasana dances his defiance. When they meet in battle, the fighting takes the form of an energetic duet to a constant clatter of drums and crashing cymbals. Linked hand to hand, the combatants wheel about the stage, each propelling the other to new heights of rage. Inevitably, Good triumphs over Evil; with his mace Bhima knocks Dushasana to the ground. But now it is clear that Bhima's emotions have gotten out of control, a serious violation of the code of the warrior as expressed in the *Mahabharata*. Bending over his foe, the long fingernails of his left hand quivering with the passion of the moment, Bhima buries his face in Dushasana's torn belly, rips out his enemy's entrails, and drinks his blood. The deed completed, Bhima begins to return to his senses; the bloody entrails fall from his mouth as Lord Krishna enters. Suddenly aware of what he has done, Bhima falls on his face before Krishna to beg forgiveness. As he receives the lord's benediction, Bhima's entire manner changes; anger visibly drains from his body, to be replaced by the tender mood of pathos.

The entire scene encapsulates one of the great moral lessons of the *Mahabharata*: Without self-control a man is no better than a beast. To the rasikas in the audience, one of the transcendent experiences of the kathakali stage is the moment when the expression on Bhima's face changes, signaling a shift from the rasa of anger to the rasa of pathos under the influence of Lord Krishna. At such moments, kathakali fulfills its purpose as a stage where the workings of divinity are made manifest through the vehicle of the human body.

An Ottan Tullal performance outside a village
temple near Trichur, Kerala, October 1991.
This one-man show blends elements of kathakali
and even older dance dramas into a form of
popular entertainment.

Lankalakshmi (left) is a malevolent incarnation of the Hindu goddess Lakshmi, according to this kathakali actor from Kerala, India, who plays this role, although many devotees of the goddess might dispute the existence of such an alter ego. He has blackened his face with lamp-black and reddened his eyes with the juice of a seed to heighten his facial expressions.

Below, a kathakali performance by a traveling troupe from the Kerala Kala Mandalam. The play is The Dice Game, an episode from the Mahabharata in which a dispute over control of a kingdom leads to an epic battle between two sets of cousins, the Pandavas, seen here, and the Kauravas.

Chapter 3
Dance of the Realm

The professor is dancing. With a kind of dignified gusto, he leans into the music, the moonlight catching in his white hair, his bent knees taking up the strain as his sandaled feet palpate the ground and his bare arms carve almost visible waves in the dense air. He is a heavyset man who moves like an athlete. Wrapped around his waist and torso is a green, black, and gold-striped Asante robe, a long rectangle of cloth with one corner thrown over his left shoulder. When his fluid but vigorous body movements shake this corner loose, he flings it back over his shoulder without missing a beat; the gesture becomes part of the dance.

Professor Albert Mawere Opoku is seventy-six years old. He is dancing to the music of a small group of musicians in the garden behind the Hotel Georgia in Kumase, the second largest city in the west African nation of Ghana. Thirty years ago the professor founded Ghana's national dance ensemble. He has taught at universities in Ghana and

in the United States. For the last month he has been helping to organize a major festival of his people at the palace of the Asantehene, the elected king of the Asante (pronounced ah-Shan-ti). Now the professor is making eye contact with the group's lead drummer, a man who has been playing three drums more or less simultaneously. In response to the professor's glance the drummer picks up the pace, adding yet another layer to the intricate mix of percussive patterns that speak to dancers in a language understood by all those who participate in Asante culture. "You're looking good so far," the drumming seems to say, "now let's see what you can do with *this*." And the professor, his joy transparent, responds with his whole body.

During a break in the music Professor Opoku chats with the leader of the group, a musician and composer named Ko Nimo. The word is that tomorrow's festival will bring together more than fifty thousand Asante from all over Ghana to reaffirm their identity as a

people. Ko Nimo acknowledges "the prof" as his mentor, referring to him as "a library on fire" because he is one of the last of his generation with a comprehensive knowledge of Asante traditions. The professor, Ko Nimo says, comes from an Asante clan with close ties to the palace: "He knows who we are and what made us. He wants to make sure that all this outlives him."

One of the Asantehene's proudest titles is "master of the music and the drums," which is another way of saying "master of the dance," since drumming and dancing are all but synonymous to the Asante. Drums in Ghana come in all shapes and sizes and tonal variations, but the largest and most impressive, called fontomfrom drums, are the perquisites of chieftaincy. If, as the Asante say, "drums are what make a chief," the deep-toned fontomfrom is the chief of drums. Fontomfrom drums may be playable for more than a hundred years. Each is hollowed out from a single, carefully seasoned tree trunk and stands

about five feet tall with finely carved fluting all around like a Greek column. Stretched across one end is a thin slice of elephant ear whose tension is controlled by wires attached to seven wooden pegs. The drumsticks are cut from springy branches, with short tips that slant back at a forty-five-degree angle.

Fontomfrom drums are used for warrior or heroic dances. In the hands of accomplished drummers, they can be made to "talk." The Asante language is one of a family of west African languages that use pitch to distinguish meaning. By rhythmic and tonal mimicry the drummer can carry on an elaborate dialogue with the dancer, who may be a member of the Asantehene's entourage, a lesser chief who has come to pay homage to the Asantehene, or the Asantehene himself.

At one time, being a good dancer was one of the qualifications for election to the post of Asantehene. The king of the Asante is expected to dance before his people on certain occasions to display

his royal virtues and to honor his ancestors who are also the heroes of Asante history. In one dance, the fontomfrom beats out a challenge heard and understood by all: "Some men fight, some run away. Which kind of man are you?" The Asantehene responds with a choreographed display of strength and virility that says, "Try me and see!" He jumps in the air, hops on one foot then the other, shifts his weight from side to side, plants his left foot and pivots around it, stamps the ground. He extends his right arm in a sweeping gesture whose meaning is clear: "You are my people; I gather you all together." Then he clenches his right hand into a fist and brings it down on top of his left hand, which signifies "I sit on you, I am your chief." His movements, while energetic, are never hurried or jerky because, as the professor says, "a king is more majestic when he moves slowly, elegantly. It was the same at the court of Louis XIV."

For his most impressive entrances the Asantehene rides in a palanquin woven of wicker and carried by members of his court. But this does not hinder his dancing since in west Africa, as in most of the world, dance involves the whole body. Seated in his palanquin, the Asantehene dances to remind his people of the victories that he and his ancestors have won, beginning with the Asante war of independence against the kingdom of Denkyera in 1700. Holding a sword in his right hand and a musket in his left, he mimes an entire campaign in which the Asante, dividing their army into three columns, confused the Denkyera with deceptive maneuvers, feigning attacks on first one, then the other flank, before striking a decisive blow where the enemy was weakest. Staring first to the right, then to the left, the Asantehene rears back in the palanquin before thrusting his upper body forward and slashing out with his sword.

Dancing at court is not the Asantehene's responsibility alone. Chiefs at every level maintain ensembles of drummers and dancers to do honor to their own position and to pay homage to those higher up in the hierarchy. And theoretically, anyone can step out of the crowd and dance before the court. But critical standards are high; a dancer who fails to live up to them—by making an inappropriate hand gesture or by failing to bare his shoulders in respect or by thrusting the pelvis forward and backward in a lascivious manner instead of moving it decorously from side to side—may fall victim to "drum censorship." Suddenly, in midbeat, the drummers cease playing. In the awful silence, the inadequate dancer has no choice but to shrink back into the crowd and make

way for the next soul brave enough to try his or her best before the caretakers of Asante culture.

In the history of its people, the court of the Asantehene—like other royal courts around the world—has been a center of power, patronage, and pageantry. Wherever rulers have gained dominion over large territories and large numbers of people, communities of the talented and ambitious have sprung up to help them rule. These communities were typically organized in a pyramid of power, with the ruler in the royal palace at the top and his or her ministers, advisors, retainers, and hangers-on arrayed in more or less clearly defined ranks below. In one sense, all these courtiers enjoyed a life of privilege, abundance, and leisure; wealth was one index of a ruler's power, and life at court was often a lavish round of feasts, sports, and other pleasurable activities. But in another sense, a courtier was always on duty. In the days when a position at court was both a mark of royal favor and a badge of authority over the less fortunate, a courtier's clothes, speech, manners, and bearing attested to his or her status at all times. Indeed, virtually every event at court, each solemn ritual, each entertainment, was an occasion to demonstrate rank. On many of these occasions, dancing of some kind was central to the display of power. Dancing at courts everywhere tends to be deliberate, dignified, measured, hierarchical; training is required to do it properly, and, throughout history, public embarrassment (or worse) has awaited those who fail to meet the court's high standards.

Most of the courts that once deter-

mined the destinies of entire peoples have either vanished entirely or lost their hold on the levers of power. Some—like the Asantehene's court in Ghana, the royal courts of central Java, and the emperor's court in Japan—have survived the transition to other forms of government because the ideals of behavior embodied in their court rituals came to be viewed as emblems of a cultural, even a national, identity. In other cases, courtly ideals survived the demise of the court itself; this is what happened in Western Europe where the court dances of the kings of France evolved from an instrument of political control to become the basis of theatrical and social dancing in the West; long after the fall of the Bourbon dynasty, the legacy of elegant movement passed down from the ballrooms of Versailles can be seen on ballet stages throughout the world.

A thousand miles north of Kumase, at about the time the Asante were banding together to throw off the yoke of the Denkyera, a courtier at Versailles described the shattering embarrassment of a young man who had suffered the French equivalent of drum censorship: "This young man, who up to then had attended court little or not at all . . . had been asked if he danced well and had replied with a smugness that made everyone eager to find fault. They were satisfied. He lost his countenance at the first bow: He was out of step from the start. He tried to hide his mistake by drooping to one side and waving his arms: This proved even more ridiculous and prompted laughter which soon came in bursts and then turned to jeers

despite the respect owed the presence of the King, who could hardly keep from laughing himself. The following day, instead of fleeing or keeping silent, he claimed that the presence of the King had upset him, and promised to outdo himself at the ball to follow. . . . As soon as he began to dance at the second ball, everyone stood up pushing to see, and the jeering grew so loud that it led to clapping. Everyone, even the King, laughed heartily, and most of them explosively, in such a manner that I doubt whether anyone else ever suffered the like. After that, he disappeared, and did not show his face for a long time."

The year was 1692, the king was Louis XIV, the dance was the minuet, and the would-be courtier's failure was no minor contretemps. Louis had found a way to control the obstreperous nobility of France, by structuring his court

quite literally around the dance floor.

The use of dance as an instrument of political power in Europe had roots in the court spectacles of fifteenth-century Renaissance Italy. The newly invigorated study of classical literature provided mythical characters who were immediately recognizable to educated audiences and endlessly adaptable stories that could be recast into allegories with contemporary significance. The spectacles performed at the courts of Italian princes came to be called *balli* (from the Italian word for "dance," *ballare*). Like all such entertainments, the *balli* required enormous expenditures of time and money; the talents of painters, set designers, costumers, musicians, librettists, and dancing masters were brought together to produce a spectacle that might never be repeated after a single performance. The dancers were

Louis XIV may have started coming to his father's hunting lodge at Versailles in 1661, when he was twenty-three years old. The renovations that created the grand chateau we know today were begun in 1668, when Pierre Patel painted this bird's eye view in which the king's carriage, followed closely by the queen's, is seen arriving for a visit. At this time the chateau was still a modest country estate; it had about twenty rooms and a dormitory for men.

The Ballet Comique de la Reine *(1581)*
at the Louvre is considered to be the first court
ballet. It was choreographed by Balthasar de
Beaujoyeulx, an Italian violinist, composer,
and choreographer, who came to Paris with a
group of violinists about 1555, and made a
career of organizing fetes at the court. He
became a personal servant to Catherine de
Médicis.

courtiers whose participation in these
extravaganzas was a public display of
their own status as well as an acknowl-
edgment of their dependence on the
prince of the realm. To succeed at court,
a man of ambition had to be as accomplished in dancing as he was in riding,
fencing, and fine speech. The proper
bearing for a courtier, according to
Baldassare Castiglione, who wrote the
book on it (*Il Cortegiano*, 1528), was to
"preserve a certain dignity, albeit tem-
pered with a lithe and airy grace of
movement."

Like Renaissance music, painting,
and literature, dance evolved under the
stimulus of the new humanistic scholarship. Dance manuals with detailed
instructions on how to perform the
new, complex ballroom dances began to
appear as early as 1444. Some of the
postures that courtiers struck in the
court spectacles consciously imitated
models from classical sculpture. The
taste for elaborate court spectacles,
along with the know-how to produce
them, was brought to France by
Catherine de Médicis, daughter of the
pageant-loving Lorenzo II, duke of
Urbino. In 1533 she married the man
who was to rule France from 1547 to
1559 as Henry II; after his death she
remained a power behind the throne for
another thirty years during the reigns of
her three sons. It was an era of dynastic,
religious, and civil wars. Legitimacy was
in the eye of the beholder. No prince
with pretensions to greatness could
afford to maintain a less lavish court
than his rivals. In a competitive frenzy,
the royal houses of Europe were soon
emptying their treasuries to outdo each
other in the production of court specta-

cles, which in France were known as *ballets de cour*.

The spectacle that set the standard for all subsequent *ballets de cour* was the "Ballet Comique de la Reine," which was staged for a royal wedding at the Louvre on October 15, 1581, during the reign of Catherine's son Henry III. Grateful to be chosen for a part, courtiers rehearsed for as long as two weeks under the eye of the king's dancing master. Combining steps also used in the ballrooms of France and Italy, they worked their way through complex floor patterns that held symbolic meaning for knowledgeable spectators: for example, two equilateral triangles within a circle signified Supreme Power.

Alternating with these dances were interludes of music and songs, declaimed poetry, mime, acrobatics, and ingenious theatrical effects created by specially constructed mechanical devices. One memorable device was a three-tiered gold and silver fountain on wheels, lit by a hundred candles and spouting perfumed water, that carried the queen and eleven gorgeously costumed high-born ladies, representing naiads, around the dance floor. Later that same evening a courtier impersonating Mercury, messenger of the gods, descended from the ceiling in a mechanical "cloud" accompanied by a clap of thunder, followed in due course by Jupiter, king of the gods, mounted on an "eagle," to do honor to the monarch of France. Some ten thousand people of quality are said to have packed the Louvre's Great Hall to see this performance, which began at ten in the evening and lasted till half past two in the morning.

Until the second half of the seven-

teenth century little distinction was made in Europe between what we call theatrical and social dancing. By the age of two the future Louis XIII could already do "all sorts of dances to the music of a violin"; at four-and-a-half he donned a mask "to dance a ballet" for his father. The pressures of ruling did not dim Louis's enthusiasm for dance. After succeeding to the throne in 1610 the king undertook a number of roles, noble and comic, male and female, in *ballets de cour* that he himself helped write.

His son, the future Louis XIV, was similarly groomed to take his place in the center of the dance floor; gossips noted that the young Louis loved dancing so much that he spent more time at his dancing lessons than his grammar lessons. He was four years old when he succeeded his father as king in 1643; his widowed mother was regent, but for the next eighteen years the real power in the land was the prime minister, Cardinal Jules Mazarin, who also supervised the young king's education. In 1649 opposition to Mazarin's policies took a violent turn, the mob took to the streets, and the court, with the young king in disguise, fled Paris. Once the rebellion against the regime was suppressed, Mazarin orchestrated a court spectacle designed to impress all of Europe—but especially the restive nobility of France—with the pre-eminence of the young monarch whose name was soon to become synonymous with the "divine right" of kings. A medal minted at his birth had proclaimed him "Orbis Solis Gallici" ("The Risen Sun of Gaul"). Fourteen years later he appeared in "Le Ballet de la Nuit"

performed at court during Carnival season in February 1653. Among his roles, which he repeated six times in succeeding weeks, was Le Roi Soleil (The Sun King), around whom masked courtiers circled like so many planets revolving around the sun in the still controversial cosmology of the late Nicolaus Copernicus.

Of course, the young Louis was actually portraying Apollo, the Greek god who had passed into the allegorical conventions of Christian Europe. But the intent of the symbolism was lost on no one; to the end of his reign Louis XIV was apostrophized as the Sun King, and he lived his life as if the universe revolved around him. "In exercising a totally divine function here on earth," he wrote in his memoirs, "we must appear incapable of turmoils which could debase it."

What Louis did, in practice, was to enshrine himself as an object of worship, not just for the common people but also for the higher nobility who had long been accustomed to thinking of the king of France as no more than "first among equals" atop the feudal system. Louis built a number of elegant palaces where his world might do him homage, but the central temple of the Sun King cult was Versailles, which he constructed in a drained swamp eleven miles southwest of Paris, at a safe distance from the fickle mobs of the capital. A new city was created to house the twenty thousand people attached to the court. But anyone who was anyone fought for the privilege of living in the palace itself, which had apartments for a thousand titled gentlemen and ladies and some four thousand servants. And

Opposite: The fourteen-year-old Louis XIV as Le Roi Soleil (The Sun King) in Le Ballet de la Nuit, performed at court during Carnival season in February 1653. Although this was the role that came to symbolize his reign, he also danced other parts in court ballets, including a gypsy fortune teller, a village maid, and a monkey.

This page: The choreography of large groups need not be limited to dancers. Louis XIV's "Grande Carrousel" (left) celebrated the birth of his son, the Dauphin, in 1662, and gave the Place du Carrousel in Paris its name. The festivities, seen here in a contemporary painting, involved hundreds of horsemen riding in carefully designed formations. The Tuileries Palace, in the background, was destroyed by fire in 1871. Court spectacles that are direct descendants of the Grande Carrousel are still found in Europe. An example is this military tattoo in front of Edinburgh Castle (below). In the United States, holiday parades and pageants like the half-time festivities at football games carry forward the tradition of mass choreography established in the Renaissance courts of Europe.

In the branle (left), which opened all formal court balls before the eighteenth century, couples joined a linked line in order of social rank, with those of highest rank coming first. In the danses à deux that followed, one couple danced at a time before the critical eyes of the assembled guests. This engraving, by Israel Silvestre in the second half of the seventeenth century, shows a branle at the Louvre.

The allemande (below left), a sixteenth-century court dance probably originating in Switzerland and Germany, was characterized by a figure in which the gentleman turned the lady under his arm, and vice versa. This is an illustration from Simon Guillame's dancing manual of 1770. The allemande step familiar from American square dancing may have been suggested by this dance.

Jean Ballon (1676–1739; below right) began choreographing the ballets of Louis XIV from about 1700. Before then, he had been a dancer and, since 1691, a member of the Paris Opéra Ballet. It was Ballon who choreographed the ballet in which Marie Camargo made her debut in 1726.

A wedding reception at the French court for the sister-in-law of Henry III, in a painting of c. 1582 by an unknown artist. The couple in the rear to the left is dancing a lively volta, in which the man lifts the woman off the floor. This was a favorite dance of Queen Elizabeth I.

what did the courtiers lucky enough to be granted such an apartment actually do within the palace grounds? They danced—both figuratively and literally—in attendance on the king.

By force of personality, by ruthless operation of the machinery of power, by clever manipulation of a system of rewards and punishments, Louis drew the lords of the realm to Versailles and kept them there as hostages to ambition, forcing them to spend fortunes they did not have to keep up with the extravagant ways of the court. The actual work of government was in the hands of ministers chosen from the bourgeoisie. When the king went to war, which was often enough, the job of the aristocrats was to fight; during interludes of peace they fought for positions close to the king's person. To hold a candle for the monarch as he climbed into the royal bed was a much-desired plum; to be evicted from an apartment in Versailles by the king's order was a devastating blow; to be invited to dance at a ball in the king's presence was an honor that might launch a fledgling career. Louis himself first danced in public at age seven; he was a portly forty-one when he

took his last recorded turn around a ballroom floor.

While the king was in residence at Versailles and no war claimed his attention, he hosted as many as two or three balls a week. The protocol governing these social occasions was as rigid as the laws governing the planetary orbits that Johannes Kepler had worked out at the beginning of the century. The balls invariably opened with a double-file dance known as a branle, in which the men lined up behind the king, the women lined up behind the queen, and the company circled the floor one couple after another. The order was so strictly by rank that anyone observing the branle knew immediately who stood above whom at court.

The branle was followed by the first of the *danses à deux* or couple dances. These were also hierarchical and pitilessly judgmental, since only one couple danced at a time while everyone else watched from chairs or from temporary bleachers erected around the walls of the ballroom. First the king and queen danced together, then the queen danced with the highest ranking gentleman; that worthy then danced with the high-

est ranking lady, and so on down the social ladder.

In Louis's youth, the dance that followed the branle was the solemn and dignified courante, his favorite, whose varied figures he practiced several hours a day and, according to an early eighteenth-century dancing master, "danced . . . better than any member of his Court, and with a quite unusual grace." The machine of fashion that was the French court required regular infusions of novelty; as many as four new dances were introduced each year. By the 1690s a new genre of formation dances known as contredanses (possibly adapted from English models) were popular. Resembling the reels and square dances of today in form, they allowed two, three, or more couples to take the floor at the same time.

Meanwhile, the minuet, a name apparently derived from the French for "small step," replaced the courante as the first couple dance after the branle. The minuet was a flexible *danse à deux* in which facing partners went through a kind of ritualized courtship—approaching, passing, retreating in S or Z figures, presenting their hands to each other at

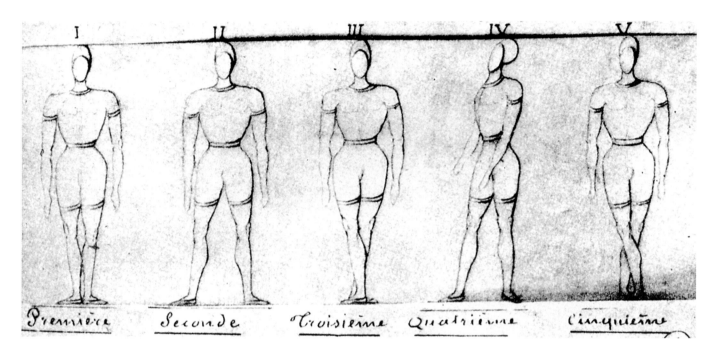

Première   Seconde   Troisième   Quatrième   Cinquième

arm's length while exchanging discreetly flirtatious glances. To dance a proper minuet required schooling at the hands of a dancing master, who typically also taught fencing and etiquette to would-be courtiers. It was important to maintain a "noble carriage," to keep the torso upright as a still center of gravity while movements of the head, forearms, wrists, fingers, legs, and feet flowed into each other without awkward breaks. Even the "reverences," or bows, which the lady and gentleman exchanged to begin a dance were highly stylized. As time went on, the minuet grew slower, more sedate, and more mannered until it became (for eighteenth-century commentators like Voltaire) the very model of the effete amusements of a terminally decadent court.

When the young Louis XIV danced the role of the Sun King in 1653, he was expressing the pretensions of the House of Bourbon to absolute power. The reality, as we have seen, was something else again. Cardinal Richelieu, prime minister to Louis XIII and Mazarin's mentor, had spent nearly twenty years bolstering the royal authority. But neither civil wars nor administrative reforms could strip the nobility of its feudal prerogatives until Louis XIV built Versailles. By detaining the peers of the realm in an elegant playpen-cum-prison, the king cut them off from their natural bases of power in the provinces. These strong-willed men, quick to take insult and ever ready to avenge their honor at sword point, became in effect wards of the state. It is not clear that Louis set out to emasculate an entire class of titled troublemakers by ensuring their attendance at an endless round of court fetes and hunts and balls and ballets. But it is on record that he believed "people love spectacles; by these we

hold their minds and hearts more often perhaps than by rewards or benefits."

It was Louis XIV who drew the first clear line between amateur and professional dancers. In 1661 he established a Royal Academy of Dance to systematize the rules governing the kind of virtuoso dancing that he admired and that he lamented "few among those of our Court" were able to do. Pierre Beauchamps, the king's own dancing master, stressed the five basic positions of the feet on which classical ballet technique rests. (The precise placement of the feet has varied over the years, but the fundamentals of the technique are traceable to Louis's academy.) To make it easier to train new dancers and teach new ballets, an entire hierarchy of steps and sequences was worked out and assigned names like balancé and entrechat that have survived to this day (although the movements they refer to may have

changed). The opening of the Paris
Opéra in 1671 gave the newly codified
court dance a public showcase under
the direction of Beauchamps and Jean
Baptiste Lully, an inspired music master
(and celebrated dancer) whose librettists
included Corneille, Racine, and Molière.

Even as the French aristocracy began
to lose its purpose and vitality as a
class, the ideal of the manly courtier
was transferred to the professional stage
in the figure of the *danseur noble*, who
typically portrayed heroes or gods out of
Greek and Roman mythology. In amateur productions at court, female roles
had often been played by young boys; in
1681 professional female dancers made
their debut at the Opéra and were an
immediate hit, a ballerina named La-
Fontaine being acclaimed "queen of the
dance" in her first season.

The political system centered on
Versailles survived the death of Louis

XIV in 1712, but without his commanding presence the center could not hold.
Having reduced the nobility to the
status of supernumeraries, the French
monarchy was exposed to the anger and
frustration of the middle and lower
classes whose taxes supported the structure of the state. The Revolution of
1789 swept away much of the old order.
Never again would a European monarch's person be accorded semidivine
status. Late Bourbon manners, dress,
and diction, once considered the touchstone of Europe's rulers, became proverbial in the next century for ineffectual foppery. Yet the ideal of the courtier,
as expressed on the dance floors of Louis
XIV's France, endured as a model of
noble deportment in painting, sculpture, opera, and ballet—a model from
which succeeding generations in post-
Revolutionary Europe drew both
pleasure and inspiration.

*Louis XIV attends the theater at Versailles.
The production is* Les Fêtes de l'Amour et
de Bacchus *(1678). Here, one can see the
origin of the relationship between performer
and audience that came to characterize
classical ballet. The king's position is central
and unobstructed, and the action is oriented
toward that central viewing point.*

It was always an exciting and dangerous place. The great officers of the kingdom, even the King himself, were subject to rapid changes of fortune. Their patronage was a way to power and wealth, attracting supplicants and followers, but patterns of alliance were ever-shifting, and a prosperous group might quickly find itself in difficulties. Around the King and court, men maneuvered, calculated, spied on each other and were spied upon. Alliances by marriage, trade or favor were made and broken. A large number of supporters showed a man's power; they also cost him money."

These words might have been written about the Versailles of Louis XIV and his successors. In fact, they describe Kumase, the capital of the Asante, as it was in its heyday in the early years of the nineteenth century.

A century earlier, a confederacy of small states calling themselves Asante gained control of the region around Kumase. The survival of the Asante as a distinct people is due not only to the legendary prowess of their armies—whose emblem was the many-quilled porcupine—but also to their genius for political organization. One of the founders of the confederacy was a priest named Anokye, who along with the first Asantehene, Osei Tutu, constructed a strong but flexible polity that combined elements of centralized empire, feudalism, and representative democracy. The Asante ruled their confederacy without benefit of an indigenous written language (although they staffed their treasury with literate Muslims). They made a fetish of cleanliness; European travelers commented on the broad, well-swept streets of their villages and towns. The official currency of the land was gold dust. Expanding by war or by diplomacy backed by the threat of war, the Asante established dominance over most of the area of modern Ghana; only the encroachment of the better-armed British in the late nineteenth century ended their power.

Above: Reception for the British Embassy at Kumase, 1817, *from T. E. Bowdich, Mission from Cape Coast Castle to Ashantee (London, 1819). Bowdich wrote that upon entering the city, "more than a hundred bands burst at once on our arrival, with the peculiar air of their several chiefs."*

Opposite: Asantehene Kwaku Dua II receiving a British official at his palace, 1884 (left). Each chief has his own umbrella; and, as at Versailles, the closer a courtier is to the king, the more status he has. As is the tradition in many royal courts, the ruler is seated on a raised dais. The Asantehene's palace, constructed of wood and clay, was the largest building, or rather group of interconnected buildings, in Kumase. It was not only the primary residence of the king and many of his wives and servants, but part of it also served as the forum in which the council of the realm decided important matters. At right, the great courtyard, c. 1890.

The umbrellas used to shade the Asantehene and senior chiefs and signal their appearance in public are among the most striking articles of Asante regalia. Their purpose is not only to keep the chief physically cool, but to signify his spiritual coolness, or dwo, as well. The umbrella-bearer makes the umbrella "dance" to the music of the drums and horns in the chief's entourage. At a Big Adae in Kumase in 1991, the Asantehene Otumfuo Opoku Ware II (right) and a group of senior chiefs (below) are shaded by umbrellas.

A chief and his court (left) arrive at the assembly ground in Kumase for a Big Adae. Each chief wears his most ornate robes and gold jewelry (below right). Almost as conspicuous as the umbrellas among Asanti regalia are linguist staffs with elaborate gold finials (below left), which are carried as a badge of office by chiefs' spokesmen among the Akan peoples. These elaborate gold staff tops are of relatively recent development, and among the Asante were not used until 1924, but the custom of providing messengers—that is, translators or linguists—with such staffs to vouchsafe their authority can be traced back to the silver-topped canes that European merchants brought to the Gold Coast in the seventeenth century.

When the British got their first glimpse of Kumase in 1817, they were impressed by its generous layout, and by the golden treasures of the Asantehene and his court: "The sun was reflected, with a glare scarcely more supportable than the heat, from the massy gold ornaments, which glistened in every direction." Modern Ghana, which achieved independence in 1957, took its name from an ancient west African kingdom that was first mentioned in the eighth century by Arab travelers who knew it as "the land of gold"; they described the king of Ghana holding court literally weighed down with gold necklaces and bracelets; the hair of his attendants was "plaited with gold," and even his watchdogs wore collars of "gold and silver."

Most of the land under Asante control at the beginning of the nineteenth century was tropical rain forest, so dense that sunlight penetrated to the forest floor only where the Asante had cleared farms and living spaces and the narrow footpaths that connected their smaller villages to the larger towns. They built their capital Kumase on a hill overlooking a river. In the early nineteenth century it supported a population of twenty thousand. Of its twenty-seven major streets, the largest was half a mile long, and fifty to a hundred yards wide, and lined with clay-and-wattle buildings whose outer walls were sealed with white plaster. These were maintained by leading chiefs and court functionaries who conducted business in airy rooms entered directly from the street. The most impressive buildings, some of them two stories high, belonged to the palace of the Asantehene. Formal audiences and council meetings took place in a Great Court, which was connected to other courts and buildings by passageways and galleries. As at Versailles, numerous attendants, court officials, royal consorts, and servants had apartments in the palace complex.

The unity of the Asante nation was symbolized by a Golden Stool, carved in wood and encased in sheets of gold, which, according to tradition, descended from heaven in 1700 onto the knees of Osei Tutu, who became the first Asantehene. No one, not even an Asantehene, has ever sat on the Golden Stool, which enshrines the spirit of the Asante people. Although he combined in his person the powers of head of state, head priest, and commander in chief, the Asantehene was never an absolute monarch. Any man who belonged to the royal clan by descent on his mother's side was a candidate for succession. When the office fell vacant, a new Asantehene was named by a council of subordinate chiefs, who were themselves named to their positions by councils of lesser chiefs, who in turn owed their authority to lesser councils on down to the village level. On each level a place of honor was reserved for a woman known as the "queen mother," who represented the women of her community, played an important role in nominating new chiefs, and often served as a power behind the chief, in the manner of a Catherine de Médicis. If the performance of any chief, including the Asantehene, was found wanting, he could be removed from office by the vote of those who had elected him.

On certain occasions fixed by the Asante calendar the entire hierarchy of chiefs, subchiefs, elders, and court functionaries gathered in Kumase at the palace of the Asantehene. They came with their retinues, resplendent in their best robes and finest gold jewelry, to ratify the ties of political and religious authority that held the community together—a web of mutual obligations made manifest through the exchange of gifts and services, ritualized flights of rhetoric, and the display of objects of symbolic value like the Golden Stool, but most of all through the dynamic symbolism of dance. The festival that the current Asantehene, Otumfuo Opoku Ware II, has declared to be a Big Adae (Ritual Day) continues this centuries-old court ceremony; it takes place at the hilltop palace complex in the center of Kumase, a modern city with a population of four hundred thousand.

A century after the British subdued the Asante (they sacked Kumase twice, in 1874 and 1896), the court of the Asantehene remains a force to be reckoned with. The national government in Accra, Ghana's capital on the Atlantic coast a hundred miles south of Kumase, recognizes the authority of the traditional institution of chieftaincy in certain legal and cultural matters. But while the Asante region is the country's most prosperous, comparatively few Asante have been welcomed into politics on the national level. As a result, the last few years have seen a renewed interest in chieftaincy among the Asante, a development that Professor Opoku views with some skepticism: "Successful Asante have money and few outlets for their ambitions. So they want to be chiefs even if they know nothing about our traditions. At the same time the court has money problems, so you get people buying a stool, buying their way in. Not only do these people not know how to dance, they don't even know enough to appreciate good dancing. Without knowledgeable patrons who understand the culture, how can the best survive? Happily, there are still a few chiefs with close ties to the people who take their political, cultural, and spiritual responsibilities seriously." The professor also worries that the dances that helped to define Asante identity for nearly three centuries are being forgotten by a younger generation that is more interested in imitating the moves of Michael Jackson: "I don't mind telling you, we are in deep trouble. The British couldn't stop us from dancing, but the TV might."

The present Asantehene, a British-trained lawyer who was taught the requisite dances after his elevation, has invited all Asante to join him in observing the Big Adae; and he has called upon all Asante chiefs to reaffirm in person their allegiance to the Golden Stool. The public display of the stool and other regalia is designed to reassure the assembled nation that their hallowed treasures are in good hands.

The public part of the ceremonies will be held adjacent to the palace complex on the assembly ground, a fan-shaped expanse of red-brown earth with two low rostrums at one end: a circle of whitewashed concrete for the Asantehene and a smaller concrete square for the queen mother. Other than these and a few red and yellow canvas canopies along the periphery to keep the sun off visiting dignitaries, the area is without decoration. No flags, no banners, no posters, no triumphal arches, no frills of any kind. The only markings on the bare earth are parallel lines of white lime laid down around the perimeter at right angles to the outer edge, as if to define so many parking spaces. Between each pair of lines a small wooden sign on a stake bears the name of the particular chief whose entourage will soon occupy that space: "Amantinehene," "Agogohene," "Adansihene," "Kenyasehene 2," "Essumejahene," "Acherensuahene." Each of these men will sit surrounded by his own entourage, including musicians and dancers. But when the moment comes to pay homage to the Asantehene, each will know exactly where in the hierarchy he fits, with lesser chiefs going first and the most powerful and prestigious going last—the exact opposite of the progression at Versailles, where the king danced first and others followed in decreasing degree of status.

According to the professor, every courtier has a responsibility to pass along the traditional songs and dances to the next generation. The Asantehene's head drummer, a man of eighty-two who carries the entire court repertoire in his head, had a son who showed promise on the drums but ended up as an accountant in Chicago; the head drummer is now training his two youngest boys, twelve-year-old twins. Even before they learn the dances of their people, the professor says, Asante children are told stories that make plain the central role that dancing plays in their world: "There's the one about a greedy chief who thinks only of himself and who is cautioned that his stool has a taboo against dancing. So he says, 'Don't worry, I understand, no dancing.' His sons, who have been so neglected by their father that they are starving, dig a tunnel under the palace, and one day while the chief is taking a bath, they start drumming; he can't help himself, he starts moving to the beat and someone says, 'What are you doing?' and he says, 'Oh, the water was so cold I was just shivering.' And the person telling the story mimics the drum with his voice and acts out the chief's movements, and the children learn to imitate him. The whole idea of a chief who can't dance is so silly, it makes them laugh."

There is a quality of life known and prized throughout tropical Africa that the Asante call dwo. This can be translated as "spiritual coolness" or "inner peace" or just plain "cool." It does not refer to air or body temperature, although a metaphoric connection to the large-leaved shade trees that dominate the main streets of even the smallest Asante villages can hardly be accidental. The professor remembers gathering under such a shade tree as a child with a group of friends to learn new dances. His grandniece Esther Boateng, who at the age of five danced for Queen Elizabeth II when that monarch visited Ghana in the 1950s, says that when you dance at court (or for that matter anywhere else) the important thing is to be relaxed, to stay flexible, to remain cool. "The opposite of cool is nervous," she says. "When you start dancing and you feel cool, you feel like the whole world belongs to you."

The Buddhist monument of Borobudur (c. 800) in Central Java manifests the cosmic mountain in mandala plan. The massive structure has nine levels, or terraces, with bas-reliefs lining the galleries that surround each level. The images relate the story of the Buddha's life and the lives of his disciples; some depict dance postures that suggest the astonishing continuity of dance forms in Indonesia.

Java, the fourth largest island in the island nation of Indonesia, is one of the world's most densely populated areas, with over 1500 persons per square mile. Six hundred and twenty miles long and 125 miles across at its widest point, its population of over a hundred million shares the mountainous land with over fifty active volcanoes, seventeen of which have erupted in recent years. Mt. Merapi near Yogyakarta in central Java erupts every five years or so, causing death and destruction, but also coating the all-important rice fields with fertile volcanic ash. The devastating eruption of Krakatoa, which blew up in the strait between Java and Sumatra in 1883, was heard two thousand miles away. Earthquakes and tidal waves are all-too frequent occurrences. What these disasters have in common is that they are recurrent, yet, unlike seasonal storms and floods, there is no way to predict when they will occur next. Perhaps it is not surprising that people who live at such close quarters with natural violence should cherish a court aesthetic that is rooted in the cultivation of a profound tranquillity.

Following a dynastic split in the eighteenth century, two competing royal courts were established in central Java fifty miles apart, one at Yogyakarta and one at Surakarta. Each court has evolved its own versions of the classic Javanese court dance, the sublimely tranquil bedoyo. This dance commemorates a three-hundred-year-old tradition according to which a Muslim ruler of the state of Mataram, the ancestor of both Javanese royal courts, was ritually married to the goddess known as the Queen of the Southern Sea, who taught

Bedoyo performance (above) in the main pendopo of the sultan's palace at Yogyakarta, Central Java. This court dance commemorates the ritual marriage of the sultan's ancestor to the deity known as the Queen of the Southern Sea. The identically dressed dancers, who usually move in unison, represent aspects of a single person, concept, or theme. Top, the sultan's palace guard.

him this dance. Javanese traditions linking royalty and divinity go back even further, to the god-kings of the ninth and tenth centuries who developed a unique blend of Buddhism and Hinduism and built the island's two greatest monuments, neighboring temple complexes at Borobudur (Buddhist) and Prambanan (dedicated to the Hindu deity Shiva.) A thirteenth-century ruler of Java was extolled by a court poet as an incarnation of *both* Shiva and Buddha. After adopting Islam the rulers of Mataram were provided with genealogies linking them to all previous gods as well as to the line of Mohammed.

As a danced ritual attributed to an indigenous ocean deity, performed at a Muslim court and incorporating Hindu myths with overtones of Buddhist quietism, bedoyo appears to be a typical product of the Javanese aptitude for combining disparate, even opposing, elements into a harmonious whole. While some bedoyos are considered more sacred than others, all are performed to proclaim the glory of the ruler, to affirm the court's ancestral ties to a divine source of power, and to embody clear teachings about the Javanese way of life—how to compose your inner life, how to present yourself to others.

Everything about bedoyo suggests the public projection of the disciplined self. It is danced by nine identically dressed women whose synchronized movements and indistinguishable facial expressions signify that they are not nine individuals but rather nine different aspects of one individual or of some abstract idea or theme. Nine is considered a "perfect" number. Depending on the commentator, the dancers are said to represent

the nine orifices of the human body or the nine human desires or nine constellations or the nine ceremonial gates of the palace.

A focal point of every Javanese palace is a permanent structure built especially for court dance and spectacle. So important is the enactment of rituals of legitimacy in this part of the world that one scholar has referred to the traditional nations of southeast Asia as "theater-states." The courtiers of Louis XIV would have had no trouble understanding the connection between statecraft and stagecraft. In Yogyakarta court dances are performed in an open-sided rectangular pavilion—called a pendopo—with a high peaked roof supported by carved black and gold pillars; similar structures can be found in bas-relief on the walls of ancient Javanese temples, along with carved figures of dancers whose graceful postures are similar to those seen in today's court dancers.

As with all court dance, preparations for bedoyo are elaborate and time-consuming; it takes several hours just to dress the dancers in the costume of a royal bride. Each dancer wears a velvet bodice embroidered in silver-gilt thread, a scarf secured around the waist by a gold belt, silver-gilt or gilded leather armlets in the shape of dragons on the upper arms, a gold or silver-gilt breast plaque set with tiny diamonds, and, tightly wound around the legs, a length of diagonally striped batik whose free end falls to the floor and passes between the ankles like a train. The dancer's bare feet move soundlessly over the marble tile floor to the fluid sounds of a court gamelan—a predominantly per-

cussive orchestra that includes a variety of tuned gongs, cymbals, xylophone-like instruments, a drum, a flute, and a two-stringed lute.

The essence of bedoyo is balance or equilibrium, which is a quality the Javanese prize highly. Much of the time the nine dancers move in unison. To initiate each slow-motion step, a dancer arches her instep and curls her toes upward as she lifts one foot just perceptibly off the ground. Knees turned out and slightly bent, she replaces this foot on the ground heel first and shifts her weight forward to the toe in a continuous movement that seems to invest the everyday act of walking with aesthetic significance. As in ballet, the basic steps are highly stylized and are referred to by name; in the *gedruck*, for example, the dancer balances on one foot while scooping her batik train back out of her way with her other heel and then tapping her toe on the floor behind the supporting foot.

Like the geometric figures of Louis XIV's *ballets de cour*, the stylized movements and smoothly flowing floor patterns of bedoyo have symbolic significance: for example, the transition from asymmetrical to symmetrical grouping (three rows of three dancers each) represents a change of inner state—from a conflict between flesh and spirit to a reconciliation of all aspects of the human being. At other times the dancers may depict scenes from the history of the dynasty or from the classic Hindu epics, the *Mahabharata* and the *Ramayana,* which have never lost their currency in Muslim Java. But even when two of the dancers separate from the other seven to enact a love duet be-

Opposite: *Pendopos at the early-seventeenth-century royal palace of Kasephuan in Cirebon, West Java. In Indonesia, the pendopo is used in architectural settings ranging from modest homes to elegant palaces, as well as in Hindu temples and Islamic mosques. At Yogyakarta and Surakarta the main pendopos, built in the early nineteenth century, are much larger and more elaborate than the ones shown here.*

tween the ruler and the Queen of the Southern Sea, bedoyo dancers betray no emotion; they remain exemplars of Javanese demeanor—calm, inwardly focused, deliberate, modest, restrained.

In other court entertainments, such as the wayang wong spectacles in which both men and women perform, two radically different styles of male dancing are found: one employs abrupt, forceful, expansive movements to portray robust warrior types and ogres; the other, marked by smooth, flowing, refined gestures, is reserved for thoughtful heroes like Arjuna and Rama, protagonists of the classic Hindu epics. While unrefined characters may fight on the side of Good against Evil, it is significant that the most revered heroes are invariably refined types. In bedoyo, all hint of

The Water Palace at Yogyakarta was originally built by Sultan Hamengku Buwono I in 1758 and once had underwater corridors leading from women's bathing pools to a partly underwater mosque; the water motif recalls the dynastic connection to the locally revered sea goddess.

91

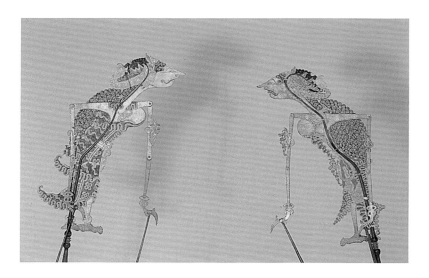

No account of the performing arts patronized by the royal courts of Java would be complete without a mention of wayang kulit, or shadow play. The puppets (left), made of buffalo parchment, are manipulated by a lone puppeteer so that an overhead lamp throws their lacy shadows on a white cotton screen. The stories come from Indic, mostly Hindu, sources as well as indigenous legends. As can be seen from these two nineteenth-century examples from Cirebon, West Java, the stylized form of the puppets reveals a kinship to both bedoyo and wayang wong.

The elaborate dance drama called wayang wong (below and opposite) was first described in the eighteenth century; during its "golden age" in the early decades of this century performances at court could last up to four days, with long scenes of ritualized combat based on episodes from the Mahabharata. The influence of the shadow puppets is strong: the sultan is considered the puppeteer of the performance, and some sultans actually collaborated with their court literati in writing the stories, composing the music and choreographing the strictly disciplined movements. These are performances at the Yogyakarta palace.

East of Java in the Indonesian archipelago is the far smaller
island of Bali, which, unlike its larger neighbors, never forsook
Hinduism for Islam. Bali is known for its astonishing variety
of dance forms, some of which overlap with Javanese dances.
The destruction of the royal courts of Bali in the early twentieth
century led to the dispersal of court dancers into the villages
and countryside. Here Balinese wayang wong dancers, c. 1930,
perform a scene from the Ramayana.

conflict has been submerged in an elegant style of movement that once served as a standard against which the bearing and manners of Javanese nobility might be measured.

From the early nineteenth century, when Dutch commercial interests consolidated their political and military hold on Java, the two royal courts redoubled their competition in the only arena allowed to them: the arena of culture. The language and etiquette of the courts became ever more refined; beautiful pools and gardens (symbols of heavenly bliss in Islam and emblems of the rulers' association with the Queen of the Southern Sea) were constructed; and the custody and ritual display of the royal heirlooms, considered to have great spiritual power, became even more important. These heirlooms, or pusaka, which had been divided between the two courts when the dynasty split, range from gold crowns to gold-leafed umbrellas to ceremonial daggers to classic court dances like the bedoyo.

There is a deep-running paradox in Javanese culture concerning the nature of power. On the one hand, power is connected to specific possessions; in a battle over succession in the late seventeenth century, a contender for the throne whose father had lost both his army and his treasury nevertheless triumphed because he possessed certain pusaka. On the other hand, true (i.e., spiritual) power is held to be invisible, all-pervasive: if you need to flaunt it, you must not have it. In striking a balance between these two opposing attitudes, the Javanese courts competed as patrons of what was held to be the best of ancient Javanese culture. With

material resources unmatched elsewhere in their society, and with the leisure to study the traditional arts and embellish them, the courts of central Java focused attention on a history and a spiritual heritage that all Javanese could look to with pride.

Unlike the court dances of the Asante and Bourbon France, the dances of the Javanese courts were not originally open to outsiders, even those associated with the court. Until 1918 the bedoyo at Yogyakarta was performed only by female relatives of the sultan; it was even forbidden to teach classic dance outside the palace walls. In fact, other than invited guests, few Javanese ever saw the court dances. Their performance was considered a sacred trust, necessary to the well-being of the people and the continuity of the dynasty, but out-of-bounds for all but the highest dignitaries; even the costumes and seating arrangements of the spectators were hierarchically coded. Those of lowest rank wore black and sat nearest to the palace kitchen; those of highest rank wore white and sat nearest to the ruler—whose throne was elevated so that his head was higher than any spectator's or performer's.

Commoners have never been allowed to view or learn the court dances of Surakarta. But during the reign of Sultan Hamengku Buwono VIII (1921–39) the court dances and spectacles of Yogyakarta were opened to the people. In a momentous step analogous to Louis XIV's founding of his Royal Academy of Dance, a school was created outside the Yogyanese court where anyone could study what had once been the exclusive province of the nobility. The goals were

to invigorate court arts by exposing them to new influences; to raise the standards of popular dance forms by bringing them into contact with highly developed court forms; and to reinforce an historically rooted Javanese consciousness against the modernizing pressures of Western colonialism. Hundreds of performers were recruited from the domain of Yogyakarta to learn the dances and the movement styles associated with such spectacles as wayang wong. The most accomplished of these performers became full-time servants of the court; and many thousands of Javanese got their first look at the centuries-old treasures of their culture that the court of Yogyakarta had maintained.

The next sultan, Hamengku Buwono IX (1940–88), was a leader in the fight for independence against the Dutch. The struggle brought together leaders from Java, Sumatra, Bali, and the other islands that now make up the nation of Indonesia. But it was by no means certain in 1945, when independence was proclaimed, that the different islands, with their distinctive peoples, histories, and cultures, would continue to seek a collective future. Although the sultan was a lover of dance and a choreographer himself, he worried that local traditions like the court dances at Yogyakarta would weaken his people's allegiance to the central government, so he suspended all performances at the palace. Deprived of their principal patron, dances like the bedoyo might have died out except for the efforts of former palace servants who now taught outside the court.

The present sultan, Hamengku Buwono X, has revived performances at

This page: The classically trained Javanese court dancer Sardono Kusumo has created a modern dance inspired by temple bas-reliefs. In these photographs, one can see dancers covered with mud, which, when dried, gives them the look of carved, stone figures. The relief figures—monkeys from the Ramayana—come alive and dance with contemporary bedoyo dancers.

Opposite: As in Java, traditional dance in Bali has spawned contemporary interpretations that adapt elements of ancient Balinese culture. Here, a Balinese dancer personifies the oldest of Balinese divinities, Sanghyang Tjintiya, with fire-energy issuing from the junctures of his limbs. The dancer, in a meditative posture, stands in the middle of a lotus pond whose flower is a symbol of the cosmic womb. This deity is the Balinese counterpart of the Indian god Shiva Nataraja.

the palace and given new life to Javanese dance in general. He believes that classic dance, especially bedoyo, is an indispensable asset of his court. In his view, such dances represent a "tool of legitimacy" because they express values—a code of behavior and a spiritual heritage—that "continue to color the life and customs of Javanese society today." Taking the dances out of the palace has inevitably led to changes. Some have been shortened and simplified to appeal to modern tastes; the performing arts in general, and dance in particular, have become major tourist attractions in Java. Innovative choreographers have mixed stylistic elements from different regions (and even combined them with Western steps and music) to create new hybrids that excite some audiences while dismaying traditionalists like Romo Sas, choreographer and dance master to the Yogyakarta court.

Romo Sas, who considers himself first and foremost a palace servant, deplores the new emphasis on crowd-pleasing physical virtuosity in dance, at the expense of traditional content that the Javanese see as both practical and spiritual: "Dance is tending to become a form of entertainment, when it should be a means of education. For example, anyone who learns how to dance automatically knows how to sit the *sila* way, decorously, legs crossed and fingers crossed Javanese style. The etiquette of the dance tells us how to sit, how to walk, how to kneel, how to get along with other people, how to adapt to our situation in life."

*Bugaku performed by a Shintō priest
on the terrace of the Itsukushima-jinja
shrine, Miyajima Island, Japan.*

Tadamaro Ono is also a palace servant. His job is to play gagaku ("elegant music") at the Imperial Court of Japan. The austere, stately dances performed to this music are called bugaku. Members of Ono's family have been performing at the emperor's behest for close to twelve hundred years. His is the thirty-ninth generation in an unbroken line of court musicians.

Gagaku and bugaku represent the world's oldest continuing tradition of court music and dance. For centuries, these performances were a closely held secret of the palace, heard and seen only by members of the aristocracy, government officials, and official guests. Since the end of the Second World War performances have been open to the public in a theater on the palace grounds. Even for the Japanese, the glacially paced gagaku and bugaku are an acquired taste. Yet more than fifteen thousand people apply for admission each year. Since the performance hall holds only seven hundred and there are only about thirty performances a year, a lottery is held to determine the lucky ticket winners. The losers can console themselves with a compact disk of the music, sales of which have been rising. In Ono's words, "there is a boom, something like nostalgia," for gagaku and bugaku.

Outsiders who try to understand modern Japan are struck by the apparent contradiction between the Japanese appetite for the new (whether in electronics, economics, or politics) and their concern with preserving the past. This contradiction is itself nothing new. Except for a three-hundred-year period of isolation from the world that ended in 1868, the Japanese have characteristi-

cally adopted new ideas without letting go of tradition. Often, today's novelty becomes tomorrow's tradition and takes an honored place in the ever-expanding gallery of Japanese culture. A classic example is the way Japan enthusiastically adopted Buddhism, imported some thirteen hundred years ago from the Asian mainland, while keeping up the rites of Shintō, the indigenous religion. Many Japanese families maintain two household shrines, one Shintō and one Buddhist. At the Imperial Court, the same impulse can be seen in the survival of gagaku and bugaku, which bonded native traditions and exotic foreign novelties into something fundamentally Japanese.

The word Shintō can be translated as "continuity." Shintō has no founder and no set scriptures, no myth of creation-out-of-nothing, no apocalyptic world-ending. From the first Japanese historical records in the fourth century, Shintō is already there, channeling the energies of its people toward the worship of myriad divinities, ranging from tutelary spirits and deified ancestors to personalized forces of nature and abstract concepts such as purity and truth. The first Japanese emperors known to history were both political and religious leaders; and through centuries of political upheaval in which the Imperial Court was often little more than a pawn of powerful warlords, the religious role of the emperor has remained crucial to the self-image of the Japanese.

The imperial family claims descent from Amaterasu, the sun goddess, whose favor is necessary to a successful rice harvest. Disgusted by the boorish behavior of her brother, Amaterasu shut

herself up in a cave and the world fell into darkness. To lure her out, the goddess Ame-no-uzume danced half-nude on an overturned tub before the assembled divinities; her antics so amused the gods that their laughter awakened the curiosity of the sun goddess, who peeped out of the cave and was drawn back into the world. Ame-no-uzume became the patron of music and dance in Japan—the Land of the Rising Sun—and dance as "entertainment for the gods" became a part of Shintō ceremonies. But in the seventh century, when Buddhist dance-drama processions and gorgeously costumed banquet entertainments were introduced from Korea and China, the Imperial Court of Japan quickly embraced the new imports.

Over the centuries these were adapted to Japanese taste and combined with surviving Shintō rituals to make up a suite of spectator dances, known as bugaku, for performance at court functions and religious festivals. What is most remarkable is not the survival of the native Shintō elements but the preservation, in something approaching their original form, of the imported dances and music. The original Chinese and Korean forms have long since died out on the mainland, where they are known only through literary and pictorial sources. The Japanese, however, saved what they borrowed, as if to proclaim their pride in recognizing quality no matter what its origin.

In the Imperial Palace theater, gagaku and bugaku are performed on a square platform (measuring just under six yards per side) covered in green brocade and resting on a slightly larger

This page: Thirty-four figures perform Bugaku dances across an oversize screen (above) by Hanabusa Itchō, a Japanese painter who worked in Edo in the early eighteenth century. Bugaku screens were fashionable in both temples and at court since at least the fifteenth century, although no early examples survive. This is one of a pair that was probably commissioned by a rich merchant or military ruler eager to acquire the traditional trappings of the aristocracy. A hanging drum like the one visible in the screen can be seen right, behind a bugaku dancer performing in the theater in the Imperial Palace, Tokyo.

Opposite: Bugaku dancer at the Iwashimizu-hachimangū shrine, near Kyōto, Japan.

square of black-lacquered wood. A red railing runs all around the larger square. During dance performances the orchestra sits in an alcove behind the stage, between two huge drums. Some bugaku dances depict legendary battles, others enact encounters with divine personages or mythical beasts like the phoenix; one famous set-piece shows two dragons frolicking. The splendid costumes include long flowing robes of solid blue or deep crimson, gold-brocade leggings lined with scarlet silk, elaborately embroidered breastplates, black-lacquered "stovepipe" hats or golden helmets, ceremonial swords, lances, and shields, and spectacular face masks: the two dragons, for example, frolic in hairy blue masks with sharp silver fangs. But whatever the subject matter, the dancers move almost imperceptibly through simple geometric floor patterns punctuated by long pauses in which the performers strike significant poses. Although most pieces are choreographed for two to eight dancers, they are actually a series of "solos" in which a single character may be represented by four identically dressed dancers who repeat identical movements in the four cardinal directions.

Repetition is as basic to the bugaku aesthetic as is the deliberately slow tempo. One Japanese commentator has compared the performing of bugaku to the process of making color woodblock prints: "When color printing is being done, the platen revolves several times putting on colors: first yellow, then blue, then red, and in the end black. The same idea is applied in the performance, repeating the same melody and the same patterns several times . . . the element of

sound and the element of movement are piled up on top of each other and create intensity."

The musical accompaniment also works on the principle of achieving maximal effect with minimal material. Musicians are expected to play their instruments—drums, lutes, flutes, harps, reeds and pipes—as if they were themselves dancers, although they usually remain seated. For example, the player of the biwa, a short-necked, four-stringed lute, will lift his arms just so as he runs his ivory plectrum across the silk strings to produce both a pleasing sound and a pleasing gesture. And the pounder of the large drum that sets the tempo will shift his weight from heel to toe as he strikes the drumhead, making a grand gesture out of what might otherwise be a metronome-like operation. A centuries-old instruction manual gives some idea of the refinement of movement and posture that gagaku and bugaku strive for. In certain pieces, dancers are urged to emulate "tinted leaves blown about in a storm on a mountain in autumn," while in other pieces they should resemble "a willow waving in the spring breeze."

The unchanging nature of gagaku and bugaku over the centuries manifests the role that the Imperial Court has played in Japanese history. The court retainers who developed these arts had time to shape and reshape each element of each piece until they were satisfied that something of lasting beauty had been created. At the brilliant eleventh century court described in *The Tale of Genji* (recognized as the world's first novel), emperors and nobles not only attended performances but took an active part in

them. But from the end of the twelfth to the middle of the nineteenth century the Imperial Court at Kyōto functioned solely as a symbol of Japanese unity while real power was wielded elsewhere by military leaders known as Shoguns. Although some Shogunate courts sponsored music and dance performances of their own, the survival of the Imperial Court depended on the perception that the soul of Japan resided in Kyōto. The regular production of gagaku and bugaku, with due attention to all the nuances, was essential to this perception, even if only a handful of people witnessed the performances. The Japanese not only revere the past, they feel a sense of duty to keep it alive.

During the Onin Rebellion (1467–77) Kyōto itself was sacked, and court musicians and dancers scattered to take refuge in shrines and monasteries. Some stayed away even after order was restored, and to this day their descendants perform gagaku and bugaku at important shrines throughout Japan. When the Tokugawa Shogunate consolidated its power in the early seventeenth century, the third Shogun organized a gagaku and bugaku festival in Kyōto in 1626 to impress the people and the emperor with the power of the new rulers of Japan. In 1661 the Shogunate placed the production of court music and dance on a firm financial footing and ordered a competitive examination every three years to maintain a pool of talented performers.

Having preserved their Imperial Court in a kind of suspended animation for so long, the Japanese turned to Kyōto when the Shogunate lost power in the middle of the nineteenth century.

The precipitating event was the failure of government forces to defend the country against the incursions of Europeans. Rallying under the slogan "Revere the Emperor! Drive Out the Barbarians!" a broad political alliance restored direct imperial rule. In 1868 the emperor's residence was moved from Kyōto to the Shogunate capital of Edo, which was renamed Tokyo.

In the rush of modernization that followed, the Gagaku Department of the Imperial Household Agency was reorganized, and performers were required to learn Western music, including polkas and military marches. The emperor also ordered his musicians to compose Western-style music with traditional melodies; one of these compositions evolved into the Japanese national anthem.

Japan's defeat in the Second World War nearly brought about the end of gagaku and bugaku. There was agitation (which continues in some quarters) to abandon the performances as an expensive anachronism. But the Japanese reverence for tradition won out, and in 1955 the court musicians and dancers were declared Important Intangible Government Properties, more commonly known as "living national treasures." A six-week tour of the United States in 1959 brought worldwide acclaim and renewed interest in Japan itself.

Today, Tadamaro Ono sees no more reason for gagaku and bugaku to die out than for the Japanese to turn their backs on the tea ceremony or the Nō theater which also, in his view, reflect "the Japanese national character." Court music and dance continue to be passed down from generation to generation of palace servants by a time-honored process of oral instruction. The families who have been entrusted with the tradition choose the most talented boys from each generation to be trained; their training in all the details of gagaku and bugaku may begin as early as the age of five. Ono himself was skeptical about the efficacy of this early selection when his turn came to judge the younger members of the family. "However," he says, "it must be done to keep the tradition, and our family, alive."

All morning long, under the increasingly forceful African sun, the chiefs arrive at the assembly ground outside the Asantehene's palace. They arrive by bus or car or on foot from nearby houses where they have spent the night. Each chief is wearing his most ornate robes and gold jewelry, and each comes in procession with as many attendants as his rank and purse warrant. The attendants range from small boys and girls to women in high heels and white-haired men in traditional black-leather Asante sandals. In their everyday lives they are farmers, teachers, students, office workers, homemakers. Today they carry chairs and heft brightly colored umbrellas and large fringed canopies, and beat drums and strike clapperless metal bells with sticks, and dance and sing as their chief leads them toward their assigned area, where they arrange themselves in a U-shaped formation that constitutes a temporary court.

Soon there are some fifty of these courts, side by side, around the perimeter of the assembly ground. At the bend of each U, shaded by an array of fancy umbrellas held up by young attendants, sits the chief flanked by his most important counselors. The others in the entourage take their places along both arms of the U, with a row of younger children sitting on the ground and one or two rows of older people on stools or folding chairs behind them. Everyone faces the narrow aisle between the arms of the U and everyone sits as close together as possible, which reduces the distance between the people on the far ends and their chief, whom everyone addresses with the honorific "Nana."

The drummers and other musicians stand in a knot behind one arm of the U and lay down interweaving rhythms; a few people at a time—a man and a woman, two men, three women—get to their feet, slip off their sandals or high heels as a sign of respect to the chief, and begin dancing in the space within the U. They bend their knees and elbows, turn slowly clockwise in place with their eyes closed, take small steps that keep contact with the ground, shift their weight gracefully from hip to hip, and move in a counterclockwise direction between the open end of the U and the closed end where the chief sits, while making arm-and-hand gestures that proclaim: "I depend on you" and "Wherever I go, I belong to this land" and "We are one people." From time to time, the chief stands up and dances down the aisle toward the musicians, whose efforts he rewards with a handful of paper money while the rest of his entourage claps and cheers. If a chief is derelict in his duty to his musicians, a drummer may beat out a complaint: "Nana, I have been drumming all morning, I need a drink."

Royal drums (left) in the entranceway to the Asantehene's palace, c.1890. The skulls and bones decorating the drums are of defeated enemies. Prior to the British subjugation of the Asante in the late nineteenth century, war was one of the most important activities of the state, as it was for Louis XIV. Below, Asante dancers (on the left a queen mother) on the grounds of the Asantehene's palace, 1991. Behind the dancers are the fontomfrom drums of the Asantehene.

Asante dancers (above) in Kumase dressed in red during the mourning period for a recently deceased chief, 1972. Dancing plays a significant role in funerals among the Asante. Left, the Asantehene's head drummer in white, then in his early eighties, dances on the grounds of the Asantehene's palace, 1991.

Adults and children alike practice dance moves at the Big Adae in Kumase.

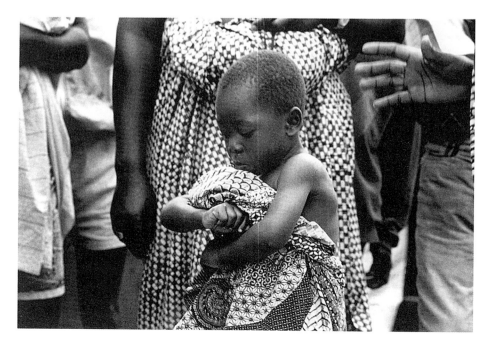

At first it may appear that each little court is an island of dance and music apart from all the others. But as the day progresses, a surprising pattern emerges: the entire assembly area, which holds more than fifty thousand people, has become one huge dance floor. Processions of lesser chiefs (accompanied by their musicians and dancers) wind through the packed crowds to pay respects to their superiors in the hierarchy; when two processions encounter each other, their heralds shout "*Agoh! Agoh!*" ("Make way!") and the attendants who hold the largest and most colorful umbrellas over the most important chiefs twirl them like pinwheels and flap them up and down in a kind of dance within a dance. The sound of drumming comes from all directions. Only when the Asantehene finally makes his appearance in his palanquin, in a grand procession accompanied by all the court regalia, do the events of the day come into focus. Significantly, the place of honor at the head of the procession goes not to the Asantehene himself but to the Golden Stool, the symbol of the nation, which is held aloft by its own bearer and shaded by several umbrellas and its own fringed canopy. Once the Asantehene has taken his seat on his rostrum, the exchange of visits between lesser and greater chiefs—and the sharing of dance and music that is an essential part of Asante life—resumes.

Professor Opoku is sitting in the dining room of his hotel, sipping a cold beer and looking back over the day. Despite his apprehensions about the future of Asante traditions, he is not at all displeased with what he saw. One moment especially stays in his mind. A young man was dancing a very expressive adowa—a dance named after the graceful movements of the pigmy antelope—before the queen mother and her court. Seeing how well he danced, the queen mother got up to join him. Immediately, the young man began dancing in a properly respectful, subordinate position. With her hand gestures the queen mother said to him: "Brother, support me, and let's do it well." And the young man linked his two index fingers in front of him, like two links in a chain, to indicate: "We are together, we cannot be separated, we are one people." Then came the moment that the professor relished. When sweat broke out on the queen mother's face, one of her women attendants took a cloth and wiped the queen mother's face while she danced. "And what was really so beautiful," the professor says, "was that the way she did it, it too became a part of the dance."

Courts come into existence as instruments of political, military, spiritual, and cultural authority. Their primary purpose is to manifest power. While this may be accomplished in the short run by brute force, long-term survival depends on the ability of a court to reflect the needs and aspirations of the population at large. By providing a secure home for those who look after the society's spiritual and cultural well-being, a court may outlive its military and political power. In its administrative structure and in the content of its performances, court dance typically embodies the hierarchical organization of the court itself. Court dances, like other court arts from painting to architecture, tend to be conservative in the literal sense; they conserve attitudes about life that were deemed essential to the society in the past. But depending on the attitude of the court, they can also change in response to major changes in society.

Courts and court dances are expensive, and ultimately it is the people who pay the bills. Where court forms, like ballet and bedoyo, are encouraged to migrate outside the court, new participants, spectators, and patrons become involved. Schools and academies, museums, orchestral societies, public grant-giving agencies assume the burden of support that was once the monopoly of the court. Ballet might have died with the Bourbon dynasty if Louis XIV had not entrusted its future to his Royal Academy of Dance in 1661, and if the ballets offered to the public had not found an enthusiastic audience among the middle and upper classes of eighteenth-century France. The subsequent development of ballet into an art of worldwide appeal raises the question of whether other court forms may follow a similar course. In Yogyakarta, the establishment of a dance academy outside the court has let loose creative energies whose impact on the classic court dances cannot be predicted. Bugaku has appeared on Japanese television and toured the world, but its protected status as a "national treasure" would seem to restrict opportunities for further development. The court of the Asantehene continues to provide a focus for the self-image of the Asante people; adaptations of court dances figure prominently in the programs of Ghana's National Dance Company, and a community of Asante who live in New York City has organized around an elected chief who takes his place proudly in the hierarchy that culminates in the court of the Asantehene in Kumase.

Whether or not courts and their dances survive would seem to depend on how successful they are in holding up a mirror to their society. The power of dance to communicate the past glories of a community—and by so doing to bind that community closer together in the present—is eloquently expressed in the words of Professor Opoku: "All our public occasions end in dance. When you hear the drums, it sweetens the inside of your head, as we say in the Asante language, like sugar, and you become aware that you belong to a great people."

Chapter 4
Social Dance

Social dancing socializes. This may sound like a tautology, but it points to a powerful mechanism of social control that is rarely acknowledged; we only become aware of how much our social dances reflect the values of our society when we come into contact with a society whose dances differ greatly from our own. For most people, social dancing begins in pleasure; if they must dance to please the powers that be or to earn a living or to avoid ill consequences of one sort of another, it's not social dancing. Of course, people sometimes feel pressure to dance in ways that are otherwise associated with pleasure; social dancing can serve many functions in a society. The point is, even when people get up and dance for their own pleasure, what they do and whom they do it with is of vital interest to the society at large. To see why, we have only to look at the social occasions on which people dance. These occasions often have to do with rites of passage; for example, in the Middle East, people dance at circumcisions; in

Africa, they dance at funerals; in Puerto Rico, they dance at baptisms; and virtually everyone dances at weddings. There are also rites of passage that are not tied to a particular time and place: whenever and wherever young people seek each other out for companionship, music and dancing are almost always part of the scene.

Few societies pass up the chance to monitor and regulate activities such as these, which bear directly on the perpetuation of the group. New generations must be nurtured and educated along socially approved lines; and dance, which displays the body in public, is one of the channels of communication used to pass along important social skills from one generation to the next. Through dance, young people can be taught how men and women behave in their society; through dance, they can practice gender-specific behaviors and attitudes. Dance also provides an arena where people can negotiate challenges to group values posed by minorities or a

new generation or behaviors imported from other societies. And all this can be accomplished not through threats or coercion but in the name of pleasure.

The people of Rarotonga, an island in the South Pacific twenty-one hundred miles northeast of New Zealand, take great pleasure in dancing. They also take their dancing seriously. They dance on all social occasions and on their major holidays, like Constitution Day (August 4). The constitution in question is New Zealand's. Previously a territory of New Zealand, Rarotonga and the thirteen smaller islands that make up the group known as the Cook Islands became self-governing in 1965. The population of Rarotonga is ten thousand; the native language is Maori, but everyone learns English in school.

Portuguese explorers were the first Europeans to visit these islands, at the beginning of the seventeenth century, but not until Captain James Cook, the English navigator, made three separate trips between 1773 and 1777 did the island culture come under pressure from outside influences. This pressure grew severe after Protestant missionaries (sent out by the London Missionary Society) began arriving in 1823. As elsewhere in the Pacific, the missionaries were deeply disturbed by what they saw as the indecent dances of the natives. They were hesitant to describe these dances in so many words, but if the movements at all resembled what today's Cook Islanders call "traditional" dance, the focus was on the lower part of the body: side-to-side hip-swinging by the women and vigorous knee-flapping by the men. Some sources also indicate that, as in Tahiti, dancing could lead directly to copulation. To the missionaries this was sufficient evidence that Satan ruled here unopposed. (The abundance of god-images with prominent phalluses did nothing to allay their suspicions.) The missionaries' attempts to convert the populace to Christianity were remarkably successful, but their campaign to discourage traditional dancing was not. Like many other Polynesians, the Cook Islanders were more willing to give up their fertility deities than their pelvic-centered dance.

Sir Thomas Davis, known throughout the islands as Papa Tom, is a former space scientist who returned to Rarotonga from the United States in 1975 and served as prime minister for nine years. In the 1930s he had been one of the first islanders to go off-island for an education. When he took up duties on Rarotonga as a medical officer in 1945, he found that the New Zealand authorities had banned all native dancing in favor of what he refers to as "the cheek to cheek and the breast to breast and the belly to belly and the thigh to thigh." Papa Tom, who had competed with the best dancers in the Cooks as a young man, led a protest that reversed the ban and revived the traditional dance style.

In traditional Cook Island dancing, which is performed by highly trained teams, men and women never touch

Votive figures like this one (left), representing the god Te Rongo from the island of Rarotonga, discomforted missionaries. One missionary sent such a sculpture back to London with an apologetic note regarding this "object of veneration to the deluded Rarotongans."

Below, daily class at the Avarua School on Rarotonga. The occasion is a dress rehearsal for a trip to New Zealand, which is why the boys are wearing grass skirts. Normally, the boys wear shorts and T-shirts and the girls wear muumuus.

each other. They line up in alternating rows, by gender, and execute choreographed sequences of body movements and hand gestures in unison. Successful choreographers gain great prestige in the community. In the dances called drum dances, which are thought to go back to training exercises for warriors, the men take the lead; in the so-called action or story-telling dances, the women are often featured. The men's sequences tend to be vigorous and athletic, the women's smooth and graceful. All team dancing is directed toward an audience: the teams perform for some large social unit, such as the extended family or the assembled community or, in recent years, a group of paying tourists. But even when Cook Islanders dance one-on-one at parties, men and women avoid body contact; they may come very close, in a teasing display of gender-specific movements, but good dancers take pride in their ability to fit their bodies together in matching curves without actually touching.

Papa Tom believes that the primary function of Cook Island dancing is the same as dancing everywhere: "It's the world's way of letting boy meet girl." But the emphasis on dancing in orderly rows separated by gender, rather than couple by couple, also expresses something basic to Cook Island culture: "Here, the nuclear family has absolutely no importance. The extended family is everything. Without the backing of an extended family, you are left out of everything." Team dancing contributes to the islanders' sense of belonging to a large, cohesive social group. Through carefully coordinated movements and gestures, the dancers draw out "hidden" meanings in the lyrics of songs that tell familiar stories or express commonly shared emotions, often about love:

At the touch of your loving hands
I love it so much.
You're just like a Queen
Your beautiful body
You're such a beautiful Queen
Your beautiful body
O turn your eyes to me
O your soft and loving hands . . .
You're such a beautiful Queen
Your beautiful body
O I love it so much . . .

Throughout Polynesia, the impact of Christian missionaries on dances and dance attire was strong. The effect of missionary pressure is obvious in the clothes worn by the hula dancers (below) in Hawaii, c.1875. By 1910, as the ceremony at Waikiki commemorating an event in the reign of King Kamehameha I, bottom, suggests, the hula was becoming a symbol of national identity in Hawaii.

Instruction in this kind of dancing is built into the school curriculum; regular classes run as long as two hours a day. Along with teamwork and the proper movements for each gender—women swing their hips but don't flap their knees, men flap their knees but don't swing their hips—school children learn the fine points that distinguish Cook Island dancing from other Polynesian styles. For example, no matter how vigorously a Cook Island woman swings her hips from side to side, her pelvis should never move in a circular fashion and her shoulders should remain motionless. Cook Islanders are known throughout the Pacific as fine dancers. Among their rivals in this respect are the people of Tahiti, where the women rotate their hips in a full circle. Cook Islanders refer to this rotatory motion as "the washing machine dance."

While formal classes are necessary to train dance teams, no one has to teach Cook Island youngsters the rules and customs that govern one-on-one social dancing. These they pick up by observing their elders at parties, where gender-specific movements are important but so are changing attitudes about sex and the sexes in what was once a polygynous, male-dominated society.

Women were among the first converts to Christianity in the Cook Islands. The new religion offered women an alternative to a religious-political system that limited their freedom in ways both minor (they were forbidden to eat certain foods or be seen in certain places) and fundamental (in a land-based economy, they were forbidden to own land). The high chiefs and priests enforced the laws of tabu, which prescribed death for many infractions. Obedience by men as well as women was ensured by fear: the survival of society was thought to hinge on adherence to the sacred laws. The arrival of the Europeans cast doubts on the sanctity of this system; here were people who, ignorant of the islanders' gods and tabus, not only survived but prospered.

Over the last quarter century, the traditional division of labor in the Cook Islands—between men who farm and fish, and women who keep house and care for children—has given way to an economy in which the majority of women on Rarotonga hold salaried jobs and more women than men are pursuing university-level education. A woman can now inherit land. But men retain most levers of economic and political power; and when it comes to gender roles, many men still profess belief in a double standard, which defines house-keeping as the exclusive responsibility of the woman (even when she brings home more money than her husband) and encourages men (but not women) to pursue sexual encounters before marriage and to "run around" after marriage.

Even active feminists who are working to extend women's rights on the job and in the home see no problem in teaching their children gender-specific dance movements. Poppy Apera, a health education officer in the islands, puts it this way: "Cook Island men maintain their masculinity by dancing the way a man should dance, and the women maintain their femininity by dancing the way a woman should dance here in the Cook Islands." In team dancing, she points out, "there are certain times when the man leads and the women have to follow, or the woman leads and the men have to follow." But informal social occasions are something else again. At parties women typically get up and ask men to dance. And no one leads. "No way," Apera says. "When it's just socializing, I'll do my own thing. I never want any man to lead me in my dancing."

The importance of dance in defining a Cook Islander's identity is something both men and women can agree on. John Jonassen, a well-known composer of songs, says that the origin of the distinction between knee-flapping for men and hip-swinging for women is unclear. He does not think that it heightens sexual excitement. But as the father of three daughters and a son, he would not want his children learning the dance movements appropriate to the opposite sex: "I'd like my son to pick up the techniques of male dancing. . . . I'd like him to dance as a boy and be seen in the minds of the public as a boy. So as part of growing up, I would probably tell him off if I saw him swinging his hips, because that's how girls dance. Boys don't dance that way."

Halfway around the world, in the Moroccan city of Fez, the rules governing social dance convey different messages about the way men and women should interact. The population of Morocco reflects a history of invasion and assimilation that is characteristic of North Africa in general. Living side by side are descendants of the Arabs who brought Islam from its Middle Eastern homeland after the Prophet's death in 632; descendants of the indigenous Berbers who adopted both Islam and the Arabic language soon after the Arab incursions; remnants of a once flourishing Jewish community; the largest French presence in North Africa; Spaniards and other Europeans.

Among Moroccan Muslims, encounters between the sexes are traditionally regulated by laws and customs that trace their authority to the Koran, which conservative Muslims take to be the literal word of God. In fact, local practices, which may predate the arrival of Islam, have played an important role in determining when, where, and how people dance. No text in the Koran explicitly condemns or endorses dancing, although religious authorities have penned a great deal of commentary on both sides of the issue. Some minority sects, like the so-called Whirling Dervishes, move in ways designed to bring the worshiper into communion with God, but these movements are not usually referred to as "dance." In general, dancing has no place in the devotional practices of observant Muslims. But in Morocco, as in all Islamic countries, many communities maintain vigorous dance traditions—from all-male "combat dances" to all-female wedding dances—outside the boundaries of worship. Since the Koran is mute on the subject, attitudes toward dance have been largely shaped by attitudes toward gender embedded in the local culture, which itself reflects Arabic and Islamic influences.

The Koran gives men authority over women and enjoins women not to display themselves before men other than blood relations. At the same time the Koran spells out the rights of women (even slaves) in a detailed way that was

The Mawlawi fraternity of Dervishes (left) in Konya, Turkey, gave music an important place in religious ceremonies. Their whirling ceremony is one of the few forms of danced worship in the Islamic world. The dance involves complex choreography, and revolves around the sheikh, or leader of the congregation, in the middle of the room. This fraternity was suppressed in 1925, but an annual festival is held with government approval, and other groups in Turkey and elsewhere continue to incorporate ecstatic dancing into their worship.

Perhaps because dancing in Arab countries tends to be segregated by gender, there is an undercurrent of male dancing that parodies the social dancing of women. The male dancers (below) impersonating women in Luxor, Egypt, are performing in a café while the onlookers clap in time. Such dancing is considered slightly disreputable, but it requires skill and practice.

The French Romantic painter Eugène Delacroix (1799–1863) traveled to Morocco in 1832. While there, he visited a Jewish wedding where a female performer entertained the guests in the dance style indigenous to the country. Jewish Wedding in Morocco *was painted about seven years later.*

unusual for its time. Islamic scholars cite the relative freedom that women enjoyed in the society of Mohammed's day: they took an active part in public affairs, even engaging in religious debates with men. Only as Islam expanded into the larger Mediterranean world and came into contact with other faiths and cultures did the role of women grow more circumscribed, especially in cities where the streets were filled with strangers. Here, public life was reserved for men; women were obliged to concentrate all their energies on home and family, which is to say on the tasks of reproduction and nurturing.

In contrast to the deeply ascetic strain in Christianity, however, orthodox Islam has always celebrated the sexual nature of men and women; it regards the sexual act as a God-given joy as well as a procreative necessity, and holds each partner responsible for the other's pleasure and fulfillment. This acceptance of the body as a source of pleasure is not far from the traditional Polynesian view. But whereas Polynesian

society conspires to bring the sexes together through dance, Islam has insisted on a strict separation of men and women in many parts of the Muslim world. In essence, women were considered dangerous to the social order because men were thought to be vulnerable to female charms. There is an Arabic word, *fitna*, that refers to the loss of control an unwary man may experience in the presence of an attractive woman. If physical attraction leads to sexual activity outside the approved channel of marriage, the men who are legally responsible for the woman's behavior—her father, her husband, her brothers—will be dishonored in the eyes of their community. One way for these male guardians to avoid disgrace is to keep their women hidden from the eyes of any man who is not a member of the extended family. This is the rationale behind the face-concealing veil, the various types of garments that conceal the entire body, and, more drastically, the secluded women's quarters known as the harem. As for dance, the Islamic view of sexuality

The vast majority of Yemenis are members of tribes, and for Yemeni men, to be able to perform the barᶜa (below) is synonymous with belonging to a tribe. While not a combat dance, the barᶜa requires at least a dagger, and often a rifle, to be danced properly, and the way the dagger is wielded varies from tribe to tribe. The dance embodies tribal values of valor and cooperation and is danced at weddings, important tribal occasions, and on religious holidays. In the 1980s, the barᶜa became a symbol of Yemen as a nation.

has found expression in two related dance traditions in Morocco, each of which acknowledges, in its own way, the power of the female body and society's need to keep it under control.

For pious Muslims, the male-female couple dancing that originated in the West and spread to many other cultures around the world is not an option— at least not in public. But alternatives exist, especially for women. While some of the devout avoid dancing altogether, they are the exceptions. Even in a city like Fez, which is famous as a center of religious studies, it is perfectly acceptable for Muslim women to dance at all-female parties and celebrations.

At such a gathering, a married woman may get up and dance before her peers to the music of hired female musicians or to recordings of popular Arabic songs. She may have arrived at the party in a traditional outer garment that covered her entire body. But among her friends she will take off this garment to reveal a stylish silk dress, gold bangles on each wrist, high-heeled shoes, and a shawl tied around her hips. This is her dancing outfit. As she dances, her upper torso shimmies from side to side while she rotates her hips in a series of circles that seem to radiate outward from her pelvis and up the trunk of her body. Most of the time she keeps her eyes demurely downcast, but once or twice a smile plays across her lips as she glances up at the circle of onlookers, who comment openly on her physical attractiveness and skill. When one dancer sits down, another stands up and tries to outdo the first in a frank exhibition of the female body that is no less sensual for being addressed to an all-female

audience. Through the movements of the dance, each woman demonstrates— even boasts about—her ability to fulfill the traditional role of wife and mother that society has assigned to her, using body language that might be paraphrased as follows: "I am beautiful and sexually appealing; therefore I am secure in my husband's affection and protection."

At wedding celebrations, unmarried young women may perform similar dances before family members and invited guests, including married couples and unmarried young men and their mothers who are on the lookout for prospective daughters-in-law. Among the qualities that enhance a young woman's matrimonial potential is the ability to dance well.

There is no masculine equivalent to the dance that Muslim women practice among themselves. In the countryside, following traditions that may be older than Islam itself, men in many Muslim countries take part in dances that emphasize athletic prowess and often employ warlike props such as swords, daggers, and rifles. But in the cities, dance for Muslim men is more of a spectator sport. At parties in private homes or in public rooms hired for the purpose or in hotel nightclubs, groups of men gather to watch female entertainers sing and dance; in form the dancing of these professionals closely resembles the spirited movements of the amateurs at all-female parties and celebrations. Despite the fact that this dance is indissolubly associated with women, some

male spectators will get up and dance along briefly with the entertainers. These men undulate their shoulders and hips in what looks like a self-mocking parody of traditional gender roles, combined with a sheer delight in rhythmic physical movement.

The tradition of the dancing girl in the Mediterranean world is certainly older than Islam. Precursors can be found in Egyptian tomb paintings from the days of the pharaohs. The dancers of Cadiz, a Roman colony on the Iberian peninsula in the first century A.D., were noted for a vigorous dance in which they sank down "with quivering thighs to the floor." In A.D. 527 a former dancing girl married the Emperor Justinian and became Empress Theodora, co-ruler of the Eastern Roman Empire. Dancing girls were a fixture of Persian courts before and after the arrival of Islam; and when Muslims from central Asia estab-

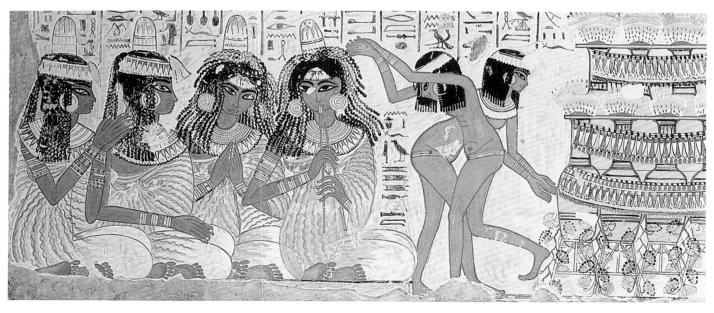

When Muslims from central Asia established the Mughal Empire in northern India, they brought with them a taste for dancing girls. This Mughal miniature of 1588 (right) shows a dancing girl entertaining a prince.

Opposite top: While he was in North Africa, Delacroix was eager to see a harem, that cloistered part of a Muslim house in which the women lived. Through connections in Algiers, he was finally to get his wish, and one of his traveling companions reported his delighted response: "It's beautiful! It is as if in the time of Homer!" Two years later, he painted Women of Algiers (1834), basing the work on notes and sketches from his travels. About the picture, he wrote, "This is woman as I understand her, not thrown into the life of the world, but withdrawn at its heart, as its most secret, delicious and moving fulfillment."

Opposite bottom: Fragment of a banqueting scene of c. 1420 B.C. showing dancing girls, from the Tomb of Nakht, Thebes, Egypt. The guests to the left, observing the dance, are wearing perfume cones on top of their wigs.

The West has been fascinated by North African and Middle Eastern dancing girls. This Bedouin dancer, named Rabah, was brought from North Africa to Nice to play a role in Rex Ingram's film The Garden of Allah; *if the studio's publicity unit is to be believed, she actually sought a divorce when her husband refused to permit her to appear in any more pictures. The 1927 movie starred Alice Terry and Ivan Petrovich.*

lished the Mughal Empire in northern India, they brought with them a taste for dancing girls that later gave rise to the dance style known as kathak. Although orthodox Islam frowns on the public display of the female body that is the dancing girl's stock in trade, the tradition has flourished in North Africa, where nineteenth-century Europeans found relief from their own society's moral austerities in what the French referred to as *"la danse du ventre"* and Americans called the "abdomen dance" or the "stomach dance" before settling on the "belly dance." Perhaps inevitably, Westerners unfamiliar with the dance focused their attention on the performers' pelvic movements, although in North Africa the mark of a good dancer is how she moves her shoulders, and the dance is seen as sensually evocative rather than provocative.

Through accounts of travelers like Gustave Flaubert, North Africa became fixed in the Western mind as a realm of exotic voluptuousness, populated by dancers who aroused men's desire with undulating bodies and then satisfied that desire with those same bodies. On a trip up the Nile in 1850, Flaubert's imagination was inflamed by a dancer who called herself Kutchuk Hanem, which is Turkish for "little princess." Flaubert characterized her in a letter to a friend as "a very celebrated courtesan . . . a regal-looking creature, large breasted, fleshy, with slit nostrils, enormous eyes and magnificent knees." An American journalist who was entertained by the same dancer described her performance as "a curious and wonderful gymnastic" in which every limb was animated with "the soul of passion. . . .

Her hands were raised, clapping the castanets, and she slowly turned upon herself, her right leg the pivot, marvelously convulsing all the muscles of her body . . . in time to the music. . . . Kutchuk fell upon her knees and writhed, with body, arms and head upon the floor, still in measure. . . ."

Reports such as these paved the way for the importation into Europe and the United States of "exotic" dancers from North Africa and the Middle East in the late nineteenth century. The most popular attractions at the 1893 World's Columbian Exposition in Chicago were dancers from Algeria, Syria, Egypt, and Palestine. While most of these shows were actually quite chaste according to present-day American standards, the belly dancers gave rise to a new genre that became a staple of burlesque; the prototype was a near-nude entertainer who danced at Coney Island under the name "Little Egypt."

In Arabic, the *danse du ventre* is known as *"raks al-baladi"* ("dance of the people") or *"raks-al-Misri"* ("Egyptian dance"); the Egyptians themselves call it *"raks al-sharqui"* ("dance of the East"). (It is possible that the English term "belly dance" came from a misunderstanding of the word *"baladi."*) In its Middle Eastern homeland the dance is not considered lascivious per se— although for pious Muslims any woman who exposes her body before strangers in public has placed herself outside the bounds of respectable society. Some of the dancers in the biggest hotels and nightclubs are actually Europeans or Americans. Moroccan women who perform for male audiences typically come from socially marginal groups or

communities in which dance is considered an acceptable route out of poverty.
Their dances, usually improvised solos,
mingle smooth pelvic undulations,
hip shimmying, and fast, syncopated
footwork with jumps and percussive
stamping.

In recent years, the desire to dance
has also found expression in the
Western-style discos that have opened
in some North African cities. Here,
men and women dance as couples to
Western-style music in a manner that
would not be out of place in the dance
clubs of New York, London, or Paris.
The young couples typically arrive
together; it is still rare for a man or a
woman to go to a disco alone and dance
with a total stranger. As in Polynesia,
pressure for change in relations between
the sexes has come largely from educated women; according to Fatima
Mernissi, author of Beyond the Veil, one
third of all university-level teachers and
scholars in Arab countries, including
the Gulf states, are women. For many of
these women, dance has become a symbol of personal liberation; a woman who
dances (even in the traditional manner)
at a mixed gathering like a wedding
or a large party is declaring her opposition to age-old constraints on social
interaction.

Elsewhere in Morocco, these constraints remain in effect. Just a hundred
miles from the urban discos (and from
the Mediterranean beaches where
sunbathers in bikinis display their tans),
women in traditional communities veil
their faces, girls are married at the age
of twelve or thirteen, and the idea of
couples dancing in public Western-style
is still unacceptable.

In the West, couple dancing has not only reflected society's changing attitudes toward relations between the sexes, it has sometimes foreshadowed them. When European men and women first began dancing as couples at social gatherings in the late Middle Ages, the primary social unit was still the extended—as opposed to the nuclear—family. Several generations lived under one roof or in closely adjoining dwellings; marriages were typically arranged to bring benefits (economic and social) to both families; children were treated as assets in the larger family enterprise.

As we saw in previous chapters, Christianity's attitude toward the primary biological unit—the male-female couple—had been ambivalent from the

days of the early church. The Virgin Mary, as the mother of Christ, was available as a model of behavior for Christian women; but the example of Eve, who brought sin and death into the world by succumbing to temptation, weighed heavily on the minds of Christian thinkers. The perpetuation of Christian communities obviously required closely knit families with many children; but the early church fathers were worried about the effect of unrestrained sexuality, especially female sexuality, on those same communities. The position articulated by Paul—abstinence is best for the soul but it is better to marry than to burn with uncontrollable desire—pointed to the compromise eventually adopted by the Western church in the

late Middle Ages: those who wished to pursue a life devoted to Christ (as priest, monk, or nun) were enjoined to choose celibacy; everyone else could reproduce within the bonds of holy matrimony.

It might seem paradoxical that a civilization that excluded both dance and sexuality from its central mysteries should come to emphasize the male-female couple in its social dance. But one of the factors behind the new attitude toward the dancing couple in the late Middle Ages was precisely the European tendency to divide daily life into two separate realms—the sacred and the secular. While liturgical dance came under close scrutiny from the church hierarchy, dance on unconsecrated ground was relatively free to express nonreligious concerns; it was these concerns that later contributed to the emergence of the nuclear family as the focus of Western society.

The new attitude toward women and dance, which surfaced sometime in the twelfth or thirteenth century, was strongly influenced by the Crusades. For one thing, great numbers of men left their homes to fight the Muslim enemy in the Holy Land or Spain; in many cases the women they left behind had to learn, out of necessity, to manage affairs that had formerly been thought of as men's business. As a result, European women gained new status in the secular life of their communities, despite the fact that legally they remained the wards of their fathers and husbands.

When the Crusaders returned to their homes, they brought back with them a respect bordering on envy for the wealth and sophistication of Islamic civilization—a civilization that had in fact borrowed and preserved much of the West's own heritage of Greek and Roman thought. What made the greatest impact on European ideas of gender, however, was Islam's attitude toward women, as expressed in its songs and poetry. Because they were seen as irresistibly attractive, all women—except for the slave-dancer-singer-courtesan—had to be hidden away from the view of non-kinsmen. Inevitably, seclusion heightened their appeal, which a school of Arabic poetry arose to celebrate. The poems addressed by distant admirers to the women of another man's harem extolled a love that was considered "pure" because it could never be satisfied in the flesh.

When a similar conceit of "pure" love was adopted by the troubadours of southern France, the walls of the harem were replaced by the more abstract barriers of female "virtue." In the troubadours' hymns to the beloved, the already married object of the poet's affection always preserves her virtue, her most precious possession, intact; her body may belong to her husband but her soul is free to soar with her lover's. Whether or not this distinction was observed in real life—where flesh-and-blood courtiers wooed the flesh-and-blood wives of absent lords— the conceit of courtly love encouraged a new way of looking at the role of women in Christendom. The beloved was in no way subordinate to her lover. She was seen as a highly esteemed individual in her own right, worthy of being pursued, worthy of being adored by men of the highest social rank, worthy of assuming a new role as partner to a man on the dance floors of Europe.

In many parts of the world—including Polynesia, North Africa, and the Middle East—public dancing that focused on a physically linked couple would have been unthinkable, a violation of communal propriety. But the group dances of the European countryside had long included passages in which a man and a woman came together briefly for a few steps or turns; these may have provided models for the couple dancing that drew increasing attention in Western Europe toward the end of the Middle Ages. Inevitably, attempts were made to ban couple dancing; inevitably, the bans were ignored. In providing an arena for a man and a woman to stand out from the crowd, late medieval social dance anticipated (and possibly contributed to) the empowerment of the individual that

Two Peasants Dancing, *woodcut by Albrecht Dürer, 1514.*

Opposite: Pieter Brueghel's Wedding Dance *(1566) portrays couple dancing in a distinctly moralistic manner, reflecting widespread concerns that the practice led to the sin of lust. Its effects on three of the men in the foreground (once bowdlerized but restored in this century) where the dancing is wildest are particularly evident. The bride, wearing a wreath on her uncovered head and a black gown, is dancing with an older man, perhaps her father.*

marked the era that historians call the Renaissance. The early Renaissance in Italy saw a reevaluation of the role of the individual in society. Renewed interest in Greek and Roman history—prompted in part by a rediscovery of many works of classical literature—found one expression in the courtly entertainments known as *balli*. These spectacles are thought to have evolved from the stately processions, jousting tournaments, and interludes of song and declaimed poetry that enlivened medieval courts. The *balli* featured costumed courtiers who acted out allegorical themes from Greek and Roman mythology, such as Jason and the Golden Fleece (performed at the wedding of the duke of Milan in 1489).

Before long, to play a role in such a spectacle was the ambition of every courtier, not just in Italy but in France and England as well. Success at court had always entailed mastery of three skills: riding, fencing, and "fair" speech. To instruct the nobility in the new and increasingly complicated dances—and in the proper ways of talking and walking required to make a mark among the well-bred—a new profession of dancing master sprang up. Some of the earliest dancing masters were Jewish; there had long been a need for dancing instructors in Jewish communities because of the Talmudic dictum enjoining Jews to dance at weddings. It was during the fifteenth century that the first European dance manuals began to appear and the foundations of classical ballet were laid. At this time, there was no clear distinction between "social" and "theatrical" dance.

The early dancing masters were high-ly educated men, versed in the newly revived classical learning and responsible for the intellectual and social as well as the physical proficiency of their pupils. They not only taught dance and deportment, they composed dances for court entertainments and often the music as well. As authorities on etiquette they were sought after by members of the lesser aristocracy, the gentry, and the middle class who wanted to gain entry to the best houses and cut a presentable figure there. As early as 1533 laws were passed in London to control the proliferation of dancing schools. In a 1588 dance manual called *Orchésographie,* Thoinot Arbeau (an anagram for Jehan Tabourot, a Catholic priest) instructed readers who wished to make a good impression in the best ballrooms:

"Spit and blow your nose sparingly. . . use a fair white handkerchief. . . . Be suitably and neatly dressed, your hose well secured and your shoes clean. . . . And if you desire to marry you must realize that a mistress is won by the good temper and grace displayed by dancing. . . . And there is more to it than this, for dancing is practiced to reveal whether lovers are in good health and sound of limb, after which they are permitted to kiss their mistresses in order that they may touch and savor one another, thus to ascertain if they are shapely or emit an unpleasant odor as of bad meat."

We have already seen how the rise of powerful women like Catherine de Médicis went hand in hand with the spread of the new kind of dancing through Western Europe. We have seen how the minuet came to represent on the dance floors of Versailles the hierarchical ideals of pre-Revolutionary Europe. We have also seen how strongly some religious leaders opposed dancing in general and dancing between men and women in particular. After the Reformation, many Protestants came to see ballroom dancing ("Mixt or Promiscuous dancing," as Increase Mather called it) as inherently sinful, an invention of the Devil. It is hardly surprising that the Protestant missionaries who set out to convert the "heathens," in the wake of European colonial expansion in the eighteenth and nineteenth centuries, showed little sympathy for the dance they found embedded in the local cultures. There are still places in the American Bible Belt where local ordinances discourage mixed dancing, especially by young people. But rules and perceptions vary: When teenagers began dancing to rock-and-roll music in the 1950s, the gyrations of the stand-alone dancers were denounced as "lewd" by some Protestant preachers who had never expressed opposition to the conventional "touch dancing" of the day.

Most people today learn social dancing through observation or through informal demonstrations by relatives and friends; this means that the social values embodied in the dances are often passed along without being made explicit. By contrast, when parents send young children to a dance school to learn ballroom dancing, the instruction typically includes lessons in how men and women of a particular social class should behave in each other's company. At some schools, like the thirty-five-year-old Walter Schalk School of Dance in New Canaan, Connecticut, great attention is paid to what earlier generations referred to as etiquette. Ten-year-old boys wear suits and ties, ten-year-old girls wear dresses and white gloves; the boys ask the girls to dance (never vice versa); the boys always lead, the girls always follow. But however important these particulars have been in the development of couple dancing in the West, they clearly do not define its essence.

The one unbreakable rule of couple dancing is that the partners must move *inter*dependently, as a unit. In the early years of the nineteenth century, when the waltz first became popular, men and women fitted their movements to one another in a public display of mutual confidence and teamwork. No one led because no one had to; the steps followed a predetermined pattern, the dancers always turned in a predetermined direction (clockwise) while circling around the floor with all the other couples in a predetermined direction (counterclockwise). Once the dancers had mastered the steps and

Court balls in the eighteenth century featured dances with precise sequences of steps whose proper performance required prior instruction and rehearsal under the eyes of a dancing master. This engraving by François Nicolas Martinet shows a costume ball held during the Carnival season at Versailles in 1763. The dancers, in rustic attire, perform a maypole dance, one of those European customs whose roots go back to the pre-Christian era.

In this late-seventeenth-century engraving (right), a dancing master wears a sword and is playing a pochette, a small violin.

Discipline and training, not spontaneity, were the prerequisites of ballroom dancing in the early nineteenth century. The dancers (below) are executing the "three forward and back" section of the pastourelle figure of a quadrille, in an English etching of the 1820s.

THE DANCING SCHOOLE.

John Playford's The English Dancing
Master: or, Plaine and easie rules for the
Dancing of Country Dances, with the
tunes to each dance of 1651 was published during the Commonwealth, the period
of Oliver Cromwell's strict Puritan rule of
England. The frontispiece (above), however,
was quite blunt about the advantages of
being able to dance: Cupid himself presides
over the dancing school.

While people of all ages take dancing
lessons, instruction in dancing has been considered especially important for young men
and women whose parents want them to
acquire the skills they need to succeed in
society. George Cruikshank's The Dancing
Lesson of 1835 (left) shows a dancing
master playing his pochette as a boy and girl
dance the minuet, and off to the side another
girl stands in a box to improve her turnout.

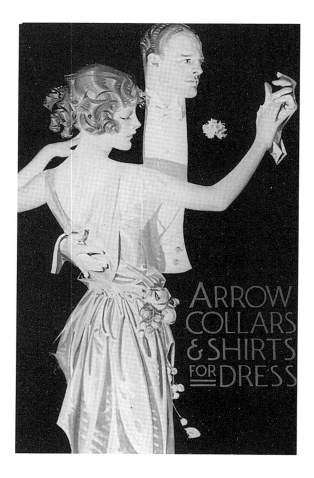

ARROW
COLLARS
& SHIRTS
FOR DRESS

The American illustrator J.C. Leyendecker's famous advertisement of 1913 for Arrow Shirts provided a perfect image of the ideal dancing couple of European and American society: the man is commanding and strong, the woman demurely responsive to his will.

Opposite: Fred Astaire and Ginger Rogers: together, and apart, and together again, in a sequence from the film Top Hat *(1935).*

learned to synchronize their movements with everyone else on the floor, the waltz was a very egalitarian dance.

But since fewer and fewer men had the leisure or inclination to take lessons from a dancing instructor, by midcentury it had become necessary to simplify the steps; at the same time each waltzing couple was set free to move and turn as they wished without reference to the rest of the dancers. With the new freedom, however, came new problems: How were the partners to synchronize their movements with each other? How were they to decide when to turn and in what direction? How was each couple to avoid bumping into other couples? Fortunately, there was a simple solution to all these problems: One partner had to lead the other. The leading partner was responsible for steering a safe course around the ballroom, and the other partner had to follow the leader. The leading role, it goes without saying, fell to the man.

The late-nineteenth-century waltz revealed a lot about the society that engendered it. The man was in charge—but if he tried to dominate without taking his partner's reactions into account, he could cause an awkward stumble and so cut a foolish figure before his peers. If, on the other hand, he and his partner performed as a well-knit team, they would not only look good but could pay more attention to the business of romance, which was likely to be the motive that had drawn them to the ballroom in the first place. The romantic ideal of ballroom dancing is beautifully expressed in the dancing sequences in Fred Astaire movies, where the choreographed steps appear to flow spontaneously not from the flashing legs of Astaire and his partner but from their lovers' hearts—so perfectly attuned that they seem to be beating as one.

The need for continuous communication between the partners is built into the very structure of couple dancing. But the rule that the man must always lead is not; as in all dance, the role of the genders in a waltz or a Lindy or a fox-trot is determined by the culture. If they wished, the partners could conceivably take turns leading or flip a coin before each dance to see who leads. When, at the beginning of the 1960s, couples around the world separated and began dancing as individuals to rock-and-roll music, they were choosing a third option that spoke directly to the social issues of the time: if no one leads, no one has to follow.

Chapter 5
Classical Dance Theater

All art holds a mirror up to the society that produces it. The longer an art endures, the more confident we can be that the mirror reveals something important about the society—and that the society itself has been changed by what it sees. In its 400-year history, ballet has come to embody for audiences who share a European heritage (as well as for many who do not) a blend of spectacle, music, and physical virtuosity in pursuit of a highly stylized ideal of social behavior. Halfway around the world, Japan's 400-year-old kabuki theater presents a different kind of spectacle that revels in contrasts; with elaborate costumes and utilitarian props, vivid sound effects and ethereal musical accompaniment, grand gestures and subtly modulated expressions, kabuki explores the conflicts that arise between desire and duty in a convention-bound society.

Both ballet and kabuki are considered "classical" forms of dance theater. Classical in this case means not merely that something is old, but that it has

been endorsed by powerful forces in the society. The label, of course, is no guarantee of survival. Ballet and kabuki, like southern India's kathakali, Java's wayang wong, and Chinese opera, have at times been threatened with extinction through official disapproval, audience apathy, or artistic sterility. If they have survived to earn a place of honor in their societies, it is because, whenever these forms are endangered, a devoted core of performers, patrons, and spectators has refused to let them die.

Classical dance theater is an expensive, time-consuming endeavor. Since each form depends on a particular relationship between performers and spectators, not just any theater will do for performances; the size and design of the stage and the nature of the seating arrangements are essential to a proper production. So are the right kinds of costumes, props, and sets—and the availability of skilled people to make and maintain them. There must be stories that excite and inspire perform-

ers and audience. Most importantly, no classical repertory can be sustained without a critical mass of well-trained and enthusiastic dancers and musicians.

Wealthy and powerful patrons can help perpetuate a classical form, but they cannot call one into being by fiat. Audiences must be willing to invest time and money by attending the theater and subsidizing schools and companies; and successive generations of performers must be willing to invest time and effort to master the skills that stamp each new performance, however freshly conceived and executed, as being in the classical tradition. Ballet and kabuki offer twin mirrors that reveal, beyond the specifics of time and place that shaped them, the underlying processes through which theatrical dance forms evolve into classics.

A t the end of an advanced class at the School of American Ballet in New York City's Lincoln Center, fifteen would-be ballerinas file into the carpeted corridor outside the studio. They are sixteen, seventeen, eighteen years old, dressed in black tights and black or pastel-print tops and flimsy wraparound skirts that barely brush their thighs. Aside from the scarcity of baby fat, this could be any group of teenagers chattering about what they did last night, what they will be doing tonight, what is happening this weekend. But once they undo the satin straps of their smudged pink toe shoes, part of the price they pay for wanting to dance with the effortless grace of Suzanne Farrell or Sylvie Guillem is clear.

Their feet look old and battered. An assortment of bandages, gauze pads, and cotton wadding separates and cushions corns, calluses, and bunions. The conversation is all about injuries and remedies. The latest panacea for suffering toes is "a tiny little Ace bandage wrapped around a soft gumdrop-like material that makes a *wonderful* cushion!" But it is expensive, so most of

the students make do with Band-Aids. A girl whose painful shin splints forced her to drop out of the morning's class receives the sympathy of her friends. Another girl holds up one ballet slipper to display its floppy bottom: the layers of glue and fabric that stiffen the sole broke down in the middle of class but the dancer "worked around it," which put an extra strain on her leg muscles.

In another studio a teacher introduces two young dancers to George Balanchine's *Tchaikovsky Pas de Deux*. The teacher is Suki Schorer; as a principal with Balanchine's New York City Ballet from 1968 to 1972, she danced this particular pas de deux several times. At one point the choreography calls for a "fish dive," in which the ballerina dives headfirst into her partner's arms, he catches her, and they both freeze, her backward-arching body steadied on his left knee, her legs bent up behind her in a graceful figure that ends above his left shoulder, and a confident smile on her face which is turned toward the audi-

Former ballerina Suki Schorer teaching a class at the School of American Ballet in New York City. The school was founded by Lincoln Kirstein and George Balanchine in 1934, and it is now the official school of the New York City Ballet.

ence and suspended a few inches above the floor. Like all such moves the fish dive gets easier with practice. To show her students what it looks like when done right, Schorer uses the example of the pas de deux danced by Merrill Ashley and Adam Luders; their fish dive is a breathtaking triumph of artistry over gravity. Done the first time by unfamiliar partners, it is an exercise in faith; even the teacher winces when the boy, grunting aloud with the effort, catches the girl and strains to keep her face from doing a cheek-to-cheek with the linoleum floor.

That same night, during a New York City Ballet performance of Jerome Robbins's *Dances at a Gathering*, one of the company's principal dancers slips on stage and falls to the floor with a loud crack. There are audible gasps from the audience, but the orchestra keeps playing; the dancer jumps to her feet, finds her place in the intricate four-couple formation, and the dance goes on as before. During curtain calls the applause for the dancer who fell is unusually warm and sustained, as if the audience, aware of its role in preserving ballet's magnificent illusion of "effortless grace," were eager to reaffirm the mutually beneficial partnership that spans the footlights.

The sweaty physicality, the sinewy strength, the ever-present risk of injury, the strain of maintaining balance and control, the exacting precision required for smooth partnering—these are aspects of the dance that ballet dancers expend great energy to conceal from view. The royal courts that nurtured ballet are either gone or stripped of their political power, but the courtly ideal of

making the most difficult feats of prowess look easy has become an integral part of the ballet aesthetic. George Balanchine warned his dancers at the New York City Ballet to avoid any interruptions in a movement sequence that might give away the fact that they were getting set for a major leap or turn. Even the sound of ballet shoes striking the stage is considered a distraction that audiences politely ignore; the floor is treated either as a neutral support for movement or as a launching pad that dancers exploit to achieve the highest possible elevation. In kabuki, by contrast, no attempt is made to minimize the physical nature of the performer's art. Quite the contrary. The "wind-up" to each momentous gesture or pose is an important part of the performance. When a kabuki performer stomps down a wooden runway to make a spectacular exit from the stage, an attendant beats wooden blocks against a board to accentuate the impact as each foot makes contact with the floor.

In order to turn their bodies into finely tuned instruments capable of making the most demanding choreography look easy, ballet dancers start stringent training around the age of ten. (To start earlier is to risk damage to still maturing bones and muscles.) Their training does not end when they are hired by a ballet company or even when they achieve stardom. Throughout their career they continue to attend class six days a week, to keep their bodies limber and responsive.

Work in class begins at the barre, a hip-height wooden rail that runs along the walls of the classroom. Students rest one hand lightly on the barre for sup-

port. The first exercise is usually the deep knee bend known as a plié. Different teachers employ slightly different progressions of exercises, but all are designed to warm up, stretch, and loosen muscles, make joints more flexible, and prepare the body for the work that follows. After finishing at the barre, the dancers move to the center of the room where they perform similar exercises without support, followed by slow combinations of steps and then more rapid combinations; finally, the women practice steps on point and the men practice jumps and turns; in some cases they pair up to work on partnering.

During his thirty-five years as ballet master of the New York City Ballet, George Balanchine taught the ninety-minute company class every morning. He used this time to correct errors of form he had spotted during performances, weed out bad stylistic habits that might interfere with performance (and even lead to injuries), and explore new combinations that might later be included in new ballets. The classroom was his laboratory, the trained bodies of the dancers his tools. Balanchine's classes incorporated the lessons of over three hundred years of ballet masters before him. His choreography was called "neoclassical" because it built on an inherited vocabulary of positions, steps, gestures, and poses to create something new. He cleaned up, speeded up, sharpened up the classical technique. He directed his dancers' attention to what he called "the small parts of our bodies"; he showed them how a slightly misaligned instep or an imprecisely curled index finger could destroy the beauty of a step or pose. His choreography was

Ballerina Larissa Lezhnina with her coach in a rehearsal studio at the Kirov Theater, St. Petersburg, 1991.

always guided by the music he had chosen. To bring out what he called the "shape" of the notes, he might set more steps to a single phrase than any of his predecessors would have dared; or he might explore the intricate give-and-take of partnering through what appear at first glance to be slow-motion acrobatics but which are actually classical steps decelerated, taken apart and recombined in unexpected ways. Out of these experiments he devised ballets that struck his contemporaries as profoundly expressive of their time and place.

Ballet's vocabulary of movement evokes an ideal of beauty derived from what Havelock Ellis called the "social discipline" common to societies shaped by a European past. This past was dominated by a hierarchical class system that converged toward a single point—the sovereign. Performers in early court entertainments, whether aristocratic amateurs or trained professionals, were careful never to turn their back on the royal "Presence." When ballet moved from ballroom to theater, the Presence took up residence in the royal box. The ballet dancer's turnout from the hips (which ensures maximal opening of the body toward the front), the strongly frontal orientation of ballet staging, even the proscenium stage itself can be traced to the European court tradition that directed the performance toward the sovereign in attendance. Classical ballet "in the round" is almost a contradiction in terms.

When European courts lost their power, the upper- and middle-class patrons of ballet assumed the place of the sovereign. They came not just to see

but to be seen; their presence at the theater was one way of demonstrating their place in the social hierarchy. Even the traditional organization of ballet troupes, with grades of dancers carefully ranked according to experience and ability, reflected the hierarchical structure of preindustrial European society. While modern ballet companies have dispensed with much of this organizational apparatus, direction from the top down remains the norm.

Yet for all its ties to an unapologetically aristocratic and specifically European tradition, ballet has found avid audiences around the world. Among the rewards that ballet offers theatergoers who fall under its spell are passages of transforming beauty, when a dancer's body, molded by an aesthetic of perfection, seems to approach the superhuman. The excitement that such moments can provoke is well illustrated by the reception accorded ballet during the last century in the United States, a country founded in opposition to everything the royal courts of Europe stood for.

Long before there were any resident ballet companies in North America, touring artists from Europe were greeted with a fervor bordering on hysteria. When Fanny Elssler, Austrian-born

star of the Paris Opéra Ballet, arrived in New York in 1840, the city was gripped by what the local press called "Elsslermania." Symptoms spread to Washington, D.C., where Congress adjourned for a day so that no one in government need be late for her performance. Admirers fought to drink champagne from her slippers; they unhitched the horses from her carriage and pulled her through city streets. Watching Elssler dance in Boston, Margaret Fuller, a leader of New England's Transcendentalists, turned to her companion and said, "Ralph, this is poetry." To which Ralph Waldo Emerson replied, "No, it is religion."

What did they see that prompted such comparisons? The first half of the nineteenth century was the heyday of Romantic ballet, when dancing on toes—*en pointe* in ballet's technical vocabulary of French words and phrases—became the hallmark of the female dancer, and the female dancer became the unrivaled star of the ballet stage. Behind the scenes, men remained in charge, determining the choreography, the casting, the choice of music and librettos, and, most importantly, the selection and instruction of the dancers. Young girls went through arduous train-

By the early 1870s, when Edgar Degas painted The Rehearsal of the Ballet on the Stage (below), the Paris Opéra Ballet was almost entirely the preserve of star ballerinas—it had at times no male dancers—and a corps of young girls who were eagerly pursued by male admirers from the audience. The company, long the world's most prestigious, began a decline in the mid-nineteenth century that was arrested only after the arrival of Léo Staats (right), who was named ballet master in 1914. Staats (1877–1952) made his debut as a dancer at the age of ten and choreographed his first ballet six years later. Here he is seen with his dancers in a rehearsal studio.

Jerome Robbins, seen here coaching Broadway dancer Allyn Ann McLerie, is an American dancer and choreographer. His first ballet, Fancy Free (1944), which he choreographed to music by Leonard Bernstein when both were twenty-six years old, was a huge success, and led to a dual career choreographing and directing both for the musical theater and for the ballet. McLerie danced for Robbins, Agnes DeMille, and George Balanchine in various Broadway musicals.

A contemporary of Léo Staats, Mikhail Mordkin (1880–1944) was a Russian dancer, ballet master, and choreographer. As a dancer, he starred in Moscow in his youth and, after a short stint with Diaghilev's Ballets Russes, toured with Anna Pavlova. He settled in the United States in 1924 and formed his own company that eventually became the American Ballet Theater.

Fanny Elssler in the Shadow Dance, *a popular lithograph published in New York in 1846, shows the Romantic ballerina in her element.*

Opposite: Reinforced point shoes began to appear during the 1860s. Dancers customarily sew on the ankle ribbons themselves. Alexandra Danilova, whose point work is seen here, studied in St. Petersburg and joined the Maryinsky (now the Kirov) Ballet, where she became a soloist in 1922 at the age of eighteen. She left Russia with George Balanchine and had a long career in the West, principally with the Ballets Russes de Monte Carlo.

ing to be able to go up on point and stay there. The heavily blocked and steel-shanked toe shoe had not yet been invented. Ballerinas danced in heelless slippers with a bit of protective wadding stuffed inside and some extra stitching on the outside to improve traction. To achieve the leg strength that allowed her to seem to float across the stage, Marie Taglioni—the original, the quintessential Sylphide—drilled for hours under the exacting eye of her father; it was reported that after each exhausting lesson on point she fell into a faint and had to be coaxed back to consciousness. Fanny Elssler projected a more physical image; her energetic star turns were inspired by the folk dances of Spain, Italy, Poland, Hungary. To Théophile Gautier, a regular ballet critic and the librettist of *Giselle*, Taglioni was a "Christian dancer . . . she resembles a happy angel who scarcely bends

the petals of celestial flowers with the tips of her pink toes," whereas Elssler was "a quite pagan dancer; she reminds one of the muse Terpsichore."

Whatever their specialty, the ballerinas of the Romantic era came across the footlights as more than merely human; by using the body to transcend the body, they symbolized the yearning for release from everyday reality that exemplified the Romantic sensibility. The fact that the stars of nineteenth-century ballet were typically women of modest social background whose backstage lives often stretched the bounds of respectability only added to their appeal; critics like Gautier rarely failed to include an appraisal of the ballerina's physical charms in their notices. Ultimately, however, what held the attention of ballet audiences was the dancer's ability to project an image of the human body in the service of

a higher ideal. In *La Belle au Bois Dormant (The Sleeping Beauty)*, a ballet that has come to be regarded as the acme of nineteenth-century classical dance, the ballerina in the title role of Princess Aurora embodies a vision of purity, of invincible innocence in the face of evil, that remains close to the heart of Western culture.

While a classical art is by definition respectful of tradition, ballet is also daring, ambitious, as restless as the culture from which it springs. Ballet honors its past by periodically reinventing it, as Balanchine did with the legacy he inherited from the nineteenth century. Under changing circumstances, ballet continues to find beauty in the struggle of the human body to overcome its limitations, to rise (often literally) above all constraints, and to leave a clear imprint of its improbable triumphs in the mind of the beholder.

Bandō Tamasaburō rehearsing out of costume at the Kabuki Theater, called the Kabuki-za, Tokyo.

Opposite: Tamasaburō in Musume Dōjōji (The Dancing Maiden at Dojo Temple), *one of the classical dance pieces of the kabuki stage.*

Japan's kabuki theater achieved classical status by a diametrically opposite route from that of ballet. While ballet percolated down through the social structure from the aristocracy to the middle class, kabuki worked its way up the ladder of acceptability from the bottom. Kabuki traces its origin not to the stately bugaku of the Imperial Court but to the pay-as-you-go tumult of popular entertainment. The word kabuki originally meant "out of kilter" or "off center." Pulled this way and that by government censors, public taste, and the aspirations of its dancer-actor-impresarios, kabuki has pursued a zigzag trajectory from raunchy outlaw-theater to corporate-sponsored classic over the last four hundred years, a span of time that roughly parallels the ascendancy of ballet. During this time the image of female beauty projected on the kabuki stage has left a deep imprint on Japanese culture, just as the image of the ballerina has on the West. In both societies respectable women have gone out of their way to emulate the looks and deportment of performers considered (often with some justification) to be prostitutes of one kind or another. In the case of ballet, the onstage icons of femininity have been largely molded by men; in the all-male world of kabuki the icons of femininity *are* men.

The Japanese word for a kabuki performer who specializes in female roles is onnagata, or "woman person." The transformation of a mature male actor into a beautiful young woman is accomplished in part through masklike make-up and costuming—a process that may take up to an hour. But the key to the onnagata's art lies in the gestures, voice,

and bearing of the performer, who must not only move like a woman on stage but think like a woman. Some kabuki performers are acclaimed for their versatility in playing male as well as female roles. But the finest onnagatas have been specialists. In an early example of mass marketing through sex appeal, leading onnagatas of the eighteenth century lent their names to feminine beauty products such as incense, face powder, kimono patterns, hair oil, and hair ornaments.

Today's onnagatas reach even larger circles of admirers. The delicate features of Bandō Tamasaburō, a tall, slender man in his early forties, are instantly recognizable to most Japanese from television and advertising posters. As one of kabuki's most popular and highly paid performers, Tamasaburō surrounds himself with the trappings of a rock star: outsized automobiles, a retinue of business associates and personal servants. He has appeared in Western-style dramas playing male as well as female parts—among them Shakespeare's Lady Macbeth and the Idiot in an adaptation of Dostoevsky's novel—but his fame rests on his ability to create the illusion of a beautiful woman in such kabuki classics as *Musume Dōjōji (The Dancing Maiden at Dojo Temple)*. When he turns his heavily made-up face (chalk-white base, bright red lips, red-highlighted eyes) toward the audience, his adoring fans, mostly women, cry out, "*Kirei, Kirei!*" ("Beautiful, beautiful!").

For any classical theater to exist, there must be a means of passing from generation to generation the vocabulary, outlook, and repertoire that have been deemed worth preserving. Ballet has

schools, the best of which are under the control of the leading ballet companies; through such schools, each generation responsible for preserving the legacy is ensured a supply of young dancers trained in the classical style. In Japan, the establishment of formal kabuki schools is a recent innovation. Traditionally, young performers have been trained by older members of stage families, who control the production and presentation of kabuki and who pass along to the younger generation the family's distinctive style of dancing and acting. Instruction is typically one-on-one; a pupil rehearses a role or a portion of a role until he has mastered every movement, every expression, every line; only then does he proceed to another role. Training begins as early as age five; stage debuts by six-year-old apprentices are not uncommon. This method of instruction is typical of Japan's traditional arts, which tend to be family monopolies. Only if talent seems thin in the family's ranks is room made for outsiders who are adopted into the family.

An onnagata's apprenticeship typically begins with instruction in walking. He practices with a sheet of paper between his knees, feet slightly pigeon-toed, elbows at the hips, fingers close together, body swaying slightly from side to side; if the sheet of paper slips to the floor, he knows he has not yet learned how to walk like an onnagata. Tamasaburō was introduced to kabuki when he was six years old; a doctor suggested that lessons in traditional dance might help him overcome the effects of a mild case of polio. He was adopted into a kabuki family at the age of six. After studying

the classic onnagata roles, he spent time observing the great onnagatas of the older generation, such as Nakamura Utaemon VI, who in his mid-seventies still plays young girls on stage and has been named a "living national treasure" by the Japanese government. Tamasaburō has also pored over videotapes of Greta Garbo, Katharine Hepburn, and Marilyn Monroe. Learning female patterns of behavior, he says, is like learning a foreign language: "To do it well, the patterns and expressions must become one with your thoughts and feelings."

Ichikawa Ennosuke III, perhaps kabuki's most versatile performer, is famous for both his male and female roles. Although his innovative staging of kabuki classics has earned him a reputation as an iconoclast, he cannot imagine a kabuki theater without onnagata. Reformers in this century have proposed letting women play female roles, but the idea was rejected by the traditional kabuki troupes on the grounds that actresses would inevitably perform onnagata-style—and do it less well. Women have performed kabuki outside the classical venues; women's clubs that specialize in kabuki dances are popular throughout Japan; and women appear as actors and dancers on the modern Japanese stage, especially in the famous Takarazuka theater. But the

onnagata's place in classical kabuki seems secure. Purists argue that the stylized theatricality of kabuki, which is the essence of its appeal, would be undermined if women played women. In the words of Ennosuke: "What makes kabuki a great art form is the invention of onnagata." This invention, like so much else in kabuki, grew out of a series of clashes between entertainers who made a living by pleasing crowds and government officials whose principal task was to maintain public order.

Some time around the turn of the seventeenth century a young woman named Okuni, who claimed to have danced at a shrine near Kyōto, began attracting new audiences by dancing in the dry bed of Kyōto's Kamo River. The riverbed was home to an ever-changing cast of street entertainers, fortune tellers, and vendors of pleasure in one form or another. Okuni's first performances may have been based on the dances staged at temples and shrines to please the gods, attract pilgrims, and raise money. These dances were not necessarily models of chaste devotion; the women who performed them, especially those who traveled around the country to solicit funds for the repair of temples, were known by a number of names, the least derogatory of which can be translated as "singing nun." But Okuni's

appeal was evidently broader; in 1603, according to one account, she was invited to perform for the emperor in the Imperial Palace.

It is not known what she did there or how she was received by an audience whose tastes had been honed on the classic Nō dance-dramas, which were sparse in staging, slow in pace, and contemplative in mood. What Okuni did to please the large crowds that clamored to see her out-of-doors is better known. She organized a troupe of dancers and began to embellish her performances with props, plots, and musical instruments borrowed from the Nō theater but used with a new freedom; at the same time she added lively songs and steps from popular street dances. Her almost blasphemous blending of elements from a centuries-old aristocratic theater with the latest moves from the street created a sensation.

A painted folding screen from the period captures the spirit of these early seventeenth-century performances: An alluring young woman (who may be Okuni herself) poses alone in the center of a small stage, leaning on the hilt of a long sword. She is dressed as a rakish man-about-town, in a fashionable multicolored kimono that leaves her arms bare. A fan dangles from her fingertips, her hair falls over her temples and fore-

Okuni, the renegade shrine priestess who is credited with founding kabuki, performing a roguish male role. The picture shows a typical seventeenth-century kabuki theater; the outdoor stage resembles that of the Nō theater. The musicians play percussion instruments but the samisen has not yet been introduced. In the crowd to the right are foreigners watching the performance.

head; a second sword is thrust through her sash from which hangs a Christian cross, possibly a gift from a Portuguese admirer. (Europeans were not banned from Japan until 1639, a year after the massacre of nearly all Japanese converts to Christianity.) The sexual charge of Okuni's pose is unmistakable. She is dressed as a man because one of the staples of early kabuki was the assignation scene, in which a young dandy accosts, importunes and eventually wins over a resident of what the Japanese called the "pleasure quarter." In such scenes, female performers typically played both men and women; occasionally, male performers assumed the female roles.

This early kabuki, which some observers labelled "prostitutes' kabuki," inevitably attracted the attention of the authorities. Audiences tended to be rowdy, and fights among admirers of different dancers were common. Even worse from the government's point of view, people from different social classes were mingling at kabuki performances; this violated official policy, which tried to ensure communal stability by locking everyone into a predetermined place in the social hierarchy.

The government banned women from the kabuki stage in 1629, nine years after Okuni's death. The ostensible motive for the ban was to uphold public morality; another possible reason was that the growing popularity of kabuki gave the women who controlled it a source of income and power that discomfited the rulers of Japan's rigidly patriarchal society. Indeed, kabuki was so popular that after women were banned from the stage, the shows continued with young boys playing all the parts, an arrangement that audiences apparently found even more titillating. In 1652 the government intervened again, this time decreeing that only adult men could perform kabuki. No one thought it strange for men to play women's roles onstage; this was already the rule in traditional forms of dance-drama like Nō and bugaku.

Kabuki arose during a time of historic change in Japan. After more than a hundred years of civil wars, the Tokugawa Shogunate had emerged triumphant at the beginning of the seventeenth century. While the emperor continued his symbolic reign in Kyōto, attended by an ineffectual court nobility, the Shoguns established their military capital in Edo (now Tokyo). The word Shogun can be translated as "barbarian-subduing great general"; in fact, the Shoguns saw their task as subduing an entire unruly nation. By midcentury the government had virtually sealed off Japan from the rest of the world; the same impulse led to rules and regulations that discouraged fraternizing between Japanese of different occupations, regions, and social backgrounds. While their efforts to isolate the Japanese from one another were less successful than their campaign to close Japan to all foreign influences, the Shoguns did succeed in building a social order that kept the peace, at whatever cost to personal freedom, for more than 250 years. The inspiration for the rigid caste system the Shogunate imposed on the country was clearly military. The head of every household had to post his rank outside his home; on the street you could tell a man's caste by the way he cut his hair. Dominating the social structure were the daimyo, the landowning feudal lords; just below came the samurai, the warriors (identified by a distinctive topknot) who had fought the wars and were now eager to reap their rewards. Together, these made up a privileged class whose right to rule was based, according to a model borrowed from Chinese Confucianism, on an assertion of moral superiority.

Below the samurai, and separated from them by a great divide, came three ranks of commoners: the farmers whose productive rice fields supported the whole structure; priests and artisans; and lastly the merchants, whose profit-

This page: A print of c. 1780 (left) shows an actor applying his makeup backstage as another actor watches. The standing actor is an onnagata, but his carriage betrays his masculinity. Behind the actors are props and scenic pieces in storage. Two hundred years later, the kabuki actor applies his makeup in much the same manner, seated on the floor in front of a small vanity. Below, Ichikawa Ennosuke III prepares to go onstage in his dressing room at the Kabuki Theater, Tokyo.

Opposite: Masakado, first performed at Edo's Ichimura Theater in 1836, is a shosagoto play, that is, one that emphasizes dance. This is the climactic tableau struck at the conclusion of a spectacular battle on a castle roof between a samurai, played by Ichikawa Danjūrō XII, and a princess with magical powers, played by Nakamura Utaemon VI. When the princess recites a spell, the old castle collapses, a special kabuki scenic technique called yatai kazushi (scenic destruction).

making and money-lending activities were officially disdained but tolerated as necessary to the economy. As in all caste systems, there were gradations within gradations, sanctioned by both law and custom. Situated at the bottom of the social pyramid was an entirely separate group (with its own internal distinctions of rank) that included workers in the less savory trades, like skinners of dead animals, tanners of hides, prostitutes, and kabuki performers. Efforts were made to minimize contact between these people and the rest of society. The government began licensing prostitutes and confining them to special neighborhoods (which became known as "pleasure quarters") before the end of the sixteenth century. After 1657, kabuki performances were prohibited outside a clearly marked theater district; the performers were forbidden to live or even to move about outside this district. The purpose of the restrictions was to avert what one official called "the collapse of the social order."

The social order of the Tokugawa Shogunate rested on the twin pillars of family loyalty and feudal loyalty. The most important virtue was obedience. If a family fell into debt, for example, the head of the household might choose to sell his wife or daughter into prostitution to discharge his obligation. While the more accomplished residents of the pleasure quarter were widely admired, the life of a courtesan was hardly a desirable end for a woman of respectable family, and the unhappy consequences of enforced prostitution became a staple of the kabuki stage. Yet virtually no voices—on- or offstage—were raised against the custom itself or the social code that sanctioned it. For an individual who could not endure his or her lot there was a socially acceptable way out: suicide. But to openly disobey the head of the household and go on living was to bring dishonor to one's family—a fate considered far worse than mere personal unhappiness.

Samurai and other retainers of the powerful feudal lords had yet another level of obligation that superseded even family loyalty. A samurai swore an oath of loyalty to his lord. If obedience to the lord conflicted with family loyalty, the oath to the lord came first. The worst fate that could befall a warrior was to be severed from his lord's service, to be reduced to the status of a "masterless samurai." The anguish this caused also became a staple of the kabuki stage. In fact, the "masterless samurai" was an increasingly familiar figure in a warrior society that fought no wars and that was gradually transforming itself from a feudal to a cash-based economy. Like the "code of the cowboy" in the American West, the warriors' code of honor took on a romantic appeal even as its social utility faded. As an ideal of manly behavior, it could be admired even by commoners who had reason to fear the actual samurai they encountered daily in the streets of the city; all members of the warrior caste had the right to carry two swords and to cut down any commoner who showed them disrespect.

By the end of the seventeenth century, the lower social classes, and especially the merchants, had adopted the morality of the warrior caste as their own. To carry out one's duty according to the social code was good; to put personal desires ahead of social obligations was bad. To ensure that everyone in

Japan would remain, in a formulation attributed to the first Tokugawa Shogun, "content with one's present lot," the government tried to curtail conspicuous consumption. The style of a person's clothes was regulated by caste; for example, merchants could wear only somber colors. Houses had to be unostentatious. In time there was even a law regulating the decoration of cakes. Like the rules restricting the whereabouts of kabuki performers, these sumptuary laws were constantly reissued, a sure sign that they were being honored mostly in the breach.

Indeed, the pursuit of luxury seems to have been the order of the day in Edo, a city whose million-plus population made it possibly the largest in the world by the middle of the eighteenth century. As Louis XIV did at Versailles, the Shogun maintained an elaborate court and kept the most powerful lords near him in Edo for part of each year. Even when a lord returned to his domain, members of his family re-

mained behind to ensure his loyalty. No high-ranking household in the capital could afford to look shabbier than its rivals; and no phalanx of laws could keep the idle ladies of these households from spending their days at a kabuki theater in their latest finery. Also in the audience were some of the city's half-million samurai, many of them masterless, who lived on a kind of government subsidy that did not begin to cover the costly diversions of city life which included gambling, drinking, and frequenting the pleasure quarter. When samurai ran out of cash, they ran up bills with the merchants, who were getting rich serving as middlemen between farmers and artisans and providing luxuries and loans to the overextended upper classes.

Not far from Edo's pleasure quarter stood the theater district, where kabuki was officially tolerated (except during outbreaks of "moral reform"). Performances started early in the morning and lasted till dusk; they constituted a kind

of year-round festival of delights that must have seemed all the more delightful for being officially frowned upon. Like most Asian theater, kabuki made no rigid distinction between dance and drama. Words, music, spectacle, and movement were welded together in plays that dealt with unruly passions, violent revenge, mistaken identities, supernatural events, lamentable (and sometimes comic) misunderstandings. Staging was an amalgam of realistic effects and theatrical conventions. The huge papier-mâché temple bell in *The Dancing Maiden at Dojo Temple* looked like a real bell; trapdoors and mechanical lifts were used for mysterious appearances and disappearances; the onstage attendants who manipulated props and costumes during the performances were considered "invisible" to actors and audience alike.

This was a people's theater. Beggars got in for free; others, who typically arrived in groups, paid admission that varied with the popularity of the play.

Opposite: The Nakamura Theater, Edo, in the mid-eighteenth century. The architecture reveals many elements of the Nō stage, including a roof, from which the kabuki stage derives. According to the signboards posted on the stage pillars, the play being performed is Yanone (The Arrow Maker), one of those in the mostly aragoto collection called the "kabuki eighteen." The men at the upper left and right of the picture operate the sliding windows which are the main sources of light. There have since been many revisions in kabuki architecture.

The Shintomi Theater, Tokyo, in 1878. The print shows two runways, the main one (left) and a temporary one (right). Most of the audience sits on the ground in little boxed-off areas. A vendor can be seen selling food from the main runway. Daylight enters through the windows over the tiered seating at the sides, but there are gas chandeliers over the auditorium, a major innovation. The large banner to the left of the stage signifies that the show is sold out; beneath it is the room in which the musicians, hidden behind rattan blinds, play.

For a big hit, spectators were "pressed together like human sushi," according to a contemporary account. Since performances lasted all day, people brought their own meals or purchased food and drink from roaming vendors or patronized the teahouses that surrounded the theater building. There were no chairs; everyone sat on straw mats. The cheapest tickets were for the pit, the area that extended back from the stage (where the orchestra in a Western opera house would be). For more money, spectators could sit in two rows of raised boxes that ran at right angles to the stage on either side of the pit. When demand warranted, theater managers even packed spectators into stalls at the rear of the stage, where they saw only the backs of the performers. By mid-eighteenth century Edo's biggest theaters were accommodating audiences of more than a thousand.

Despite its size, everything in a traditional kabuki theater is arranged to heighten a feeling of intimacy between audience and performers. The stage is wider, and the rear of the auditorium closer to the stage, than in a typical Western theater; this brings more people close to the action, which tends to be dispersed across the entire width of the performing area. Lighting is uniform throughout the theater; the house lights are not dimmed when the performance begins. The most important entrances and exits take place on a raised runway that runs through the pit from the rear of the auditorium to the front of the stage. A performer on this runway, surrounded by the upturned faces of theatergoers, is exposed to view on all sides. Because spectators have to keep turning their heads from one part of the stage to another and from the stage to the runway and back again, watching kabuki is an active, participatory experience. The effect is different from watching a ballet, where the performance is entirely contained within the proscenium arch and all sightlines tend to converge to a single focus on the stage. In kabuki, as scholar Earle Ernst has put it, "the focal point of the performance is created in the midst of the audience."

There have been times when members of the audience preferred to do their kabuki-watching incognito. Barring unusual circumstances, no one would attend a ballet in disguise; to be seen at the ballet has always been a mark of culture and refinement. But kabuki has had to live down its plebeian origins. Although the law barring samurai from the theaters (where they might rub elbows with the lower classes) was enforced only sporadically, they often wore straw hats to hide their faces and cover their distinctive topknots. When government regulations permitted, the more expensive boxes on both sides of the pit were fitted with wooden screens; hidden behind these the wives and daughters of respectable families could spend the day watching their favorite performers and picking up pointers on the latest fashions in dress and coiffure

from the onnagatas, who had themselves been instructed in the arts of femininity by the courtesans of the pleasure quarter. (Given the close proximity of the pleasure quarter and the theater district, it is not surprising that the world of the courtesans and their patrons was a favorite subject of kabuki playwrights.) The screened boxes also concealed high government officials and landed aristocrats whose interest in kabuki was piqued by plays that chronicled the deeds and misdeeds of the high-born.

Kabuki's most avid fans, however, were the merchants for whom the theater district, like the pleasure quarter, offered a temporary respite from a tight-ly regulated existence. In the city proper, all but the richest merchants had to defer to the sword-wielding samurai. In the theater district, money talked. By the end of the eighteenth century a first-class ticket to a hit show cost enough to buy rice for two adults and a child for six months. The merchant who bought such a ticket might arrive at the theater wearing the drab kimono prescribed by law; once inside, he could turn back his outer garment to reveal a brilliantly colored silk lining. On stage, kabuki offered lavishly costumed spectacles that reflected the tastes and opinions of its audience (within the limits decreed by government censors). Drawing inspiration from ancient leg-

ends, traditional Nō plays and contemporary events, kabuki conjured up a cast of characters whose confrontations with society's rules and rulers never overstepped the bounds set by a social code to which everyone, no matter what their caste, subscribed.

Kabuki audiences today come to see many of the same characters in many of the same plays that attracted audiences two hundred years ago. A heroic commoner (often a "good" samurai in disguise) turns the tables on an insufferable bunch of "bad" samurai. A quick-witted outlaw, as loyal to his Robin Hood–like gang leader as any samurai to his feudal lord, holds off battalions of constables. A woman of respectable parentage, sold into prostitution by her husband, falls in love with a customer (perhaps a merchant's son) who returns her love but does not have enough money to buy her out of servitude; unable to give each other up, the lovers are trapped by their circumstances: If she runs away with him she will be running out on her family obligations; if he stays with her in the pleasure quarter he will dishonor his family. Having transgressed society's canons with their love, they now accept the consequences and commit double suicide on stage. Originally based on actual incidents reported in Osaka in the early eighteenth century, plays about double suicide apparently triggered new waves of suicides by distraught young lovers—a case of life imitating art imitating life. In both art and life, the moral was the same; there could be no escape from the social code except in death.

Although kabuki marshals words and music to tell its stories, its most charac-teristic effects rely on an extensive vocabulary of stylized body movements. The primary appeal of kabuki is not intellectual but sensuous; the audience comes to the theater to see a series of striking images. These images have been so molded by years of give-and-take between performer and spectator that they convey powerful emotional messages to Japanese audiences. For example, a kabuki performer never sheds real tears on stage, no matter how doleful the events being enacted. While real tears might be appropriate in a representational theater—one that invites the audience to pretend that the action on stage is a literal reproduction of reality—kabuki never lets its audience forget that the performer is a performer, the stage a stage. In the middle of a scene a kabuki performer may turn his back on the audience to drink a refreshing cup of tea brought to him by an attendant. The "reality" that kabuki offers is a theatrical construct, a selective assembly of images that have much in common with the carefully crafted movement-sequences of ballet. To knowledgeable audiences, a ballet dancer can convey sorrow or joy, pathos or passion, with body movements alone. With a rhythmical shake of the head and a precise hand gesture a kabuki performer not only signals "weeping" but brings tears to the eyes of spectators who have seen the same scene dozens of times before and understand every nuance of the situation being anatomized on stage.

As with ballet, the movement-sequences of kabuki are divisible into traditional poses, gestures, and actions that performers, spectators, teachers, and critics know by name. These dis-crete units of stage technique are called kata, which means forms or models. Kabuki manuals list hundreds of *kata*. Some involve props, like the onstage costume changes that transform a woman into a demon or a man into a fox. Some require elaborate machinery (trapdoors, lifts, and revolving stages). Other kata are defined by a particular reading of a line, a way of lifting an eyebrow or twirling a fan. A special class of kata, called roppos, are spectacular entrances or exits in which a performer hurtles down the runway that connects the stage to the rear of the theater, his costume billowing out around him, while a stage attendant beats an accompanying tattoo with wooden clappers and the connoisseurs in the audience shout out their approval: "*Matte imashita!*" ("This is what we were waiting for!").

The performers, rather than the plays themselves, have always been the focus of kabuki. The great acting families have produced dynasties of idolized stars whose stage names mimic royal lineages: Ichikawa Danjūrō IX, Nakamura Ganjirō II, Iwai Hanshirō V. Dynastic names are not given at birth; they must be earned through years of performing a variety of roles with distinction. Only after a performer has mastered a specific role with all its inherited stage business does he feel free to make small changes in this or that kata. This may not come until he is in his forties.

While all kabuki can be likened to dance because of its emphasis on body movement, the Japanese have a special name for plays in which the narrative element is less important than what might be called pure dance. These pieces are known as shosagoto, which literally means "posture-business." Unlike ballet, where the dancer typically strives to negate the appearance of weight, the movement of the body in kabuki is directed down from the waist toward the floor. Dance pieces are performed on special wooden platforms whose smooth surface facilitates the fluid, gliding steps of kabuki dance, which is usually performed in thick cotton socks that look like mittens for the feet. The hollow structure of the platforms also amplifies the occasional stamping of the dancer's feet, a sound suggestive of the goddess Ame-no-uzume dancing on an overturned tub to lure the sun goddess out of her cave and restore light to the universe. As a technical device that literally resounds with mythological meaning, the dance platform typifies the care that kabuki brings to every detail of staging. In many kabuki dances the feet can barely be seen since they are concealed beneath a floor-length costume (which, in the case of the onnagata, serves to hide any parts of the body that would detract from the appearance of femininity).

Perhaps the most famous dance piece in kabuki is *The Dancing Maiden at Dojo Temple* which is based on a Nō version of an ancient legend. The legend tells of a young girl whose love is spurned by a priest who has taken vows of celibacy. In a vengeful fury, she turns into a snake-demon and destroys both the temple's bell and the priest. *The Dancing Maiden at Dojo Temple* enacts a sequel to this event; years later, an itinerant dancer named Hanako asks permission to enter Dojo Temple to view the new bell

which is being installed. The priests admit her on the condition that she dance for them. As she dances, she keeps turning to stare at the bell. Little by little, she is possessed by the angry spirit of the earlier maiden. At the end, transformed into the snake-demon, she climbs atop the new bell to destroy it.

There are several versions of *The Dancing Maiden at Dojo Temple*. The hour-long solo version, first performed in 1753, is considered one of kabuki's most demanding roles, a tour de force in which onnagatas like Bandō Tamasaburō display their virtuosity and interpretive skills. The challenge is to express in movement and gesture a complete portrait of a woman in love. The contrast to ballet's *Sleeping Beauty* is instructive. The European fairy tale shows innocence incarnate triumphing over worldly evil. The Japanese legend looks beneath the innocent surface to reveal "demonic" forces within the individual—a recurrent theme in a feudal society that equated morality with outward deference to a social code.

In Japanese folklore it is the snake, not the cat, that has nine lives. To portray a woman's passage from the joy of first love to the pain of love unrequited to jealous hatred of the rejecting lover, the dancer goes through a series of onstage costume changes reminiscent of a snake shedding its skin. She comes on stage wearing several layers of kimonos, each held in place by a few strategically placed basting threads. At key moments in the dance, a stage attendant pulls out some threads, releasing the outer garment and revealing another layer beneath. Hanako first appears in a black

kimono decorated with white flowers; on her head she wears the white cloth that a Japanese bride wears at her wedding. At the climax of her dance, she is wearing a white kimono with dark flowers; the upper half of this kimono is folded down to reveal a silvery triangular pattern that resembles scales.

While an onstage "chorus" chants the traditional story and onstage musicians play drums, flutes, and the three-stringed instruments called samisen, the dancer illustrates and comments on the words of the text with movements and gestures. The pace is slow at first, but gradually increases in tempo as the climax approaches. At times Hanako mimes incidents from the past, using simple props like a small drum, a hand towel, and a fan. With a few waves of her fan she conjures up a long journey through high mountains; twisting the towel around her neck, she suggests the ties that bind true lovers. There are no off-the-floor pyrotechnics equivalent to ballet's leaps and lifts. One of the eagerly awaited moments in *The Dancing Maiden at Dojo Temple* comes when Hanako faces the rear of the stage and bends backward slowly from the waist until the audience can see down the back of her kimono—a pose that has strongly erotic connotations for the Japanese. Tamasaburō is famous for the long, graceful curve of his body as his head dips toward the floor.

The standard kabuki repertory consists of some 350 plays or parts of plays, some dating back to the seventeenth century. Few changes have been made in content or style since the nineteenth century. Like balletomanes who return

The onnagata Nakamura Tomijūrō I (1719–1786),
third son of the great onnagata Yoshizawa Ayame I,
in an early version of The Dancing Maiden at
Dojo Temple. *The dance had been introduced in*
Edo by Segawa Kikunojō II, but Tomijūrō soon
rivaled the other actor in the piece.

to *The Sleeping Beauty* again and again
to watch a favorite ballerina dance the
Princess, kabuki audiences go to see a
favorite performer bring his special
touch to a well-known role. Since many
of the details of production and performance are fixed by tradition, it takes an
experienced eye to distinguish between
differing interpretations, or to note how
a performer has slightly altered a gesture or pose from his last performance.

Even kabuki plays not classified as
dance pieces are distinguished by varying styles of body movement. Aragoto,
or "rough stuff," is a bravura style of acting that originated in Edo in the
seventeenth century. Many aragoto
characters represent supermen of the
Hercules type, whose physical prowess is
symbolized by vivid red "strength lines"
painted on their arms and legs to indicate bulging muscles. Aragoto heroes
often wear outsized costumes; some carry *three* swords. They strut, swagger, and
boast. They speak their lines in a high-
pitched, bombastic manner, the louder
the better; at peak moments they shout
out nonsense syllables. The contorted
postures and facial antics of aragoto
owe something to the cult of Fudō, a
Buddhist demigod whose cross-eyed,
snarling visage was familiar to every
temple-goer of the Edo period.
The inaugurator of the aragoto style,
Ichikawa Danjūrō I (1660–1704), a
devotee of Fudō, once said: "Even in
front of lords you must never be afraid,
or it won't be aragoto." Seen through
the lens of aragoto, strength, heroism,
purity, foolishness, and evil all appear
larger than life. Aragoto characters
occupy the top rung of the kabuki

147

caste-world; they are superior to other men in power and prestige and they act accordingly.

Only in matters of love are they sometimes bested. The beautiful (and often doomed) women of kabuki tend to fall in love with a type of man so different from the aragoto ideal that it calls for an entirely different style of acting, known as wagoto, or "soft style." If aragoto characters are the Clint Eastwoods and Arnold Schwarzeneggers of kabuki, wagoto characters are the James Deans. A wagoto lover sports no "strength lines"; sensitivity is his strength. His movements are refined; his way of walking incorporates elements from the onnagata's pigeon-toed shuffle. He may or may not be brave; his eagerness to give up all for love may even seem faintly comic; but it is his gentle, considerate wooing that wins the hearts of kabuki's most desirable heroines—and of the women in the audience who come to swoon over his tender ways and to weep over his often pitiful fate.

The most characteristic device used on the kabuki stage to heighten dramatic tension is the mie (rhymes with "we say"). In a mie, the performer freezes his body in a pose that may last as long as ten or twelve seconds. This is called "cutting a mie." It signifies that the character is in the grip of an overpowering emotion like anger or defiance, or is struggling for equilibrium while being pulled in opposite directions by irreconcilable motives. Some kabuki plays have as many as seven or eight mies; the narrative is designed to build up to each of these dramatic moments, which regular theatergoers await the way a ballet audience awaits a particular solo or duet. In

148

Nakamura Nazakō I (1736–1790), a great actor of villain roles, in an aragoto character. Note the mie expression with the eyes crossed and the stylized makeup.

the more spectacular aragoto-style mies the actor may fling out his arms and legs, cross his eyes, and twist his features into a grimace. Other mies achieve their effect through subtler means.

One of the most popular plays in the kabuki repertoire is *The Village School* (actually a long scene from an even longer play). Matsuō, a samurai dubbed "the heartless" because of his zeal in carrying out his cruel lord's commands, is torn between two life-and-death obligations. The nine-year-old son of his lord's enemy is to be beheaded. Matsuō is sent to verify the execution. Through family ties Matsuō also owes allegiance to his lord's enemy. He feels obligated to save the boy, but in order to satisfy his lord's command, he must produce a head that resembles the boy's. He chooses to sacrifice his own son. There comes a moment when Matsuō, acting as his lord's agent, is called upon to verify that the right victim has been executed. A box containing the severed head of his own son is handed to him. He extracts the head from the box, examines it, declares it to be the "right" head, and then turns to the audience and cuts a mie: his unblinking stare, strained face, and rigid body seem to distill the essence of his feelings at this terrible moment.

Like Hanako the temple dancer, Matsuō is not what he seems on the surface. As he explains in a scene following the head inspection, the apparently heartless manner in which he has behaved in the service of his lord does not reflect his true nature; he has a heart indeed, and it is breaking now. Kataoka Takao, one of today's leading kabuki performers, likens the mie to a movie closeup: "It's an enlarged vision shown

in frozen motion that reveals heightened emotion." During the Tokugawa Shogunate, depictions of famous performers cutting mies were a specialty of Japanese woodblock artists; kabuki enthusiasts collected them the way baseball fans today collect cards of their favorite players.

By the time of the Meiji Restoration in 1868, when a government in the name of the emperor replaced a moribund Shogunate, kabuki was well on its way to achieving classical status. It had evolved a standard repertoire played in carefully delineated styles using traditional kata that audiences came to savor. The merely faddish themes, the purely quirky mannerisms had been weeded out. What remained was a self-image that Japanese audiences enjoyed seeing enacted in public time and time again. The opening of Japan to Western influences in the late nineteenth century led to a reappraisal of all the arts of the Tokugawa era. Japanese advocates of modernization attacked kabuki for being "full of absurdity and nonsense, obscenity and vulgarity." But the militaristic government that began preparing Japan for war in the late nineteenth century recognized that kabuki had captured something fundamental to Japanese society; the plays that had survived the long winnowing process could still make audiences laugh and cry and catch their breath in wonder. Government ideologues paid kabuki the high compliment of trying to subvert it to their own propaganda objectives.

Ever since *The Village School* was first performed in Edo in the mid-eighteenth century, the schoolteacher who actually beheads the innocent child has offered this comment on his own and Matsuō's

actions: "It is painful indeed to serve one's lord!" But during the period of rampant militarism, this line was transferred to the schoolteacher's wife and the schoolteacher himself was made to respond: "It is only now that we can truly serve our lord."

After World War II, the Japanese might have abandoned or radically altered kabuki. Instead, the tradition was revived, with the reluctant approval of the American Occupation forces (who worried that kabuki would indoctrinate new generations of Japanese with "feudal," i.e., undemocratic, values). Today's kabuki theaters sell large blocks of tickets to Japanese corporations which pass them along to deserving employees. For some of these theatergoers, the stage conventions of kabuki are as unfamiliar as they would be to a Western tourist. Yet the popularity of a Tamasaburō would seem to confirm the ability of all-male kabuki, at its most tradition-bound, to speak to modern Japanese audiences. A glimpse of what it says to today's fans, who are mostly female, can be inferred from contemporary performances of *The Village School* in which the schoolteacher's line has been restored to its original sense of tragic resignation, of shouldering the heavy burden that a rigid moral system places on even its most willing adherents: "It is painful indeed to serve one's lord!"

What has gone down in history as "the yew tree ball" was a masked ball in the Hall of Mirrors at Versailles on the occasion of the marriage of the Dauphin, the son of Louis XV, and Maria Theresa, the Infanta of Spain, on the night of February 25, 1745. In commemoration of the event, Charles Nicolas Cochin made this engraving.

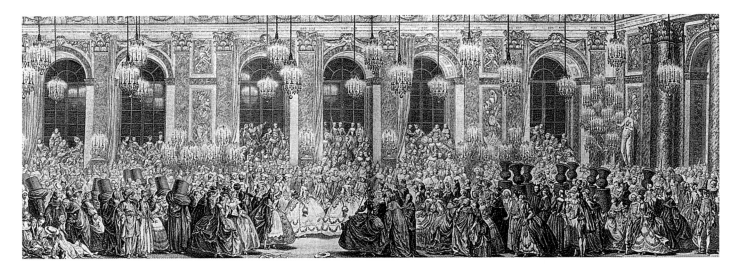

The king came to the costume ball dressed as a yew tree. All Paris knew he was looking for a new mistress. His last favorite had died the year before, and Louis XV, great-grandson of the Sun King, loved hunting, dancing, and a pretty face, not necessarily in that order. He had taken a fancy to a beautiful young woman who followed the royal hunt in her open carriage. Because of her nonaristocratic birth—she was the daughter of a financial speculator of unsavory reputation—she could not be presented at court. But balls in the state apartments at Versailles were now open to anyone who had the means and manners to dress properly. So it was arranged during Carnival season that the twenty-three-year-old wife of a wealthy commoner come to a ball in the Galerie des Glaces dressed as Diana the Huntress. Crowds thronged the brilliantly lit palace; to gain some measure of anonymity the king had commanded seven of his courtiers to be covered from head to toe, as he was, with clipped yew

branches: none of the onlookers could be completely sure which yew hid the monarch. The evening was a success. Legally separated from her husband and elevated to the title of Marquise de Pompadour, the young bourgeoise became the king's mistress; until her death in 1764 she was not only the arbiter of taste in Paris (and so to all of Europe) but also, many said, the power behind the French throne.

With Louis XV "courting" a new mistress at a crowded costume ball in 1745 we have come a long way from Louis XIV dancing as the incarnation of Apollo in a court ballet. By 1745 the French monarchy was in decline, the moneyed classes were on the rise —as they were on the inaccessible islands of Japan over seven thousand miles away. While the ability to dance was still a necessary social grace in mid-eighteenth–century France, the professional dancers who performed at the Paris Opéra were developing skills and grace that no king or courtier could

hope to match, and professional ballet masters had begun searching for a subject and an audience worthy of the technique of their dancers.

But as long as there was a court at Versailles, dancing onstage continued to reflect the values expressed in social dancing at court, and vice versa. The links between the two were most apparent in the nearly identical clothes that ballroom dancers and ballet dancers wore throughout the eighteenth century. Like the equally massive costumes of kabuki, these clothes were designed not for comfort or practicality but for show. Beneath their gaudy surfaces, they were cut to reinforce the proper posture taught by dancing masters to a clientele that now included more commoners than aristocrats. High, tight armholes set toward the back of women's gowns and men's coats forced the shoulders up and to the rear and lent a backward arch to the spine, a stance deemed necessary if one was to give a good account of oneself in the minuet.

Women were laced into boned corsets that narrowed waists and shortened breath. Yards and yards of heavy damask silks and crisp taffetas went into floor-length skirts, circular or elliptical in profile, that hung on wood, metal, or whale-bone frames called panniers. Everyone young and old wore powdered wigs. Fashionable women erected elaborate hairdos on hidden wire cores; these coiffures weighed as much as twenty pounds—about the heft of an onnagata's wig—and were undone, once a month, for delousing. Women's dancing shoes came with pointed toes and tapered heels that curved forward to meet the ground just below the instep; no distinction was made between shoes for the right and left feet.

Essentially the same opened-up stance—heels forming a right angle with one leg slightly in advance of the other—was required for the proper performance of all dances, whether in the theater or the ballroom; only children or the untutored danced with their feet parallel. Onstage, women's corsets might be a little looser, their skirts and their hairdos not quite so voluminous, and male dancers did not wear the knee-length frock coats seen in ballrooms, but in general the same conventions of aristocratic propriety applied. Ballerinas maneuvered around the stage in heeled shoes and panniered gowns that just missed brushing the floor. The standard costume for ballet heroes was a kind of pseudo-Roman armor complete with plumed helmet, leather-trimmed blouse, cape, and the male equivalent of a hooped skirt—the midthigh tonnelet that belled out over tight knickers; on their feet they wore leather-soled buskins laced to the knee. Until late in the century both male and female dancers appeared on stage in half-masks, in deference to contemporary notions of the Greek and Roman theater of antiquity. In upper-class ballrooms, masquerade balls continued the centuries-old tradition of concealing one's identity at public entertainments, especially during Carnival.

In the evolution of Japanese dance drama, kabuki performers had discarded the masks worn by Nō actors in favor of the more expressive made-up face, but kabuki costumes grew even more lavish and massive over time; the way a kabuki dancer dealt with the yards of constricting material formed an integral part of his dance. In eighteenth-century Europe, by contrast, reformers began to argue that ballet could never achieve its true potential as long as it was weighed down with all that extraneous paraphernalia. Traditionalists resisted for a while. Marie Camargo, who made her Paris debut in 1726, shocked some in the audience by shortening her skirts a few inches to show off her unusually high (for the time) leaps. Her entrechats—jumps in which the feet are crossed once or several times before landing—were especially admired by Voltaire, who said that she was the first ballerina to dance like a man. The whole idea of leaping dancers was anathema to traditionalists, who preferred floor-bound steps derived from the earlier court ballets. Camargo's chief rival at the Paris Opéra, Marie Sallé, stayed close to the floor, but in her search for emotionally expressive movement she too offended the traditionalists. In 1729 she dared to dance without a mask; five years later, in her own adaptation of Pygmalion staged in London, she appeared without pannier or wig, draped like a Greek statue in a simple muslin tunic with her hair falling naturally to her shoulders.

This was going too far. Despite Sallé's personal popularity, ballroom fashions resisted the "natural look"; and against that resistance not even the most determined ballerina could prevail. In 1760 Jean Georges Noverre, a ballet master who had more success in London and Stuttgart than in Paris, published a broadside against the state of ballet in Europe in which he exhorted professional dancers: "Take off those enormous wigs and those gigantic head-dresses which destroy the true proportions of the head with the body; discard the use of those stiff and cumbersome hoops which detract from the beauties of execution, which disfigure the elegance of your attitudes and mar the beauties of contour which the bust should exhibit in its different positions."

Noverre also railed against the practice of patching together ballets from bits and pieces of Greek and Roman myths; or inserting a ballet as a divertissement between acts of an opera without any concern for the dramatic coherence of either the dancing or the singing. On other continents, in places like India or Java, the central myths of a culture could be enacted in dance; when Indian dancers portrayed the Lord Rama or Krishna, they were assured that their audience not only knew the stories by heart but instinctively understood the issues at stake. Because of Christendom's ambivalent attitude toward the body—and therefore toward dance—reenactment of the central

The costume design (opposite), for the Queen of the Sylphs from an eighteenth-century ballet, shows the older style of ballet costume which was already giving way to the less encumbering costumes popularized by Camargo. The gown is decorated with ribbons, small clouds of gauze, and peacock feathers, and the headdress with plumes and jewels.

The French painter Nicolas Lancret painted at least four versions of La Camargo Dancing (below) in the late 1720s when the ballerina, born in 1710, was not yet twenty. The artist based his portraits on costume prints like the one opposite, and his paintings became in turn the model for a popular print of 1730. Camargo's gown permits the audience to see her feet.

The flowing Empire gown of post-Revolutionary France (right) temporarily freed the female body from the restrictive panniers used in formal dresses, and for ballerinas, at least, there was no turning back. This is the radiant young Juliette Récamier, sketched by the French painter François Gérard in about 1800.

A caricature parodying the heroic pantomime from Jean Georges Noverre's Jason and Medea (1763), which he staged in Stuttgart, where he was ballet master for a time.

myth of Christianity was forbidden to European ballet. In asserting his "divine right" to rule, Louis XIV had of course claimed the mantle of the Christian god; but since it would have been blasphemous to dance as Christ, or even as one of the archangels, Apollo was deemed a suitable stand-in.

From the beginning of the Christian era, the Olympian gods had existed in a realm of imagination known as allegory. As historically sanctioned emblems of human aspirations and follies, they had been used by Renaissance artists and princes to express attitudes not easily encompassed in Christian iconography. The allegorical links between Sun King and sun god were understood by everyone who mattered, the associations with the glory of Greece and the grandeur of Rome were favorable, and most importantly, the seriousness of Louis XIV's ambition could not be doubted. Charles Perrault, a courtier at Versailles (and author of the tale that later inspired the ballet *The Sleeping Beauty*), wrote a book arguing that Louis XIV was a greater monarch than Emperor Augustus; history might disagree but

the argument did not seem ludicrous on its face to Frenchmen of the seventeenth century.

By the mid-eighteenth century, however, the connection between classical myths and contemporary events was less secure. In an Age of Reason, it was difficult for enlightened Frenchmen to conceive of any king, much less Louis XV, as an incarnation of any deity, no matter how "allegorical." Audiences no longer collaborated in the symbolic fictions as they had just a few decades earlier. Inspired artists might still bring the old stories to life, but such people rarely wrote ballet librettos. With the exception of an underclad Pygmalion (who appealed on a more basic level than allegory), simply parading the old gods about the stage with their academic labels on display, in the manner that Noverre deplored, was more likely to trigger a bored nod of recognition than a heartfelt huzzah.

The evolution of ballet into an art capable of holding its own with painting and poetry was Noverre's dream. But it was easier to condemn the routine recycling of exhausted classical themes than

to come up with an alternative. Noverre himself staged a *Jason and Medea* and an *Amor and Psyche* and collaborated with Christoph Willibald Gluck on the opera *Orpheus*; significantly, he had his biggest success (in 1754) with an evening of divertissements based on "Chinese" themes, a concession to the public taste for mindlessly amusing and sensually arousing exotica that he himself deplored. One great problem in enacting new stories was finding a movement vocabulary that could convey complex actions and motivations to unprepared audiences. At least with classical myths, the general outline of the story was clear, so educated audiences could "read" the expressive gestures of the dancers with some confidence. To venture beyond known tales was to enter uncharted territory. Words, either sung or declaimed, could carry the plot; but this left dance in a secondary role, icing on the narrative cake, unless both performers and audience shared a common language of gesture and movement. Tantalizingly, history told of such a language, the long-lost idiom of Roman pantomimes, who were said to have been capable of communicating the most complicated thoughts and emotions without making a sound.

Contemporary commedia dell'arte troupes managed to bring to life an entire gallery of stereotypes, such as Harlequin and Punchinello (Punch) and Scaramouche, with a finite set of easily read body movements. More ambitious artists saw a need to expand the vocabulary of gestures that could be used with confidence before any audience. A 1717 English libretto for a "dramatick entertainment of dancing" entitled *The Loves of Mars and Venus* left nothing to chance. Theatergoers were informed that "Astonishment" would be mimed by "both hands . . . thrown up towards the Skies; the Eyes also lifted up, and the Body cast backwards. Neglect will appear in the scornful turning the Neck; the flirting outward the back of the right hand, with a Turn of the Wrist." As for "Detestation . . . both the turn'd-out Palms are so bent to the left Side, and the Head still more projected from the Object."

By 1750 the norms of ballet pantomime were well established. But unlike the evolution of dance drama in Japan, where kabuki performers refined their katas into tools for conveying complex emotions to knowledgeable audiences, balletic mime in the West remained a limited and somewhat awkward instrument. Mimed gestures were often seen as static interruptions in the smooth flow of the dance. The more complicated the libretto the more mime was needed, and the more mime the less dance. Having gone mute, dance drama in the West had yet to find a worthy

subject it could enact with its silent vocabulary of movement. But progress was in the air. In the second half of the eighteenth century, professional ballet dancers finally set aside their masks and their heeled shoes and buskins, and pared down their outer garments. This change in costume heralded the beginning of the end of ballet's century-long deference to the conventions of the aristocratic ballroom—and to the stage conventions that the dead hand of the court had imposed.

On July 1, 1789, two weeks before a Paris mob stormed the Bastille, a disciple of Noverre staged a new type of ballet in the provincial city of Bordeaux. It was called *La Fille Mal Gardée*. The story (borrowed from an earlier comic opera) told of a farmer's daughter whose love for a poor but honest peasant is almost thwarted by a greedy mother who wants her to marry a wealthier suitor. The plot was familiar to many in the audience. The characters were reminiscent of commedia dell'arte stereotypes, and the picturesque setting probably owed more to Marie Antoinette's quaint "dairy" on the grounds of Versailles than to life in the French countryside on the eve of the Revolution. But some of the steps, based on lively country dances with arms akimbo and much stamping of the feet, intentionally violated the conventions of the academy; and the entire production had a lighthearted freshness that struck a new chord in audiences. Compared to the stale heroic posturing of the Paris stage, even a prettified depiction of lower-class life seemed exotic and daring. *La Fille Mal Gardée* survived the downfall of the ancien régime and the

social upheavals that followed; Fanny Elssler danced it on her American tour in 1842. Versions of the ballet are still seen today, although hardly anything is left of its original music or choreography. Perhaps its most important legacy was the freedom to blend steps and gestures from folk dancing into the movement vocabulary of classical ballet, and to build entire scenes around the danced rituals and ceremonies of country life (betrothals, weddings, spring and harvest festivals); this has become a tradition in its own right.

The real revolution in dance, however, was still to come. The Paris Opéra remained open throughout the Terror and the Directoire and the rise of Napoleon. But many of its stars fled across the Channel; and English audiences were soon applauding dancers who (with a little mechanical assistance) went up on their toes and stayed there. In 1796 Charles Louis Didelot, another pupil of Noverre's, staged a one-act divertissement in London called *Flore et Zéphyre*. The classical allusions of the title were beside the point. The excitement was in the stage machinery that suspended dancers from "invisible" counterweighted wires so that they could balance on their toes—and even take off and fly across the stage. Didelot's choreography also emphasized athletic partnering, in which a strong male dancer supported and lifted his female partner, allowing her to pose, if only for a few moments, on the ball of one heelless slipper.

In response to the revolutionary currents sweeping Europe, ballroom fashions also changed, if only briefly. For a few years around the turn of the cen-

The detail (left) from French painter Antoine Watteau's Country Dance (c.1715) shows a lively country dance of the sort that enriched the movement vocabulary of ballet later in the century.

Commedia dell'arte (below) was a type of theatrical performance, full of earthy humor, slapstick, and mimicry, popular in Italy and southern France from the sixteenth to eighteenth centuries. Eventually, dances were integrated into the performances. The stories revolved around such familiar characters as Harlequin, Punchinello (Punch), and Scaramouche, and these stereotypes in turn enriched the dramatic repertoire of ballet, being particularly popular with Russian choreographers, including Marius Petipa, Mikhail Fokine, Léonide Massine, and Serge Lifar. This painting is by an unknown Italian artist of the Bolognese school after an engraving published in Naples in 1622.

Danina, or Jocko the Brazilian Ape (1826; *above*) *was a popular vehicle for Marie Taglioni just before the advent of Romantic ballet. Taglioni appeared as a beautiful Brazilian named Danina, who rescues an ape named Jocko from a snake; Jocko later protects Danina's son from kidnappers.*

Far more enduring than Danina was Giselle, written by Théophile Gautier for the ballerina Carlotta Grisi in 1846. In popular lithographs of ballet stars during the Romantic era, such as the one at right depicting Grisi in Giselle, ballerinas were often depicted floating high above the ground.

Le Pas de Quatre, *performed in London in 1845, was an all-star evening featuring four of the most popular ballerinas of the time. Taglioni is in the center, surrounded by (from left to right) Grisi, Fanny Cerrito, and Lucille Grahn.*

tury the undergirding panniers were discarded, and the female silhouette took on a less encumbered, draped look that Sallé and Camargo would have applauded. And the advent of the waltz swept away forever the rigidly hierarchical organization of social dancing; in the biggest ballrooms hundreds of waltzing couples now took to the floor simultaneously. By midcentury ballroom gowns, obeying the fickle dictates of fashion, had lengthened and swelled again. But significantly, ballet costumes did not. Just the opposite. Tights were introduced about 1810. Taglioni and Elssler danced in soft, loose skirts that came down no lower than their calves, revealing their footwork as never before. In theaters romantically lit by the new gas lamps, audiences caught their breath when these ballerinas went up on their toes, sustained not by wires or partners but even more marvelously by their own muscle power. And it was in these moments of thrilling uplift that ballet, in consonance with the emerging Romantic sensibility, found a new aesthetic mission for the technical virtuosity of its dancers: to express the beauty of the spirit that transcends the flesh.

Popular lithographs of famous ballerinas in such Romantic ballets as *La*

Sylphide and *Giselle* not only show them on their toes but, in many cases, floating high above the ground. Often, they are barefoot, an iconographic convention that clearly expressed a desire to be free of all constraints. In her apparent conquest of gravity the ballet dancer on point seemed to capture the confident spirit of Europe itself in an age of unrestrained expansion, exploration, and exploitation. Certainly there was more to nineteenth-century ballet than the illusion of weightlessness. But it was the toe dancers who held center stage. To provide them with dramatic vehicles, librettists ransacked archives of folk tales and fairy tales for stories about female sprites (Scottish sylphs, the German "wilis" of *Giselle*) who lured men away from worldly concerns; death was often the price paid by seducer and seduced, but the mood was far from tragic. In these so-called "white ballets" (named for the dancers' elegantly revealing tutus of white gauze) the focus was not on the flaws of the doomed characters but on the ballerinas' apparently effortless flights into a realm beyond.

A full 180-degree turnout was now the norm. In what is known as first position, students learned to stand heel to heel with their feet forming a perfectly straight line; this provided a stable

foundation for all the dancer's moves and gave audiences the fullest possible frontal view of every step and gesture. Eventually, the focus on the dancer rather than the dance led to excesses that required correction if ballet was to continue to evolve as an art. By the 1840s impresarios were staging all-star evenings in which the most famous ballerinas—Taglioni, Elssler, Fanny Cerrito, Carlotta Grisi, Lucille Grahn—appeared in representative snippets of dance. In Paris, which still considered itself the center of the ballet world, male dancers were largely confined to supporting roles; when it was discovered that ballet audiences (not unlike the early audiences for Okuni's kabuki) enjoyed seeing women dressed as men dance male roles, the status of male dancers fell even further. Classical ballet might have died out altogether or been permanently reduced to a kind of upper-class burlesque if the spark of creativity had not been transferred to the Russian capital of St. Petersburg in the second half of the nineteenth century.

St. Petersburg had been founded by Peter the Great in 1703 as Russia's "window on Europe." To modernize his backward country, the tsar brought architects, artists, and artisans from Western Europe to build a city (and

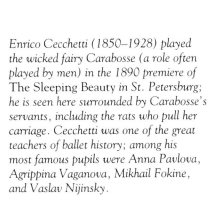

Enrico Cecchetti (1850–1928) played the wicked fairy Carabosse (a role often played by men) in the 1890 premiere of The Sleeping Beauty *in St. Petersburg; he is seen here surrounded by Carabosse's servants, including the rats who pull her carriage. Cecchetti was one of the great teachers of ballet history; among his most famous pupils were Anna Pavlova, Agrippina Vaganova, Mikhail Fokine, and Vaslav Nijinsky.*

harbor) that would rival anything he had seen on his travels in England, Holland, and Austria. To indoctrinate his nobility in European ways he compelled them to move to his new capital and build houses there. He had seen and enjoyed ballet in the West and loved dancing in masquerades; now he commanded the Russian nobles and their wives to learn French court dances like the courante and the minuet, and to dance in his presence at court. In 1735 a royal academy of dance was established. Under Catherine the Great (who reigned from 1762 to 1796) ballet masters were imported from Austria, France, and Italy to school the Russians in the fine points of classical dance. In 1801 Charles Didelot arrived in St. Petersburg; over the next twenty years, working with both imported and homegrown dancers, he brought ballet technique in Russia up to the standards of the rest of Europe. When Marie Taglioni and Fanny Elssler toured Russia, in the 1830s and 1840s they found the local balletomanes as enthusiastic as any they had encountered. In the following decades a succession of teachers and ballet masters (notably from France, Italy, and Denmark) staged the latest European ballets for increasingly knowledgeable Russian audiences.

In 1869 the French-born Marius Petipa took over the direction of the St. Petersburg ballet, which was now housed in the Maryinsky Theater. Under his leadership, and with generous government support, the Maryinsky troupe developed a company and a repertoire that had no equal anywhere in the world.

The creation of *La Belle au Bois Dormant (The Sleeping Beauty)* in 1890 is considered the high point of classical ballet. While the next era of revolution—in both politics and art—was just a few years away, the libretto of *The Sleeping Beauty* looked backward, toward a Golden Age when kings ruled by divine right and their subjects happily revered them. The original story, selected by the director of the Imperial Theaters, came from the pen of a courtier of Louis XIV. The Sun King had been a contemporary of the first Romanov tsar, whose descendant Alexander III now sat on the throne of Russia. That throne was far from secure. The tsar's government, faced with internal unrest, a threat from a resurgent Germany, and a depleted treasury, had recently secured a large French loan. The story of *The Sleeping Beauty*, which tells of innocence at risk until rescued by love, can also be read as a tale of

dynastic renewal. After a good long sleep, the court awakens and resumes its ordained role at the head of an orderly, hierarchical society.

The composer chosen to write the score was Peter Ilich Tchaikovsky. Petipa supplied him with detailed instructions that spelled out scene by scene, and at times measure by measure, the kind of music required, and Tchaikovsky responded with a score of great melodic richness, rhythmic invention, and almost symphonic texture. Some critics complained that Tchaikovsky's ballet scores were undanceably complex. But Petipa, who was accustomed to working with merely competent "house" composers, responded to the challenge of Tchaikovsky's music with equally challenging choreography. The result was a brilliant homage to the centuries-long evolution of classical ballet—from its origins as a court entertainment with a restricted range of expression to a mature art that put trained bodies to demanding tests of virtuosity and musicality in the name of an abstract beauty.

When the evil fairy Carabosse wreaks revenge on the court because she was not invited to Princess Aurora's christening, the Princess is an innocent victim of fate. (By way of comparison, it

Natalia Makarova (left) is widely believed to have danced the finest Giselle of the postwar period. Makarova was born in Leningrad in 1940 and joined the Kirov Ballet at nineteen. In 1970, she moved to the West, where she has danced principally with the American Ballet Theater in New York and the Royal Ballet in London. The young Larissa Lezhnina (right), a principal dancer in the Kirov Ballet, seen here in The Sleeping Beauty, is one of many dancers who continue to make St. Petersburg a center for classical ballet. Mikhail Baryshnikov (below) was the premier male ballet dancer of the 1970s and 1980s. Like Makarova, he studied at what is now called the Vaganova School in St. Petersburg; he made his debut as a soloist with the Kirov Ballet in 1966 at the age of eighteen. He moved to the West in 1974. The audience demands that male dancers be far more athletic than ballerinas, and Baryshnikov is known for his remarkable leaps and turns. Here he is seen in The Nutcracker, one of three Tchaikovsky ballets, the other two being The Sleeping Beauty and Swan Lake, that have never lost their broad appeal.

A publicity photo from the 1890 production of The Sleeping Beauty *at St. Petersburg's Maryinsky Theater.*

Opposite: Contrasting stage settings show how productions of The Sleeping Beauty *have evolved within a basically classical framework; above, the 1890 St. Petersburg production; below, the 1949 Sadler's Wells Ballet in their first appearance in New York.*

might be argued that the dancing maiden of *The Dancing Maiden at Dojo Temple* contains her own Carabosse within her.) Aurora's wedding is delayed until Prince Désiré breaks the evil fairy's spell and ends the court's century-long sleep. For those who seek a deeper meaning, there are echoes in the story of Persephone's descent into the underworld and other Western myths of death and revival. But by incorporating a series of variations for other fairy-tale characters, like Puss in Boots and Little Red Riding Hood, the collaborators firmly pointed the viewer's attention toward the spectacle and the dancing itself. The fairytale variations and the happy ending make *The Sleeping Beauty* quite literally an entertainment for all ages. Both Anna Pavlova and George Balanchine testified that it was their early exposure to this ballet—at ages eight and eleven respectively—that set them on their careers in dance.

In the twentieth century *The Sleeping Beauty* has become the signature piece of major ballet companies. Serge Diaghilev, who shocked and titillated Europe with his innovative Ballets Russes in the years before the First World War, chose to stage a full-length *Sleeping Beauty* in London in 1921, as if to remind postwar audiences that he and his dancers were in fact inheritors

and custodians of the great classical tradition. The Sadler's Wells production of 1939 established Britain's Royal Ballet as a national institution; and the postwar tour with Margot Fonteyn as Princess Aurora confirmed that company's international stature. The American Ballet Theater presented the first full-length American production in 1976. The 1991 revival by the New York City Ballet, with story and choreography streamlined by Peter Martins, showed that this quintessential showcase of classical ballet can still speak to modern audiences.

In the first act of *The Sleeping Beauty*, in the sequence known as the "Rose Adagio," the sixteen-year-old Aurora meets the four princes who have been chosen by her parents to vie for her hand in marriage; with each of the candidates she repeats the same slow turn on single point while steadying herself on the upraised hand of the suitor. This is classical technique at its most transparent and expressive; the image exquisitely evoked is that of a child taking her first steps, trusting that the world will not let her fall when she lifts her foot and launches herself into the future.

In striving to express his debt to the past, Marius Petipa in fact defined an attitude toward the art of dance that has made possible the innovations of

our own century—and broadened the audience for ballet in a way unimaginable for kabuki, which has remained closely bound to its cultural roots. Having survived the French Revolution, ballet survived the Russian Revolution as well, because it had abstracted from its past an aesthetic with a wide appeal. Whether kabuki might have evolved in a similar direction if Japan had not cut itself off from the rest of the world for so long is a moot point. Only time will tell whether kabuki can now find new audiences beyond its homeland and how it may be changed in the process.

Despite their contrasting histories, one area where ballet and kabuki converge is in their emphasis on charismatic performers. All the carefully honed katas, all the elegantly refined steps and combinations, would be little more than historically interesting "museum exhibits" if they were not repeatedly brought to life by performers who, during their time onstage, seem somehow larger than life. All theater strives for that paradoxical moment when performers and audience share an aesthetic experience that transcends the moment. Classical theater preserves and refines these experiences so that they can be shared from generation to generation and, under the right circumstances, across cultural boundaries as well.

Chapter 6
New Worlds of Dance

When change threatens social values and customs, dance can be a conservative force; through traditional forms of dance, individuals may reaffirm time-honored ways of relating to their neighbors, their institutions, their gods. As we have seen, the social uses of dance are sometimes quite explicit: Dance has been used to rally the faithful to religious devotions, to give public sanction to private feelings, to define community standards of behavior and to test their limits. But the importance of dance in a community goes beyond these specific functions; by dancing in a socially approved way with their peers, individuals proclaim their allegiance to society as a whole—or at least to the values that their subdivision of society holds dear.

When people leave the society they were born into, either voluntarily or involuntarily, dance is one of the things they take with them; as soon as they arrive in a new place and start dancing, they re-create, consciously or unconsciously, an important part of

their heritage. And when people from different backgrounds find themselves living side by side in a new setting, the result is often a fusion of dance forms, as people borrow from one another and transform what they borrow to reflect new social realities. Nowhere has this process been as dramatic in its consequences as in North and South America and the Caribbean, where European and African influences combined to create new dance forms of great power and lasting import.

What fueled the fusion process was the transatlantic trade in human beings that supplied captive workers for the sugar and cotton plantations of the "New World." Before this trade was outlawed in the nineteenth century, over eleven million people from west and central Africa were led in chains to the slave ships; according to some estimates, as many as half of these died on the terrible "middle passage" across the Atlantic.

The attitude of whites in the Americas toward the drumming and dancing

of the newly arrived Africans varied depending on local conditions. In North America, where whites outnumbered the enslaved Africans and (except in Louisiana) the predominant religion was Protestantism, many slave owners acted to deprive the Africans of anything that might aid them in organizing resistance. The practice of traditional African religions was prohibited. Even if the slave owners did not fully understand the religious and social significance of drumming in African societies, they were aware that the drums could "talk," so drumming was banned on most plantations. Dancing "native-style" was also frowned on, if only because it might remind the dancers of their life of freedom in Africa.

But not all dancing was forbidden. On the assumption that exercise would reduce the death rate, the captains of slave ships sought to protect their investment by having sailors lash the captives with a cat-o'-nine-tails to force them to "hump up and rattle their chains"; this form of "exercise" was called "dancing the slaves." If they survived the middle passage, Africans were sometimes forced to dance, quite literally, to their masters' tunes. After the slave trade was abolished in the United States in 1808, slave dealers turned to breeding to replenish their stocks; a former slave, who remembered being herded from Virginia to Georgia with other chained children, told her granddaughter that whenever she and her compatriots reached a town they were told "to dance through the streets and act lively" in order to attract buyers.

It was under these conditions that the transplanted Africans managed to preserve their heritage of expressive, communicative dance—a heritage that both west and central Africans shared. But instead of forming a central part of their lives, as it had in their ancestral homelands, dance for Africans in North America was regarded primarily as entertainment. On some North American plantations, slaves were allowed to hold their own dances on Saturday nights, on the grass outside their cabins, to the music of a fiddle, a banjo, or a tambourine (which replaced the prohibited drums). For amusement, the whites sometimes came down from the "big house" to watch the dancing which, to their eyes, resembled the European ballroom dances that were then popular on both sides of the Atlantic: quadrilles, reels, and cotillions. These were group dances in which four to eight (or more) dancers negotiated an intricate series of steps prompted by a leader who called out commands like: "Ladies, sashay," "First man head off to the right," "Swing your partner," and "All promenade."

When performed by Africans, these dances took on elements of traditional African dance forms. In one such form, the circle dance, shouting and clapping dancers sway, stamp, and shuffle (typically in a counterclockwise direction) while individuals detach themselves from the circle to improvise more complicated movements in the center. The

The Old Plantation (*above*), *a watercolor by an unknown artist possibly from South Carolina in the 1790s, depicts a scene that some scholars identify as a wedding ceremony in which the bride and groom jump over a broomstick to solemnize their vows; the ceremony resembles dances found in Yorubaland in west Africa. The drummer plays a drum made from a hollow piece of wood or a gourd with animal skin stretched across the end; the long-necked, stringed instrument is an antecedent of the banjo.*

The breakdown, right, was an African-American plantation dance of the Old South that eventually became one of the sources of the cakewalk, the ballroom dance craze of the 1890s. Many of the surviving images of dances like the breakdown originated as illustrations, published in popular periodicals such as Harper's Weekly *and* Frank Leslie's Illustrated Newspaper, *that perpetuated racial stereotypes even while preserving visual information about specific steps.*

THE BREAKDOWN

polyrhythmic complexity of such improvisations is acknowledged in the praise that good dancers earn from their peers for being able to dance two, three, even four rhythms in different parts of their body at the same time. Dances of this type can be seen today throughout west and central Africa—and among long-isolated communities of Sea Island blacks off the coast of Georgia.

The two traditions that came together in the dances performed by enslaved Africans under the eyes of their white masters differed in fundamental ways. Dancing in the European tradition was built on fixed steps arranged in a limited number of repeatable patterns; west African dancing featured individual improvisation against a background of basic movement motifs. European dancers tended to keep the back erect while lifting the torso up, toward the heavens; west African dancers tended to bend forward at the waist while projecting a sense of groundedness, of being in touch with the earth. European dance assigned a prominent central role to the male-female couple (as in the minuet of the eighteenth century and the waltz of the nineteenth century); the focus of African dance was typically on the group and on the soloists who emerged from the group and then merged back into it.

Yet for all their differences, the two traditions shared certain attitudes toward the dancing body without knowing it. Throughout sub-Saharan Africa, according to art historian Robert Farris Thompson, "the way you walk signals your station in life." Among the Asante of west Africa, "cool" is a highly desirable state of being that the most

venerable chiefs exhibit in the way they move. When west Africans say that a chief dances to "cool himself" and his community, they are referring to the body-language equivalent of a state-of-the-union speech. To be cool is to combine the virtues of men and women, the vigor of youth and the composure of old age. To exhibit cool by moving properly signifies power (both temporal and spiritual) and the well-being such power brings.

Modern English has borrowed the word from African-American musicians, but the concept has deep roots in the European tradition as well. In Baldassare Castiglione's *Il Cortegiano* (the courtier's "bible" first published in 1528) a gentleman who aspired to a higher station in life was advised to cultivate an air of *sprezzatura*—which has been defined as "a studied elegance and seemingly effortless grace." This courtly "cool" was supposed to be apparent in one's bearing on and off the dance floor. By the time of Versailles, the courtier's walk, with feet turned out at a ninety-degree angle, was de rigueur, while women in their floor-length skirts glided so smoothly through ballrooms and drawing rooms that they might have been wearing roller skates beneath their voluminous panniers.

So long as the social dancing of enslaved Africans did not offend the whites' notions of propriety, it was tolerated, sometimes even encouraged as a harmless diversion. On some plantations of North America, Africans could gain privileges and even a measure of fame for their ability to dance the jig, the buck, the pigeon wing, and the cakewalk. Dancing contests were staged

as betting events by the masters. Just before the Civil War a black man known as Tom became famous around Palestine, Texas: "[He was] the jigginest fellow ever was. He could put de glass of water on his head and make his feet go like triphammers and sound like de snaredrum [without spilling a drop of water from the glass]. He could whirl round and such, all de movement from his hips down."

The jig itself, as danced in North America by both blacks and whites, was a fusion of Irish and west African dance forms. Dances of animal mimicry, like the pigeon wing and the buzzard lope, probably harked back to the animal pantomimes of west and central Africa. In place of the forbidden drums, the body itself could became a percussive instrument, as in the polyrhythmic clapping and slapping routine known as "patting Juba." Where dancing was expressly denied to enslaved Africans because Protestant churches, especially the Baptist, condemned it as sinful, an adaptation of the circle dance, known as the shout or ring-shout, often took its place; although shouts could become wildly animated, they were not considered dance as long as the feet or legs did not cross.

One form of dancing that enslaved Africans probably learned from watching fancy-dress balls in the "big house" (where the best black fiddlers provided the music) was European-style couple dancing—in which the partners touched each other. Leopold Senghor, the French-educated poet who became the first president of Senegal, stated emphatically, "African dance disdains bodily contact"; and the reminiscences

This engraving from Kellom Tomlinson's The Art of Dancing Explained by Reading and Figures (1724) diagrams "The Conclusion or Presenting Both Arms in a Minuet." It is difficult to imagine that anyone could have mastered a dance as complex as the minuet from such diagrams, but Tomlinson's book was popular in places like the Virginia Tidewater, where there were wealthy families far from the centers of culture.

of former slaves indicate that so-called huggin' dances were a relatively late development on the plantations of North America. But in the early years of the eighteenth century enslaved Africans throughout the Caribbean were doing a line or circle dance called the *calenda*; according to a reliable French observer, "men and women struck their thighs together, then separated with a pirouette, only to begin again the same movement with absolutely lascivious gestures. . . . From time to time they lock arms and make several revolutions always slapping their thighs together and kissing each other. . . ."

Despite repeated attempts to ban it, the *calenda* persisted well into the nineteenth century. Like all popular dances it seemed to change with each recorded description, although pelvic thrusts and hip gyrations (said to be derived from the Congo) remained a more or less constant feature. No other account mentions men and women actually touching. The *calenda* that the Frenchman saw in the early 1700s may have been a short-lived variant which, by chance, presaged the revolutionary fusion of African and European dance styles that would come to dominate the

dance floors of the twentieth century.

Before this could happen, European dancing had to undergo a revolution of its own, with the advent of the vertigo-inducing waltz. As we have seen, dancing by couples who face each other in a formal embrace is an invention of Western Europe. No other culture focuses so much attention on men and women dancing together as physically linked partners. The reasons for this are far from clear. Among contributing factors that have been suggested are the sharp division of European society into sacred and secular spheres; the active participation of European women in the secular sphere, especially during the Crusades and after the enormous decline in population caused by the Black Death; and, most importantly, the elaboration of the cult of courtly love with its idealization of the virtuous mistress. Whatever the reasons, postmedieval European society experimented with men and women dancing together as physically linked partners, found it acceptable, and gradually allowed the dancers more and more intimate contact.

Until the latter half of the eighteenth century, couple dancing for the ruling classes remained embedded in a hierarchical social setting. Only one couple took the floor at a time. During their few minutes together in the limelight, the partners (who had been rigorously coached by professional dancing masters) went through the prescribed figures of a dance like the minuet as much to display their social graces to the discriminating audience as for the pleasure of the movement itself; the point of the dance was not to provide the partners with an opportunity for personal

The couple dances that European settlers brought to the "New World" reflected the tastes and values of their diverse homelands. This detail from a watercolor by Lewis Miller, recounting musical events in the Moravian community of York, Pennsylvania, about 1830, shows "dancing at the house of John Glepner."

interaction but to present the couple to the group.

After 1750 new group dances, like the French contredanses and the English country dances, brought a taste of social democracy to the dance floors of the aristocracy. With three, four, or more couples in each formation, the stress on "presentation" was considerably reduced. But the dance figures themselves were so complicated that prior instruction was still necessary if a dancer was to avoid looking foolish. Then, in the last decades of the eighteenth century, came a real break with the past. One of the group-dance figures—a turning movement for couples in triple time known as the waltz (from the German for "revolve")—separated from the formation and became popular on its own as a couple dance. Only this couple dance was different from its predecessors. Instead of two dancers at a time displaying their skill to an audience of their peers or social betters, the whole floor was now taken over by waltzing couples, with the partners clinging to one another for support and for their mutual pleasure.

The waltz apparently began as an amusement of the lower and middle classes, probably in southern Germany or Austria. By the beginning of the nineteenth century waltzing couples in aristocratic ballrooms were revolving around each other as they wheeled— together with other waltzing couples— in a large circle around the perimeter of the dance floor. As its popularity grew, the closed-couple waltz came under fire from guardians of public morality, who complained that the wheels- within-wheels motion was dizzying,

exhilarating, even intoxicating; the more energetic couples seemed constantly on the verge of losing control. To maintain control, the partners had no choice but to hold tightly to each other. Lord Byron professed to be scandalized:

Round all the confines of the yielded
    waist
The strongest hand may wander
    undisplaced:
The lady's in return may grasp as much
As princely paunches offer to her touch.

Ballroom dancing has been a passion in Vienna for over two hundred years. At the annual Viennese Opera Ball, the Opera House fills with some six thousand party goers. Here, at the 1960 ball, waltzers take the floor.

But once begun, there was no stopping "the waltzing mania," as it was called. At the Congress of Vienna (1814–15), where the conquerors of Napoleon met to restore pre-Revolutionary order to Europe, the delegates took to the revolutionary waltz with abandon. There were balls every night, for crowds ranging from two hundred to ten thousand. Vienna's passion for fast dancing was proverbial; good dancers prided themselves on their ability to circle the floor eight times during a single waltz. Prince Metternich, the arch-conservative champion of the ancien régime, could do it. In self-defense Lord Castlereagh, the British foreign secretary, hired a waltzing instructor; it was said that he practiced with a chair when his wife was not available.

After 1815, the triumph of the waltz was assured; Johann Strauss Sr. was invited to play his infectious music for the French, Prussian, and Russian courts. The dance itself was evolving toward a simpler form that required less instruction. By the second quarter of the nineteenth century, waltzing couples no longer wheeled all together in a uniform circle around the floor. Instead, each couple moved as an independent unit, in a manner described by Henri Cellarius, the leading dance instructor in Paris:

"Moderating or quickening their pace at pleasure, leading their lady as it pleases them, sometimes obliging her to retrograde, sometimes retiring themselves, flying from one room to another, turning to the right or to the left, varying their steps at every moment, and at last arriving at that pitch of excitement which I dare to call intoxication, with-

Magnificent formal balls are frequently associated with royalty, both in life and in literature. This newspaper engraving (above) shows a grand ball, in honor of the visit of the Prince of Wales to the United States, held at the New York Academy of Music on October 12, 1860. Under the weight of four thousand guests and one thousand gate-crashers the dance floor collapsed and had to be hastily repaired for the guest of honor's entrance.

The lively polka, seen at right in a sheet music cover of 1846 and danced in two-quarter time, came to ballrooms in the early nineteenth century; it was said to have originated as a Bohemian folk dance.

William Henry Lane, billed as "Master Juba," at Vauxhall Gardens, London. He was only twenty-seven when death cut short his remarkable career in which he introduced the dancing of African-Americans to enthusiastic audiences in both the United States and England.

out fear of contradiction by the true lovers of the waltz. . . ."

While everyone, including Queen Victoria, waltzed, other dance crazes, like the galop and the polka, came and went. Meanwhile, the constantly evolving group dances, like the quadrille and cotillion, remained popular, especially with the older crowd. The same mix of closed-couple dances and more formal group dances dominated the ballrooms of North and South America in the nineteenth century. But outside the ballrooms, even more revolutionary influences were making themselves felt.

In North America, the first unmistakable sign that European and African dance forms were fusing into something new was a bizarre social phenomenon known as blackface minstrelsy. This was first made popular in the 1830s by an entertainer known as Daddy "Jim Crow" Rice, who claimed to have built his act around the dancing and singing of an old, deformed black man with a "laughable limp" who worked in a livery stable behind a theater in Louisville, Kentucky. Blackening his face with burnt cork and dressing up like the crippled servant, Rice delighted white audiences with a comic song-and-dance routine known as Jump Jim Crow. Leading up to a funny little turnaround jump, he threw his weight on the heel of one foot and the toes of the other, then rhythmically shifted heels and toes while rolling his body from side to side and revolving in place, all the while raising one hand shoulder-high and wiggling his fingers in a "half seductive, half waggishly admonishing manner."

Marshall and Jean Stearns, historians of African-American jazz and dance,

have identified this prototypical minstrel number with a turn-in-place version of a step known to American blacks in this century as "trucking":

"Trucking is a highly individual dance with as many fine versions as there are dancers. Everybody has his own style, although the dance is usually based on short steps forward, turning the heel in after each step. Thereafter, almost anything goes. Every good dancer who 'trucks' recognizably is trying to create a unique impression. Out of an endlessly contorted and even tortured manner, each conflicting motion nevertheless dovetails with some cross-rhythm (heard or unheard), and the whole exploding combination somehow miraculously flows together and moves—a triumph of rhythm over the unorganized human condition."

The blackface minstrel show was the first indigenous American musical theater. In the dances, performers blended Old World elements—especially the taplike clog dancing of the British Isles and the straight-up, rapid-fire jigs of Ireland—with shuffle steps and loose-limbed gestures borrowed from African-Americans. In the heyday of minstrelsy, from the late 1840s to the late 1850s, all the featured performers were white with one important exception: a free-born northern black named William Henry Lane, who achieved fame as "Master Juba, the Greatest Dancer in the World," and who might have done even more to shape the course of theatrical dance in America but for his untimely death in 1852, at the age of twenty-seven, while on a triumphal tour of Britain.

The popularity of blackface minstrelsy has never been satisfactorily ex-

plained. Certainly, the minstrel shows were responsible for spreading stereotypes of plantation blacks to audiences in the North. Were the exaggerated contortions and witless comedy routines a reassurance to whites that the people they had enslaved were really childlike simpletons? Or did the white audiences take a secret, guilty pleasure in the licensed abandon of the minstrels? The diaries of whites traveling through the antebellum South are full of entries expressing amazement (or is it envy?) at the dancing ability of the enslaved Africans.

After the Civil War, the white minstrel companies crisscrossing the country had new competition from troupes of blacks—who also performed in burnt cork! One minstrel dance, originally called the Essence of Old Virginia, evolved into the soft shoe that became a staple of vaudeville hoofers. Described by a later black dancer as "a combination of shuffles," the Essence made use of the shuffling, gliding, dragging movements and toe-heel "rocking" gait that appear in so many African-American dances from the early days of Jump Jim Crow to late-twentieth-century break dancing. Moving as if "on ice skates," the dancer glides forward "without appearing to move his feet at all, by manipulating his toes and heels rapidly, so that his body is propelled without changing the position of his legs." Another dance that emerged from the minstrel shows of the second half of the nineteenth century was the Walk Around, the grand finale in which the entire cast promenaded around the stage, strutting and improvising fancy steps; the Walk Around, which owed

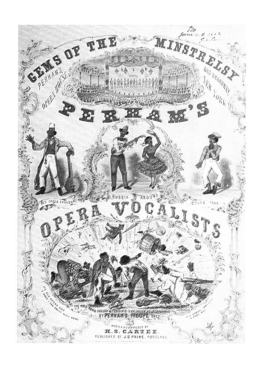

This page: "Jump Jim Crow" became a national rage after the performer T. D. Rice introduced the dance at Ludlow and Smith's theater in Louisville, Kentucky. The painting below shows Rice on stage in 1833 at the Bowery Theater in New York in a production written around the character and dance he had created. Blackface minstrel shows, in which white performers wearing burnt-cork makeup portrayed caricatures of "plantation blacks," became enormously popular in the United States during the pre–Civil War years, as the sheet music cover at left suggests.

Opposite: The cakewalk (above and below left), whose roots go back to plantation days and to the dancing of black theatrical performers, became the great American ballroom dance craze of the 1890s; the syncopated strutting evolved from black parodies of white formation dances. Bert Williams (1874–1922; below right) formed a vaudeville team with George Walker in 1895 and they cakewalked together to fame and fortune until Walker's retirement in 1909. Williams then became a regular in Florenz Ziegfeld's Follies from 1910 to 1919, performing in some of the funniest scenes: he was known for his sense of timing and his pantomime. Here, he is playing a blackbird—never for a moment was he permitted to forget his color—in a skit from the 1910 Follies.

Arthur Murray (1895–1991) and a partner demonstrate the Charleston, 1920s. A skillful ballroom dancer, the East Harlem–born Murray began teaching dancing on the faculty of Castle Hall, the dancing school of Vernon and Irene Castle. He set up his own school in Atlanta, Georgia, and moved to New York in 1924. There, he not only gave lessons, but ran a profitable mail-order business in dancing instructions, using floor diagrams that he devised. By the 1960s, he had franchised more than three hundred Arthur Murray studios. He counted among his students Eleanor Roosevelt, the Duke of Windsor, John D. Rockefeller, Jr., Cornelius Vanderbilt Whitney, and Elizabeth Arden.

something to the plantation dances of the Old South, became one of the sources of the cakewalk, the great ballroom dance craze of the 1890s.

By the time African-Americans found a place on the minstrel circuit, the format of the shows was set; black performers had little choice but to imitate the racial stereotypes that white performers had established: shiftless, pop-eyed "darkies," watermelon-chomping clowns in fright wigs, dandified con men, light-skinned mulatto heroines. (Female parts were played by men.) But the black minstrel troupes also gave work to a generation of African-American dancers and musicians, men like Bert Williams and George Walker and Billy Kersands and W. C. Handy, whose contributions would reshape American theatrical and popular dance in the twentieth century.

The cakewalk was the first American dance to cross over from black to white society and from stage to ballroom. The name derived from festival dances on antebellum plantations (usually at "crop-over," or harvest time), where enslaved Africans competed to see who could improvise the fanciest steps, and a prize, typically a cake donated by the master and mistress, was awarded to the winner. In time the steps evolved

into exaggerated parodies of the ballroom figures that the whites danced, with lots of syncopated strutting and prancing. Transferred first to black minstrel shows and later to black musicals that did without blackface makeup (one of the first, *The Creole Show*, opened in Boston in 1889), the cakewalk caught the fancy of a white public that was just beginning to enjoy the syncopated rhythms of ragtime music. By 1898 the dancing and comedy team of Williams and Walker was cakewalking to sellout crowds at Broadway's top variety theater, and William K. Vanderbilt and his wife had hired a black dance instructor to teach the new dance at their Fifth Avenue mansion. Cakewalk contests, at first for men only and then for couples, were organized throughout the country. In these ballroom contests, the white dancers threw their shoulders back, stuck out their midriffs, and did their stiff-spined best to imitate high-stepping plantation blacks parodying stiff-spined white ballroom dancers.

For most ballroom dancers, the cakewalk was a strenuous workout, but it opened the way for a whole series of less demanding if still "exotic" dances (adapted from black honky-tonks and "jook joints") that became popular in white ballrooms in the early years of

the new century. These were the so-called "animal dances": the turkey trot, the grizzly bear, the chicken scratch, the camel walk, the bunny hug, the kangaroo dip, and so on.

The impact of the turkey trot, the first of the animal dances, was felt at all levels of society. By 1910 (the same year the tango arrived from South America) audiences were cheering the turkey trot in a hit Broadway show; a committee of moral watchdogs was decrying its "unwholesome" influence on working girls; and "trotting" was all the rage among the monied youth of Newport. And that was just the beginning; in the words of one social commentator, the decade between 1910 and 1920 was "the period in which America went dance mad." Although most of the new dances were athletic and bouncy and full of self-mocking silliness (turkey trotters periodically flapped their arms to simulate an aroused fowl), their untamed energy frightened many defenders of the status quo. It was not just that the partners held on to each other while they danced; it was the wriggling, shaking, twisting motions they indulged in.

The relatively free use of improvisation that these African-American–inspired dances promoted was the real problem. What some scandalized

Vernon and Irene Castle (below) set the standards for ballroom dancing in America in the first quarter of the twentieth century; part of their self-appointed mission was to tame the wilder "animal" dances that disturbed the arbiters of social taste.

Right, an Arthur Murray advertisement from Judge magazine, January 5, 1924. Entrepreneurs like the Castles and Murray perceived that with new dances becoming fashionable at a rapid rate, the ability to do the latest steps would become important to an ever wider circle of society. Dancing lessons eased the anxiety of thousands as they stepped out onto dance floors.

observers saw as the "primitive" sensuality of the jungle was actually a vigorous hybrid: African body movements joined to European touch-dancing. Neither moral exhortation nor legal action (a New Jersey woman was sentenced to fifty days in jail for doing the turkey trot) could halt its spread. That left only co-optation.

In 1914 (just as the Vatican was officially denouncing both the turkey trot and the tango) Vernon and Irene Castle opened a school of dancing in New York with backing from influential members of high society. He was English, she was from New Rochelle, New York; their dance exhibitions (which included a toned-down turkey trot and tango) had brought them acclaim in Paris. In New York they became arbiters of ballroom taste like the dancing instructors of previous centuries. The Castles smoothed out the jazzier steps, standardized the improvisatory dances (with the help of black musicians like composer and conductor James Reese Europe), and offered their own deportment on the dance floor as a model of genteel yet fashionable elegance: "Do not wriggle the shoulders. Do not shake the hips. Do not twist the body. Do not flounce the elbows. Do not pump the arms. Do not hop—

Whitey's Lindy Hoppers in a scene from the Marx Brothers' A Day at the Races (1937; above) and on stage with the Count Basie Orchestra (opposite). What set the Lindy hop aside from earlier dances were spectacular breakaways with acrobatic "air steps" (right). The date and place of this Lindy competition is unknown.

glide instead. . . . Drop the Turkey Trot, the Grizzly Bear, the Bunny Hug. . . ."

But once the riches of African-American dance had been sampled by a wider public, there was no returning to a blander mix. The signature dances of the 1920s—the self-descriptive shimmy, the free-kicking Charleston, the butt-slapping Black Bottom, all had roots in the social dancing of American blacks, especially southern blacks, and in their music, which the rest of the world was just learning to call jazz. Although a number of musicals that appeared on Broadway during this period were produced, directed, and written by blacks, the music and the dances were often showcased to the white public by white performers.

In 1926, the same year that a white dancer named Ann Pennington scored a big hit doing the Black Bottom in a Broadway revue, the Savoy Ballroom

opened on Lenox Avenue in New York's Harlem. This was the era that became known as the Harlem Renaissance, when black writers like Langston Hughes, Countee Cullen, James Weldon Johnson, and Claude McKay gave voice to an emerging African-American consciousness. The Roseland ballroom had opened in midtown Manhattan seven years earlier to enormous fanfare and immediate success, but as with most public dance halls outside black neighborhoods, access to African-Americans was limited. Harlem itself was full of smaller halls, nightclubs, after-hours joints, and impromptu rent parties where dancing was the main attraction; but the Savoy was something else again, with its marbled stairs and mirrored walls, ornate block-long ballroom, and two top-notch bands (Fletcher Henderson, Chick Webb, Count Basie, and the like) competing with each other on

most nights. The dancing was so persistent and energetic that the management had to put down a new wooden floor every three years. From the day it opened, the Savoy was completely integrated.

The northeast corner of the ballroom, known as the Cats' Corner, was reserved for the best dancers. Here the protocol was as strict as in the ballrooms of Versailles. Dancing was highly competitive; rivals challenged each other to "cutting" contests which were judged by other top dancers. On a typical Saturday night at the Cats' Corner, couples took the floor in order of reputation, one couple at a time, with the reigning "king" cutting his steps last. In general, faster was better, and acrobatic moves (as long as they were done smoothly and without visible strain) drew the most attention. The dance that allowed the greatest license for creative improvisation was a

177

White dancers also did the Lindy hop or, as the media often referred to it, the jitterbug.

fast and furious swing dance known as the Lindy hop (after Charles Lindbergh's solo "hop" across the Atlantic in 1927).

The core of the Lindy was the so-called "breakaway." After doing a syncopated but flowing two-step together, the couples parted and went into solo improvisations to the same swinging beat; the challenge was to do something new and difficult with an air of effortlessness, and then come back together seamlessly without missing a beat. In the words of Norma Miller, who started dancing at the Savoy when she was twelve years old: "The beat is what swing dancing is all about. It's a perfect attunement between dance, movement, and music. Swing music. There's never been any music so perfectly attuned to what the body can do."

The dancers not only improvised in competition with each other but with the soloists in the bands. Lester Young, who played tenor sax with Count Basie at the Savoy, said, "The rhythm of the dancers comes back to you when you're playing." Dancer Leon James described the interplay between the best dancers at the Savoy and trumpeter Dizzy Gillespie: "Every time he played a crazy lick, we cut a crazy step to go with it. And he dug us and blew even crazier stuff to see if we could dance to it, a kind of game, with the musicians and dancers challenging each other."

Lindy hoppers practiced new steps at home, in hallways, and on the streets before trying them out for a jury of their peers at the Savoy. As competition fed innovation, the best Lindy hoppers, like George "Shorty" Snowden (who is said to have given the dance its name at a

Manhattan dance marathon in 1928), began to attract the attention of people outside Harlem. Snowden danced with Paul Whiteman's band downtown at the Paramount. But it wasn't until the head bouncer at the Savoy, a short-tempered ex–street fighter named Herbert White, organized some of the younger regulars into a group called Whitey's Lindy Hoppers that the dance made it into the mainstream. In 1935 Whitey's energetic and well-rehearsed dancers (including a fifteen-year-old Norma Miller) came away with a hatful of prizes at the first Harvest Moon Ball held at Madison Square Garden. This led to a series of professional engagements in nightclubs and dance halls around town and across the country, plus a summer-long tour of Europe and a wild dance scene in the Marx Brothers' movie *A Day at the Races.* Featured in this scene were some of the acrobatic "air steps" that the younger dancers at the Savoy had been perfecting and that some people called jitterbugging.

One of the innovators was Whitey's right-hand man, Frank Manning, who was twenty at the time. As Manning tells it, he had seen an acrobatic move where the dancers locked arms and the man lifted his partner onto his back, and he got the idea of extending that move into a real "swing step" timed to the music. So he and his partner, Frieda Washington, practiced for hours in his living room: "Finally we got a way where I would put my arms around her arms, with us back to back, and I would bend down and lift her, and at the same time she would come up off her feet and roll over my back. And she would land in front of me, facing me. And we prac-

ticed until we got it down to a point where we could do it every single time and do it on the beat with the music."

Since they had practiced in secret, no one knew what they were up to, not even Whitey, until the night they went head to head with Shorty Snowden in a Lindy contest at the Savoy. They were the last couple to dance, and they ended their routine with the new "over-the-back" step. Manning remembers it clearly: "The music seemed like it was just flowing with her as she flowed across my back. And when she landed, the music just hit like that, right on the beat. And I hugged her, and we did a jig walk backward off the floor. And it seemed like the whole Savoy ballroom, like they were jumping up and clapping hands and just hollering and screaming and carrying on. And somebody came up to me and said, 'Where'd you get that great step from? That air step you just did.' So I said, 'Oh man, well, you know, I just picked it up.'"

The Lindy hop familiarized America with the African-derived notion of embellishing a basic dance step with virtuoso improvisations. But it fused this element with the essence of European-derived couple dance, in which the partners worked together to create a unified impression. In the words of Frank Manning: "When you are dancing with your partner, for that two and a half minutes, you are in love with each other. You're corresponding with each other by the moves that you make. It's a love affair, between you and your partner and the music. You feel the music, you feel your partner, she feels you and she feels the music. So there the three of you are together. You've got a

By the 1980s, dance clubs like Studio 54 in New York (right) were jammed with crowds that mixed the young and hip with the rich and famous. Free-form dancing to rock-and-roll music became the functional equivalent of the more orderly ballroom dances of the previous century.

The international fusion of dance traditions is an accelerating trend in the modern world. Itself the product of such fusion, American rock-and-roll is now mediating cultural exchanges on a global scale. Johnny Clegg, a white South African, and his black South African band called Savuka (below) mix American-style rock with Zulu music and dance. And in Yoyogi Park, Tokyo (opposite), where rock-and-roll is king, Japanese kids have created their own street scene out of weird fragments of postwar American popular culture.

triangle, you know. Which one do you love best?"

When Benny Goodman's band played Carnegie Hall in 1936 and the press reported that teenagers were "jitterbugging in the aisles," the Lindy was officially launched in white America. Commentators worried about the effects of such abandoned dancing on the nation's moral fiber, but by 1943

Betty Grable was doing it for U.S. servicemen overseas and *Life* magazine ran a cover story on it. The black innovators took a back seat. Whitey's Lindy Hoppers were disbanded in 1942 after Manning and other members of the troupe questioned the outsized cut that Whitey was skimming from their earnings; the following year the Savoy's dance-hall license was revoked.

In the decade after the Second World War, big-band swing faded and the Lindy became a staple of the dance schools—a combination of steps to be learned and repeated on the dance floor, with little or no improvisation in the breakaway. Nevertheless, when rock-and-roll emerged from black rhythm-and-blues as a new dance music in the early 1950s, the Lindy was there.

What other dance was suitable to the revved-up back beat of performers like Elvis Presley, who was quoted as saying, "I gotta move when I sing"? Elvis not only enlivened white country music by borrowing the vocal phrasing of African-American performers, he did a passable imitation of their fancy foot-work on stage. The link between the 1930s and the 1950s is clear in news-reels and television clips; in a television documentary about the "early years" of rock-and-roll, the filmmakers mistaken-ly mixed in prewar shots of Whitey's Lindy Hoppers along with clips of white kids dancing to Chuck Berry's "Roll Over Beethoven."

The dynamic tension between impro-visation and partnering that had been the glory of the Lindy did not survive, however. In 1960, when the twist caught on, an era came to an end. In a develop-ment as revolutionary as the first closed-couple waltz, the breakaway of the Lindy broke away to become a dance all by itself. Partners let go of each other, stepped apart, and proceeded to twist, shake, undulate, and wriggle on their own. The twist was followed by the frug, the monkey, the jerk, and so on, but the principle remained the same. Like the "animal" dances of early 1900s, the "rock" dances of the second half of the century were actually bits and pieces of African-American dance routines that had evolved through improvisation and could now be broken off and passed along to a wider audience; to help the uninitiated get up to speed, the lyrics of many popular songs contained explicit instructions on how to do the dance.

The revolution on the dance floor went far beyond this, however. For many, the new kind of dancing meant liberation not only from the rules of leading and following but from rules of any kind. Arthur Murray and other dancing instructors might advertise lessons in the latest dance craze, but it was no longer necessary to "know the steps"; African-derived improvisation had triumphed over European-style touch-dancing; for whites as well as blacks, for old as well as young, for rich as well as poor, it was permissible at long last to "do your own thing" on the dance floor.

Not everyone agreed, of course. The same forces in American society that had once opposed blacks and whites dancing under one roof at the Savoy now assailed the influence of what some called "the evil beat" of rock-and-roll. For many years, radio, like so many other institutions in the United States, had been segregated; there were stations that played records by white performers and stations that played records by black performers. Audiences were presumed to be segregated as well. But in the late fifties, white teenagers began tuning into black stations to lis-ten to the up-tempo rhythm-and-blues of people like Fats Domino and Little Richard and James Brown. To appeal to these teenagers, white performers like Pat Boone began recording cover ver-sions of the more popular rhythm-and-blues songs. In 1957 a Baltimore televi-sion personality named Buddy Dean started a TV show that featured white teenagers dancing on camera to the music of black performers, who came into the studio to play their latest hits and teach the new dances. The music was integrated, but the dance floor was

not; a single day a month was reserved for black teenagers, the other days were for whites only. For several years the Buddy Dean Show was the most popular local television show in the country. But in 1964, when Dean set in motion a plan to bring whites and blacks together on the dance floor, the station abruptly cancelled his show.

However paranoid their fantasies about "white youth" being subverted by "African sensuality," the anti–rock-and-roll crusaders came closer to the truth about rock-and-roll than the Tin Pan Alley hacks who had originally dis-missed it as "just another fad." So ap-pealing was the freedom symbolized by the new kind of music and dance that by the end of the decade it had become the norm wherever the authorities per-mitted it. With the internationalization of the entertainment business, popular music and social dancing in Europe and Asia and Africa came to resemble that of North America ever more closely. Japanese pop stars shook their hips like Elvis Presley, young Englishmen put their own spin on the rhythm-and-blues of Chuck Berry, and the younger gener-ation in cities like Cairo and Nairobi began imitating the mannerisms of black American performers. Wherever people had access to radio and television and record players, African-inspired rhythms and attitudes toward dance became a part of everyday life in the last quarter of the twentieth century.

In the Caribbean and in South Ameri-ca, an earlier fusion of African and European influences had already pro-duced a different kind of hybrid culture;

here, the African drum had never been suppressed, and dance figured prominently in the religious as well as the social life of the people. The carryover from west and central Africa was especially strong in northeast Brazil, which had been the center of that country's slave trade. Some 3.5 million Africans were brought to Brazil before slavery was finally abolished in 1888. In the northeast state of Bahia, eighty percent of the population can trace at least part of their ancestry back to Africa.

Plantations in the Caribbean and South America were often run by overseers in the name of absentee owners; in many areas, transplanted Africans far outnumbered whites. Fearful of uprisings (which were common) South American and Caribbean whites reached an accommodation with their slaves, whose traditional religious practices were permitted under certain conditions. This accommodation was made possible by the attitude of the Roman Catholic hierarchy and of the Jesuit missionaries who were active throughout South America; compared to the Protestants of North America, Catholics tended to be more tolerant of pre-Christian customs so long as they could be outwardly reconciled with Christianity—as, for instance, by equating the Yoruban deities from west Africa with various Christian saints. The ocean mother Yemanjá was identified with the Virgin Mary; Ogun, the god of iron and war, was identified with the dashing St. George; Legba, the Yoruban spirit of the crossroads, whose symbol is a staff, was identified with the staff-wielding St. Peter, and so on.

For many enslaved Africans, whose religion was syncretistic (combining different elements) to begin with, this fusion was hardly disagreeable. At the same time, colonial authorities often prohibited the more explicitly African ceremonies of worship, such as the candomblé rites of northeast Brazil; their perpetuation, in forms closely resembling those of west and central Africa, is a triumph of faith akin to the perpetuation of Judaism after the destruction of the Second Temple.

In a candomblé temple in Salvador, the capital of Bahia, a group of black women in white hoop skirts dance in slow circles around the floor. The women, who may be waitresses or housekeepers in everyday life, are known here as "daughters of the saints." The spiritual beings with whom they seek communion are known as orixas (pronounced "orishas"). Like the deities invoked in Haitian voudun—and the west African deities from which both are descended—the orixas represent forces that can affect a person's life for good or ill: the sea, the wind, the forest, lightning, disease. After offering animal sacrifices to an orixa, the dancers, who have undergone extensive training for periods of up to seven years, begin to move to specific drum rhythms that are attuned to particular deities. Each woman dances to invite a deity to "enter her head" and "ride" her. Suddenly one of the dancers falls to the floor; she has gone into a trance, signifying the moment of possession by an orixa. She is led into an adjoining room, adorned with clothes and symbolic implements appropriate to her orixa, and then returned to the main dancing floor. Until her trance ends, she will be treated not as a woman possessed but as the possessing deity itself.

The orixas enjoy dancing; they "enter" their human worshipers (male as well as female) in order to join in the festive ceremony. Properly invoked, they will also help worshipers deal with personal problems. Although the dances are spontaneous, each deity not only has a specific drum rhythm but a recognizable dance style: vigorous, stamping steps for the male god associated with war; fluid, dreamy movements for the goddess of streams and rivers; and so on. The links to the west African pantheon of the Yoruba people are explicit and cherished by those who dance the dances of the gods. Candomblé spread from Bahia to the rest of Brazil after the end of slavery; the tradition of African dance that it helped keep alive has, in recent years, become part of Brazilian Carnival, a national celebration that represents a grand fusion of Portuguese and African traditions.

The European roots of Carnival go back to the spring festivals of the pre-Christian era, especially to the Roman new-year festival of Saturnalia and the even earlier revels associated with the Greek cult of Dionysus. What all such events had in common was a riotous release of the pent-up energies of winter, a public expression of thanksgiving for the return of warm weather, and uninhibited celebrations of the earth's fertility.

These spring festivals survived in Christian Europe as pre-Lenten frolics. Before the long fast began, the normal rules of behavior were suspended and even respectable citizens mocked the authority of church and state in licentious, often obscene ceremonies known

Throughout Brazil, gifts are proffered to Yemenjá, the ocean mother, on February 2. The candomblé procession (left), on the island of Itaparica in the state of Bahia, is bringing the gifts—carefully wrapped bouquets as well as doll-like effigies—to the shore, where they will be taken out to sea in a boat for the goddess.

Below, a candomblé priest possessed by Omolu, the deity that sweeps away smallpox and other dreaded diseases, being escorted through a temple in Salvador, Brazil, by an initiate who is not in a trance and functions as the ears and eyes of the orixa.

This candomblé priestess possessed by Yemenjá is wearing ornaments symbolic of the orixa.

by such evocative names as the Feast of Fools and the Feast of the Ass. Not surprisingly, both church and state tried to rein in the wilder aspects of these events; when repeated prohibitions had no effect, elegant masked balls and parades with elaborate floats were offered as alternatives to the more disorderly street processions. Despite periodic crackdowns by the authorities, a rowdy tradition known as Entrudo lasted well into the nineteenth century on the Iberian peninsula. In Lisbon, revelers donned costumes to disguise their identity, men dressed as women and women as men, servants lorded it over their masters, otherwise faithful husbands and wives dallied with strangers, and staid pillars of the community ran through the streets pelting each other with flour, eggs, mud, rotten fruit, and projectiles filled with water and animal excrement.

It was this tradition of Entrudo that Portuguese settlers brought to Brazil, where it merged with west and central African traditions of public role-reversal and socially sanctioned festivals of "release." In the nineteenth century such prodigious quantities of water were thrown about the streets of Rio de Janeiro during Carnival that the newspapers warned of impending shortages. Not until the second half of the century did the white elite of Brazil begin organizing more sedate Carnival celebrations around costumed balls and parades illustrating allegorical themes.

Carnival in Brazil today owes much to central African traditions associated with the crowning of kings in the Congo and Angola. As early as the seventeenth century, black Brazilian street processions in honor of the Virgin Mary incorporated a mock coronation of an African king and queen. The resulting

fusion, which combined elements of dance, parade, and allegorical street theater, came to be called a congada. It so happened that each Catholic parish in Portugal had a custom of crowning a "king and queen" on the feast day of Our Lady of the Rosary and celebrating the brief reign of this couple with masked dances. The Catholic authorities in Brazil—who were always looking for Christian rituals that would appeal to new African converts—may have sanctioned the original congadas because of their resemblance to this Portuguese custom.

The immediate source of today's Carnival in Rio de Janeiro is the rancho, a procession originally held on January 6, the Day of Kings, to celebrate the journey of the three Magi to Bethlehem. Stripped of its connection to Christmas and moved to the pre-Lenten period, the rancho became increasingly carnival-

esque, with marching musicians playing brass and string instruments while costumed male and female choruses sang and performed dances based on allegorical themes. To the processional pageant of the rancho, black Brazilians who had migrated to Rio from Bahia added the samba, which was originally an Angolan circle dance with solo interludes.

Out of this mix came the so-called "samba schools," neighborhood-based social clubs whose principal purpose is to organize Carnival processions. At first, the authorities in Rio discouraged the participation of samba schools from the city's poorer black neighborhoods;

in the early years of this century club-swinging police often broke up the rowdier processions. In 1935 the samba schools were recognized as official Carnival organizations; in return, the schools agreed to abide by city regulations governing the use of musical instruments and the allegorical themes around which the pageants had to be structured. From this agreement, Rio's modern Carnival, a highly organized event that leaves room for individual "acting out," was born.

The goal of every samba school is to win first prize in the officially sponsored samba contest that is the high point of Carnival. In order to compete, a samba

school must create a pageant based on a patriotic Brazilian theme, with the stress on ethnic pride and better relations among the country's racial and religious groups. There are over a hundred samba schools in Rio; each has between two and four thousand members known as sambistas. Although the samba schools receive subsidies from the city government and contributions from local businessmen, the sambistas spend most of their leisure time during the year making their own costumes, designing and building elaborate floats of wood, metal, paper, and Styrofoam, and preparing and rehearsing their songs and dances. New sambas, with special lyrics, music, and dance steps, are composed.

Today the word samba refers to a whole genre of marchlike compositions with a highly ornamented 2/4 rhythm. The singers and dancers in each pageant are accompanied by as many as four hundred percussionists, who play a battery of instruments ranging from various drums of African origin to classical kettledrums to iron frying pans struck with metal rods. The focus of all their efforts is a brief passage in front of the judges in Rio's Sambadrome, 634 yards of pavement flanked by four-story concrete bleachers that hold seventy thousand spectators—usually VIPs and tourists who can afford the high-priced seats (forty dollars a ticket and up). It takes two days for all the competing schools to pass in review before the judges.

To get to the Sambadrome the processions maneuver through the streets of the city. Precariously balanced on towering floats, singers, dancers, and musicians in gaudy costumes perform the new sambas; on the pavement around the floats hundreds of dancers move in formation while improvising fancy steps and playing exuberantly to the audience and to one another. The costumes represent what one observer has called "a living museum of Brazilian history" which reflects the population's African and European roots as well as the influence of satellite-transmitted TV and the latest movies. Depending on the theme of the pageant, the participants may represent Amazonian Indians (beaded-leather tunics and dyed-feather headdresses), African kings and queens (stylized shields, spears, and masks), international film legends like Fred Astaire and Marilyn Monroe (top hats and white tuxes, shimmering gold gowns), heroic astronauts (silver-sequinned space suits), and larger-than-life-sized caricatures of political figures, often in mock-splendid military uniforms. Side by side with the gorgeously costumed dancers are beautiful young men and women wearing nothing but the briefest bikini bottoms, their undulating bodies aglow with sweat and perfumed oil.

As each samba school passes in front of the seated judges, the performance shifts into high gear. The supreme moment is the appearance of the "standard-bearers," a man and woman who dance together while holding aloft their school's identifying flag. As "king and queen" for a day, they dress appropriately in the style of the French Bourbon court: she might wear a white lace-trimmed hoop skirt, while he appears in silk-and-satin knee-length coat, silver-buckled high-heeled shoes and powdered wig. As they dip and spin around each other, plumes of pink feathers flutter from the shiny silver armatures that rise from their shoulders like angels' wings.

Although everyone in Rio dances the samba during Carnival, many Brazilians claim that only people in touch with their African roots can get it right. Alma Guillermoprieto, a South American journalist and former professional dancer, has written a self-mocking account about learning to samba:

"1. Start before a mirror, with no music. You may prefer to practice with a pair of very high heels. Though samba is a dance that started out barefoot, and can still be danced that way, high heels will throw your spinal column out of whack and give your pelvis the appearance of greater flexibility. . . .

"2. Stand with your feet parallel, close together. Step and hop in place on your right foot as you brush your left foot quickly across. Step in quick succession onto your left, then your right foot. Although your hips will swivel to the right as far as possible for this sequence, your head and shoulders should remain strictly forward. Otherwise you'll start looking like you're doing the hora. . . .

"3. Test yourself: Are your lips moving? Are your shoulders scrunched? No? Are you able to manage one complete left-right sequence per second? Good! Now that you've mastered the basic samba step, you're ready to add music. . . . The key thing at this stage is speed. When you are up to two complete sequences per second you are well on your way to samba. Aim for four.

"4. A samba secret: Add hips. . . .

"5. Stop hopping! Keep your shoulders down! Face front! The magic of samba lies in the illusion that somebody is moving like crazy from the waist down while an entirely different person is observing the proceedings from the waist up."

In other parts of Brazil, other rhythms predominate at Carnival time. In Salvador the air is filled with the guitar-accented music of an acrobatic dance called the passo, and groups representing the city's candomblé houses play a prominent part; in the city of Recife the sound is frevo—a swinging brass-band music that brings to mind early New Orleans jazz—and the dancing in the streets owes much to capoeira, a martial art brought by slaves from Angola and transformed into innocuous-appearing dance steps. Whatever the beat, the music and dance of Brazilian Carnival blend African and European elements in a powerful cultural synthesis that virtually defines Brazilian identity. Living without Carnival, as they say in Rio, would be like "living without a soul."

Norma Miller, who learned to dance at the Savoy Ballroom, toured Brazil with Whitey's Lindy Hoppers in 1941 when she was twenty-one years old. Although she spoke no Portuguese, she says that she never had any trouble communicating with the Brazilians she met there: "I love Brazilian music. I loved it when I heard it. I used to go to black ballrooms in Rio and I would dance the samba and learn all about their rhythms. The samba and the Lindy, you could put the two of them together and . . . there's a fusion. Because it's a natural rhythm. The Brazilian black and the American black must have had the same roots somewhere in Africa. I'm sure that's what happened."

The steps and gestures of capoeira (below), as seen being danced by two men in Rio de Janeiro, are based on a form of martial arts brought to Brazil from central Africa.

This page and opposite: Samba school dancers at Carnival, Rio de Janeiro. During the pre-Lenten celebration, carefully choreographed and rehearsed dancing alternates with free-form improvisation.

Chapter 7
Modernizing Dance

n 1892, the year the first cakewalk contest was held in a New York ballroom, a woman named Loïe Fuller created a sensation at the Folies-Bergère in Paris, dancing what she called her "serpentine dance." The thirty-year-old Fuller, a native of Illinois, had been performing in burlesque and vaudeville since childhood. Her serpentine dance owed its inspiration to a prop; a few years earlier she had received from an admirer a voluminous skirt of transparent white silk. Playing around with the sensuously pleasing fabric in front of a mirror, Fuller had a vision: With dramatic lighting, she could create fantastic, evanescent, suggestive shapes onstage by agitating swaths of silk from underneath with a pair of hand-held wands.

Fuller was a born impresario with a gift for technical stagecraft. Whirling around on a glass platform, lit by as many as fourteen electric spotlights whose colors kept changing and blending, she kept yards and yards of fabric billowing around her in three-dimen-

sional evocations of flowers, butterflies, and flames. Her music tended toward the dramatic, like Wagner's "Ride of the Valkyries." To her audiences, she was a living manifestation of Art Nouveau, the decorative style that was just coming into vogue in Paris.

None of Fuller's many imitators came close to matching her technical wizardry or her theatrical sense. Her fans included poets (Mallarmé and Yeats), painters (Toulouse-Lautrec and Whistler), and scientists (Pierre and Marie Curie). In her hypnotic hold on her audience, in her ability to epitomize the taste of an entire generation, she was a successor to the Taglionis and Elsslers of the earlier nineteenth century. But unlike those ballerinas, whose careers had been formed within a long-established artistic tradition, Fuller was a self-made artist who ran her own show, literally as well as figuratively. She was not only the star dancer, she was the dance maker and the business-savvy entrepreneur. As such, she served as

precursor to a whole generation of dancers—mostly young women from America—whose fresh ideas and attitudes would prove to be as revolutionary a force in the theater as the incursion of African-American dance forms had already become in the ballroom.

The revolution we call "modern dance" was not just about how to move; it was also about how art should be made and by whom. In the West, as we have seen, dance as a serious theater art had always been a group endeavor, requiring the contributions of hundreds of individuals (from dancers and musicians to carpenters and stagehands) and substantial outlays of money. There was virtually no way to practice the art of dance, either as a dancer or a choreographer, outside the large ballet companies. Like most large enterprises, especially those that rely on the support of the wealthy and powerful, ballet companies tended to resist change. Ballet was unique in one way; although its dominant institutions (like those

of the other arts and indeed European society in general) were in the hands of men, the stars of the ballet stage were women. In no other nineteenth-century enterprise, artistic or otherwise, did women play so significant a role as they did in classical ballet. Behind the scenes, it is true, men remained in charge. Even the most acclaimed ballerinas danced, quite literally, to the tunes of men. With rare exceptions, men composed the music and the librettos, devised and staged the dances, collected and disbursed the money, and, as ballet masters and critics, set the standards and shaped the images that the dancers embodied onstage and off. A ballerina might express her personality in her dancing—the ethereal Taglioni, the pagan Elssler—but that personality was filtered through vessels crafted by men. Nevertheless, dance was one area of public endeavor in nineteenth-century Europe where women's talents were not only prized but idolized. The ballerinas whom audiences cheered were well re-

warded; they had both money and fame. They had no reason to separate themselves from institutions and traditions that had nurtured them, to strike out on their own by creating dances of a purely personal inspiration under conditions of their choosing. When agitation for this kind of freedom began, it came not from within the ballet establishment, but from women who set up shop, on their own, as self-proclaimed artists; their goal was unfettered self-expression through body movement. The freedom they won for themselves has invigorated theatrical dance in the West, including ballet, ever since.

The women who created modern dance were asserting for themselves something that poets and painters in the West had come to take for granted by the end of the nineteenth century: the right to follow personal inspiration without catering to the tastes of some private or institutional patron. This prerogative was inherent in the cultural phenomenon known as Romanticism.

The French painter Henri de Toulouse-Lautrec was often obsessive in his quest to capture the essence of a popular performer's style and personality, and he was enchanted by Loïe Fuller. In 1893, he painted Loïe Fuller in the Dance of the Veils, *a work that reveals more about the kinetic vitality of her dance than do contemporary photographs and engravings.*

Although Romanticism meant different things at different times to different people, common to all its manifestations was an emphasis on the individual as opposed to society, on feelings and intuition as opposed to rationality and calculation, on an almost mystical faith in the ability of an inspired artist to perceive universal truths and to communicate those truths to others. While genuinely inspired individuals formed a kind of natural elite, Romanticism had a built-in bias against the status quo; the artist needed no official sanction for his or her genius, and could expect incomprehension and resistance from the institutions that society had set up to monitor "good taste" in the arts. William Wordsworth, who challenged accepted taste in English poetry at the beginning of the nineteenth century, urged would-be poets to look within for their justification: "You feel strongly, trust those feelings, and your poem will take its shape and proportions as a tree does from the vital principle that actuates it." Change the word "poem" to "dance," and you have the recipe that Isadora Duncan followed in her seminal career as a pioneer of modern dance.

D uncan was born in San Francisco on May 26, 1877. The city had a verve that set it apart even in a California that was still largely frontier. The Gold Rush of '49 had left a permanent heritage of wealth, cultural aspirations, and a sense of adventure that some found intemperate: Rudyard Kipling, after a visit to California, noted, "San Francisco is a mad city, inhabited for the most part by perfectly insane people,

Isadora Duncan, not yet barefoot at twenty-one, dancing in a gown she fashioned from her mother's lace curtains, 1898.

whose women are of remarkable beauty." Duncan's mother was a strong-willed woman who divorced her husband for his philandering and financial irresponsibility; she supported her four children by taking in boarders, sewing, and giving piano lessons. As a lapsed Catholic who read atheistic tracts to her children, she believed in self-improvement through self-education, and elevated art to the status of religion; a print of Botticelli's *Primavera* became a veritable icon in the family. By fifteen Isadora was teaching ballroom dancing to Californians in need of social polish; she and her siblings also toured the state in a variety show of their own devising. Her reading ranged from Walt Whitman to Charles Darwin. Money was always a problem, and in 1895 Duncan left San Francisco to seek her fortune on the "open road" that Whitman had written about.

Duncan ended up in a New York theatrical company that toured America and England doing everything from musicals to Shakespeare. But the more she saw of the theatrical dance of the time the less she liked it. She probably saw some ballet and may have taken a few ballet lessons as well, and she liked that even less. "I am an enemy of the Ballet, which I consider a false and preposterous art, in fact outside the pale of all art," she wrote. Ballet was beyond the pale because it was unnatural; it required a "deformed skeleton" and "sterile movements" whose "purpose is to create the delusion that the law of gravitation does not exist for them." To uncover what she called "the real source of dance," she went to three places: to nature, to the art of classical Greece, and inside herself.

In Greek sculpture and vase paintings depicting figures in motion—a plump little cupid treading the ground, a gamboling satyr, a winged Hermes "with the ball of his foot resting on the wind" —she found a conformity to "natural forces" that would become the touchstone of her efforts to create what she called "the dance of the future." The Greeks only confirmed her intuition that people responded naturally to every experience with spontaneous movements of the body. Observing her own body for hours at a time in a mirror, she concluded that "the central spring of all movement" was the solar plexus, not "the center of the back at the base of the spine" as the ballet masters taught. She wasted no time informing the world of her discoveries. "I have discovered the dance. I have discovered the art which

has been lost for two thousand years," she told a theatrical producer. She was not yet twenty years old.

Duncan's claims were no more extravagant than those made by the defiant poets and painters of the nineteenth century, the Wordsworths and the Shelleys and the Baudelaires, the Van Goghs and the Monets, who had sought to reshape artistic experience (and therefore human experience itself) in their own image. But for a young woman—a woman with no credentials, no institutional backing, and no money—to challenge the artistic establishment was unheard-of. Her options were limited. There was no stage, either on Broadway or in an opera house, where she could put her theories to the test. So she turned to the only arena available to her: the salons of society

women who enlivened their leisure time by supporting Art with a capital A.

A favorite pastime in these salons was the recitation of poetry accompanied by gestures based on a system that linked specific physical movements to specific mental and emotional states. The system had been devised by François Delsarte (1811–1871), a French pedagogue with a passion for classical Greece, who was given to statements like, "Art is the telescope of the supernatural world." An American disciple, Genevieve Stebbins, codified his teachings into a regimen of what might be called aesthetic calisthenics, in which literary texts could be interpreted, line by line and even word by word, through an encoded pantomime not unlike the hand-language of Indian classical dance. The grand ambition of this form of Delsartism was satirized in the lyrics of a 1910 hit tune that proclaimed: "Every little movement has a meaning all its own/ Every thought and feeling by some posture may be shown."

Duncan's gestural vocabulary showed the influence of Delsartism, but even more important to her development was

Duncan dancers in an undated publicity photograph for a concert at the Metropolitan Opera House in New York performing Duncan's dance based on Sandro Botticelli's painting Primavera *(c.1482). A print of this work hung in Isadora Duncan's house when she was a child and seems to have made a strong impression on her. The resemblance between the postures and costumes of the Three Graces in the painting (opposite below) and the Duncan dancers is obvious.*

the fact that Delsarte's summons to free the body from all unnecessary constraints had already been heard in the salons of New York and Newport. So her wealthy patrons were in a receptive frame of mind when Duncan put on a Greek-style tunic made from her mother's old lace curtains and, to the lilt of Strauss waltzes, danced her interpretations of the *Rubaiyat of Omar Khayyam* and Botticelli's *Primavera*. Her costume, antique in its associations, was also deliciously modern. Feminists and hygienists had been campaigning for years against the painfully and even dangerously constricting clothes that fashion decreed for respectable women in the second half of the nineteenth century. From the age of three or four, girls were bound into tightly laced corsets that prevented them from lifting their arms above the head. What with corset, drawers, petticoats, dress-skirt, over-skirt, and dress-waist, the typical turn-of-the-century woman wore as many as sixteen layers of garments folded, buttoned, and belted tightly around her midriff. To such women, the loosely clad Duncan, striking poses from

quattrocento paintings and Greek sculpture, must have seemed an incarnation not just of Art and Beauty but of Freedom itself. Her dancing did not come across as erotic; "pure and sexless" is how someone later described it. She saw herself as a "Pagan Puritan, or a Puritanical Pagan."

With the money she raised at salon recitals, Duncan gathered her family and in 1899 sailed to Europe on a "cattle boat" to get in touch with the roots of her art. In London she stood "in adoration" before the British Museum's Elgin marbles and danced for the city's artistic and literary elite; among her sponsors were Henry James, the actress Mrs. Patrick Campbell, and the classical scholar Jane Ellen Harrison. On the advice of music critic J. Fuller Maitland, another sponsor, she "elevated" her choice of music from the waltzes of Strauss to the compositions of Gluck, Chopin, and Mendelssohn. For a subscription concert in an avant-garde art gallery she left off her dancing slippers and, apparently for the first time, performed barefoot for an audience. While a few expressed shock at this

gesture of emancipation from the conventions of European art dance, dancing barefoot became her trademark—and the defining characteristic of all "modern dance" in the first half of the twentieth century.

From London, the Duncan family moved on to Paris, where Duncan was enthralled by the Greek collection at the Louvre and by the performances of Loïe Fuller in a theater that had been built to her specifications on the grounds of the 1900 Exposition Universelle. When Fuller in turn saw Duncan dance, she invited the young American to join her on a tour through Germany. In the writings of Friedrich Nietzsche, Duncan found a view of Greek art that attributed its greatness to a dynamic balance between measured Apollonian beauty and irrational Dionysian frenzy; she adopted Nietzsche's *Birth of Tragedy from the Spirit of Music* as her bible.

Wherever she went, Duncan was taken seriously not only as a dancer but as a creative artist of a revolutionary kind. On a pilgrimage to Greece she paid her respects to the origins of her

Modern artists found modern dance inspiring; their goal of freeing Western art from constricting aesthetic conventions coincided with the ambitions of modern dancers in the realm of movement. The American artist Abraham Walkowitz made expressionistic figure studies of Isadora Duncan before World War I in this spirit.

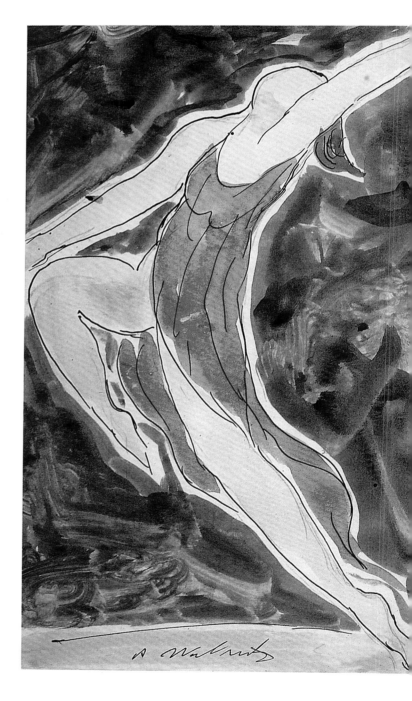

The American photographer Edward Steichen made a well-known series of images of Duncan on the Acropolis in Athens, including this one at the Parthenon. Steichen's photographs affirmed the association, so important to Duncan, of her art with the culture of classical Greece.

art by dancing ecstatically through the ruins of Athens. In the winter of 1904–5 she was in St. Petersburg, where political reformers, revolutionaries, and supporters of the tsar clashed almost daily in the streets. Her recitals, danced to a selection of Chopin preludes and polonaises, galvanized the forces of artistic reform in the Russian capital. In one of her characteristic pieces, she ran across the stage like the Winged Victory of Samothrace come to life, with her upper body and head bent backward and her arms extended behind her; some people in the audience swore they could hear the wind blowing through her hair. At the apartment of ballerina Anna Pavlova, Duncan met many of the rising stars of the Imperial Ballet, including the twenty-five-year-old Mikhail Fokine, a promising

choreographer who would be the first to put barefoot ballerinas on the classical stage; she also argued about dance with a brilliant critic and promoter of the arts named Serge Diaghilev who, four years later, would astonish the ballet world with an innovative company of Russian dancers brought to Paris under the banner of Diaghilev's Ballets Russes.

Although she certainly worked out many of her movement sequences ahead of time, Duncan liked to give the impression that she was improvising onstage. None of her dances were notated during her lifetime; with the exception of a few grainy frames of dubious provenance, no film documentation exists and the still photography of her time could capture only stagy poses, not the fluidity of pantomimic movement she was famous for. She did leave behind

students and disciples who handed down her dances in what we are assured is something approximating their original form. Even more evocative are the many drawings of Duncan by artists who thrilled to her embodiment of all that was fresh and daring in the imagination of the new century. "When she appeared," recalled one art student in Paris, "we all had the feeling that God —that is to say Certainty, Simplicity, Grandeur, and Harmony—that God was present [in] the magic of her movements."

Rodin declared: "It can be said of Isadora that she has attained sculpture and emotion effortlessly." Art historian Elie Faure confessed: "Yes, we wept when we saw her. . . . From deep within us when she danced there arose a flood that swept away from the corners of

When Isadora Duncan died in 1927, an international Isadora Duncan School was established in Potsdam, Germany, as a memorial. The school, on the grounds of Sans Souci, the former palace of Frederick II of Prussia, foundered, like other Duncan schools that had been started in her lifetime.

our soul all the filth which had been piled up there by those who for twenty centuries had bequeathed to us their critique, their ethics, their judgments. . . ."

Duncan usually danced barefoot on a soft carpet, lit by colored spotlights, against a neutral background of long draperies, wearing a light silk tunic gathered only at the breasts and hips so that her powerful legs were unencumbered. Her movements, based on the natural rhythms of walking, skipping, jumping, and running, were matched to the dynamics of the music she had chosen: familiar concert pieces by Bach, Chopin, Schubert, Beethoven, even Wagner. To dance to such music was daring in itself; before her, the works of the major classical composers were considered too "serious" to be used as mere accompaniment for any kind of dance, even ballet.

New York critic Carl Van Vechten described her interpretation of Tchaikovsky's *Marche Slave* as follows: "[Her dance] symbolizes her conception of the Russian moujik rising from slavery to freedom. With her hands bound behind her back, groping, stumbling, head bowed, knees bent, she struggles forward, clad only in a short red garment that barely covers her thighs. With furtive glances of extreme despair she peers above and ahead. When the strains of *God Save the Czar* are first heard in the orchestra she falls to her knees and you see the peasant shuddering under the blows of the knout. . . . Finally comes the moment of release and here Isadora makes one of her great effects. She does not spread her arms apart with a wide gesture. She brings them forward slowly and we observe

with horror that they have practically forgotten how to move at all. They are crushed, these hands, crushed and bleeding after their long serfdom; they are not hands at all but claws, broken, twisted piteous claws!"

Before Duncan came onstage to dance the "Liebestod" from Wagner's *Tristan und Isolde* before a full house at New York's Metropolitan Opera in 1911, conductor Walter Damrosch warned the audience: "As there are probably a great many people here to whom the idea of giving pantomimic expression to the 'Liebestod' would be horrifying, I am putting it last on the program so that those who do not wish to see it may leave." No one left, and her performance was greeted with sustained applause.

Despite her rhetoric about midwifing a new music and dance "that would express America," Duncan had no ear for ragtime or for any African-American rhythms that appealed to what she called "the appetites." She expressed a strong distaste for "the tottering, apelike convulsions" of the Charleston. "Jazz rhythm . . . rhythm from the waist down" was alien to her, the expression, as she saw it, not of her Whitmanesque America but of "the South African savage."

Like the Romantic poets who had troubled the proprieties of the previous century, Duncan made her own rules in life as well as art. Disdaining marriage as a form of slavery, she had two children by two different lovers; her young daughter and son were drowned in a freak automobile accident in 1913. When she decided to marry Sergey Yesenin, a Russian poet seven-

teen years her junior, she was reviled in America as a Bolshevik sympathizer; after several stormy years of marriage, he returned alone to Russia, where he committed suicide in 1925. By this time her dances had taken on a somber, autumnal tone; grief and suffering, not the joys of springtime or the glories of the Russian Revolution, increasingly became her themes. The girls' schools she founded in several countries to train a new generation of free-spirited, barefoot dancers failed one by one; her financial situation became precarious; she began to eat and drink to excess. In 1927, while she was riding in an open car near her home on the French Riviera, a long scarf she was wearing caught in a rear wheel and snapped her neck, killing her.

With all her misfortunes and disappointments, Isadora Duncan's achievement was epic. She defined herself and her art, controlled her own career, and forced the world to accept her on her own terms. In the history of Western culture, no woman since Sappho has been so identified with a major artistic genre. Although she left behind no institution to carry on her work, she served as a catalyst for a whole new art form—the dance known as modern. The task of securing the advances she made and of training the next generation of modern dancers fell to her contemporary, Ruth St. Denis.

St. Denis was born Ruth Dennis on a New Jersey farm in the late 1870s. Her mother was an intellectually restless woman with a strong mystical bent. Young Ruth was a natural dancer

According to Ruth St. Denis, a poster advertising Egyptian Deities cigarettes seen in a Buffalo, New York, drugstore in 1904 inspired her spiritual awakening as a dancer. This photograph, taken in San Francisco later that year, shows her in a costume and pose suggested to her by the poster.

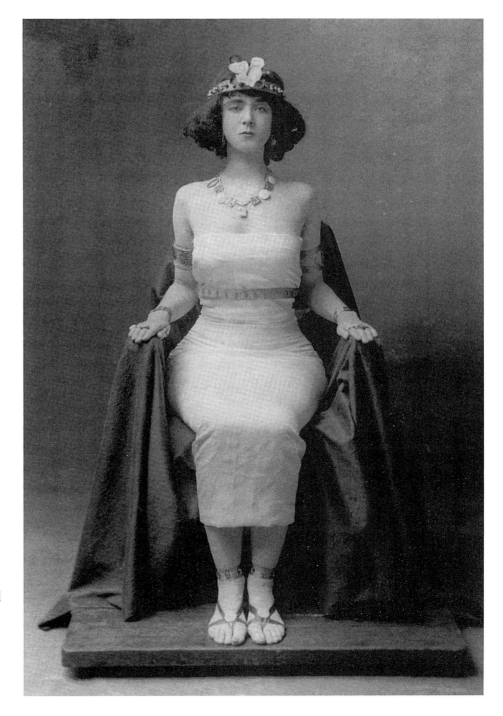

who taught herself splits and cartwheels in imitation of circus sideshows she had seen; she also took some lessons in ballet and ballroom dancing, and her mother instructed her in the rudiments of Delsarte's "expression." One of the happiest memories of her childhood was going with her mother to a lecture-demonstration by Genevieve Stebbins, the American popularizer of Delsartism. Before she was out of her teens, she was working as a show girl in vaudeville, doing what were known as "skirt dances," a free-form mix of clog dancing, ballet steps, and acrobatic kicks performed in a flouncy skirt with just enough leg showing to keep the interest of male spectators. She attracted the eye of Stanford White, the New York architect who fancied himself a patron of the arts, and of David Belasco, the Broadway impresario, who saw in her a potential musical-comedy star.

In 1900, while touring Europe with a Belasco production, she visited the Paris Exposition and saw Loïe Fuller dance; she also saw a theater troupe from Japan that Fuller was sponsoring. The star of this troupe, Sada Yacco, made a great impression on Western audiences in her role as the homicidal dancing girl in an adaptation of the kabuki classic *The Dancing Maiden at Dojo Temple*. Ruth Dennis stayed with Belasco for four more years, metamorphosing into Ruth St. Denis, a name which both her mother and her producer thought more suited to her rather refined stage presence. Then one spring afternoon in Buffalo, New York, she experienced a spiritual awakening while sipping an ice-cream soda with a friend in a drugstore. Opposite her on the wall was an eye-

catching poster advertising Egyptian Deities, a popular brand of cigarettes; the poster showed a bare-breasted woman, who was supposed to be the goddess Isis, seated in state amid pillars and lotus blossoms. Years later Ruth St. Denis described her reaction to the poster in terms appropriate to a religious conversion:

"Here was an external image which stirred into instant consciousness all that latent capacity for wonder, that still and meditative love of beauty which lay at the deepest center of my spirit. . . . I identified in a flash with the figure of Isis. She became the expression of all the somber mystery and beauty of Egypt, and I knew that my destiny as a dancer had sprung alive in that moment. I would become a rhythmic and imper-sonal instrument of spiritual revelation rather than a personal actress of comedy or tragedy. I had never before known such an inward shock of rapture."

Trying to shape her vision into a dance suitable for the stage, she recast the Egyptian goddess as Radha, Indian milkmaid and consort of the Hindu deity Krishna. A loosely defined Orientalism was in fashion during the early years of the century, and St. Denis's creation had just the right blend of sensuality and spirituality to appeal to a broad audience. In 1906 she danced as Radha in a New York variety theater and in the same society salons that had welcomed Isadora Duncan six years earlier.

A beautiful, big-framed woman with an unusually supple upper torso, St. Denis appeared as Radha wearing a gauze skirt, a bejeweled jacket that exposed more flesh than it concealed,

St. Denis (above) in a scene from the 1906 production of Radha *that reveals her "unusually supple upper torso." Right, a publicity photograph of St. Denis in* The Incense, 1916.

and some bracelets and anklets; her feet were bare. Her music was from Léo Delibes's opera *Lakmé*. According to the program notes that St. Denis wrote to explain the symbolism of her dance, Radha manipulates a series of props—ropes of flowers, a string of pearls, tinkling bells, a cup of wine—to demonstrate to the temple priests the dangerous lure of the senses. After succumbing to a transport of sinuous body movements, high kicks, and acrobatic back bends, she swoons, renounces the life of the senses, and returns to the meditative lotus position with which the dance began. Like Duncan, St. Denis had found a model for her personal approach to the dancing body in the tradition of a culture far removed from her own experience. "As I see it," she wrote later, "the deepest lack of Western cultures is any true workable system for teaching a process of integration between soul and body."

Americans had inherited from Western Europe a set of attitudes toward dance that distinguished between ballet as a serious art and other kinds of dance as popular art. This distinction was embedded in a two-tiered institutional structure: Ballet was appreciated by a relatively small group of connoisseurs and supported by a wealthy social elite, while popular dance lived or died at the box office. Convinced that what they were doing was serious art but unwilling to accept the package of cultural and aesthetic assumptions that came with ballet, modern dancers looked beyond Europe for justification and inspiration. They were hardly alone. The international expositions and world's fairs that were so popular from the latter decades

of the nineteenth through the early decades of the twentieth century fed a widespread curiosity about the cultures of non-European societies. Encounters with the art of Africa and the music of Southeast Asia helped painters like Picasso and composers like Debussy break free from the conventions of their own history. Encounters with Greece and India did the same for Duncan and St. Denis.

The fact that renunciation plays no part in the Hindu texts about the union of Radha and Krishna did not trouble St. Denis; she was not after ethnological authenticity but a way of bringing together onstage the two sides of her own personality—the spiritual and the sensual. Whether such selective cultural borrowing is legitimate and to what extent artists should acknowledge the cross-cultural roots of their work are questions that did not arise until much later in this century. The reverence that St. Denis showed for her Indian sources was certainly genuine.

With the money she earned dancing Radha in New York, St. Denis followed in Duncan's footsteps and embarked on a three-year tour of Europe. She was well received in France and Germany, but unlike Duncan, she became homesick for the United States. She returned to great acclaim, touring the country in a grand spectacle called *Egypta*, and performing "Radha" and other Oriental-flavored solos for smaller audiences. Her imagination was essentially pictorial. Among her earliest dances was one called "The Incense," in which she mimed the rippling rise of smoke with a graceful spiraling motion of one arm; in "The Cobras," her arms coiled around

her neck and body like charmed serpents.

To expand her repertoire she decided in 1914 to join forces with a male partner and form a small dance company. The partner was Ted Shawn, a former divinity student from Kansas City whom she married in 1915; the company grew into the Denishawn School of Dancing and Related Arts in Los Angeles (with branches around the country), which became the center of the modern dance world for the next ten years.

Shawn, twelve years younger than St. Denis, had even more eclectic tastes and a keener commercial sense. The Denishawn School offered a uniquely varied curriculum; among the types of dance taught were ballet, Spanish, Oriental, Egyptian, Greek, American Indian, geisha, creative, Delsarte, primitive, and folk. During the school's heyday Denishawn graduates danced to music by composers ranging from Bach and Brahms to Erik Satie and Vaughan Williams; toured the country performing everything from danced "myths" to the latest ballroom steps; and appeared in early silent movies and in the *Ziegfeld Follies* in New York. It was through its more commercial activities that Denishawn supported the serious artistic endeavors of the founders and their students. The school also trained silent-movie actors to move expressively for directors like D.W. Griffith and Cecil B. DeMille, and staged colossal costume spectacles, like the 1916 *Life and Afterlife in Egypt, Greece, and India*, which succeeded in looking exotic and wholesome at the same time.

After fifteen years of a tempestuous, on-again–off-again relationship, Shawn

Ruth St. Denis's various activities in the dance world had a strong entrepreneurial side. These pursuits found her teaching at the Denishawn schools (top) and coaching dancers in the movies (center). In the 1920s she traveled to India with Ted Shawn to see first-hand the dance tradition that had inspired her early concert dances (bottom).

Opposite: Ted Shawn's all-male dance company helped further the acceptance of men as dancers in America. Here, he performs Kinetic Molpai (1935), choreography by Shawn and music by Jess Meeker, with his troupe in 1936. Kinetic Molpai was a ballet about masculine power. Its eleven sections were called Strife, Oppositions, Solvent, Dynamic Contrasts, Resilience, Successions, Unfolding and Folding, Dirge, Limbo, Surge, and Apotheosis.

and St. Denis went their separate ways in 1931. He put together an all-male dance company to embody his lifelong conviction that "dancing is a manly sport, more strenuous than golf or tennis, more exciting than boxing or wrestling and more beneficent than gymnastics"; later he founded the Jacob's Pillow dance festival in Massachusetts. She was drawn more and more to the idea of dance as devotion, as liturgy, as "a living mantra"; she began performing in churches and founded the School of Spiritual Arts. Looking back

on her career, she wrote: "I had to be an Indian—a Japanese—a statue—a something or somebody else—before the public would give me what I craved." Yet she never renounced the solos that had made her famous, continuing to dance a "Radha" well into her eighties.

Until its demise in 1931 the Denishawn School served as a magnet for a second generation of modern dancers, first attracting them with its open-minded attitudes, then repelling

them with its eclecticism and what one of its most illustrious graduates called the "weakling exoticism of a transplanted orientalism." This illustrious graduate was Martha Graham, who came to Denishawn in the summer of 1916 and left in 1923, ready to begin her own career which would take her—and modern dance itself—into uncharted realms of personal symbolism. Although she based many of her works on incidents from the world's storehouse of myths, the truths she sought were not abstract or universal

Ted Shawn and Martha Graham in Xochitl (1920; left). She was twenty-six years old when Shawn chose her to star opposite him in this ballet, which one critic described as "a series of barbarically gorgeous pictures."

Martha Graham, in white, with her company in Heretic (1929; below). The music, a ten-bar Breton folk song, was played on the piano by Louis Horst, her music director.

but personal; each of her dances, she once said, was "a graph of the heart."

Graham was born in 1894 in a Pennsylvania town that is now a part of Pittsburgh. Like Isadora Duncan, she experienced the conflicting pulls of Puritanism and paganism. Her upbringing in Pennsylvania was sedate; but when she was fourteen her family moved to California in search of a healthier climate for a younger sister who had asthma. The brilliant sunlight and open spaces around her new home in Santa Barbara had an intoxicating effect on the adolescent Graham. She heard her father, a physician who treated mental cases, say that he based his diagnoses on the way his patients moved: "The body never lies" was his maxim. The young Martha persuaded her father to take her to see Ruth St. Denis dance. She found the performance so exhilarating that she decided then and there to become a dancer, although she could not put this resolve into practice until the death of her father, who did not approve of the theater as a career.

A year after the Denishawn School opened, Graham enrolled. She was already in her early twenties, a late bloomer by dance standards, but her intensity, intelligence, and taut, lean body caught the attention of Ted Shawn. In 1920 Shawn created a ballet called Xochitl, in which Graham played a "Toltec" maiden who ferociously defends her honor against a drink-maddened emperor. Critics called it "the first native American ballet," but its exotic costumes and sets identified it as a close cousin to Denishawn's trademark "Oriental" spectacles.

A more important influence on Graham was Louis Horst, the school's music director, whose interests lay in the work of contemporary European composers like Erik Satie and Zoltán Kodály. He introduced Graham to more challenging scores and encouraged her to strike out on her own as a dancer and choreographer. By the time she left Denishawn in 1923, she had acquired a thorough grounding in crowd-pleasing stagecraft. Moving to New York she got a job in a Broadway revue called Greenwich Village Follies, dancing what she later referred to as "sexy little things." Meanwhile, she was refining her own ideas about dance, rejecting not only the "rigidity" of classical ballet but also the movement styles of Isadora Duncan and Ruth St. Denis. She felt the need for a new vocabulary of movement that could "make visible the interior landscape" in a rapidly changing world: "Life today is nervous, sharp, and zigzag. This is what I aim for in my dances."

Graham's first New York concert in 1926 still showed traces of Denishawn exoticism (one dance featured three of St. Denis's former students as Krishna's milkmaids). But with the aid of Horst, who had come east to be her music director, she was soon showing "sharper" stuff like Danse, a 1929 solo in which she did not move her feet at all but contorted the rest of her body to music by Arthur Honegger, and Heretic, a piece for her newly formed all-female dance company, set to a marchlike Breton folk song arranged for piano and played by Horst. The song kept repeating, and, with each repeat, Graham, as the title character dressed in white,

"pleaded her case" with simple but eloquent gestures to a menacing "jury" of twelve women wearing long, dark dresses. Each time the women rejected her plea, they thumped their heels on the floor to emphasize their unwillingness to listen, then threw themselves into new postures of stiff-legged condemnation; at the end the "heretic" sank to the floor in defeat, surrounded by the triumphant conformists.

In Lamentation, a landmark 1930 solo to a Kodály Piano Piece, Graham was seen sitting on a wooden bench, shrouded in a tube of stretch jersey with only her face, hands, and bare feet showing. Rocking stiffly from side to side, she tugged and pulled and pushed at the confining fabric with her hands, elbows, knees, and shoulders, not so much trying to break free as to carve out a place of rest for her grief-wracked body in a comfortless world.

Over the next few years, Graham gave a series of recitals that drew appreciative notices from both inside and outside the dance community; in 1932 she became the first dancer to receive a Guggenheim Fellowship. Her manner was resolutely modern in a socially conscious, Depression-era way: no sets, no fancy costumes, nothing soft or pretty. "Like the modern painters and architects," she declared, "we have stripped our medium of decorative unessentials." Her themes came from Native American rituals, from a mythologized American history, from her own responses to newspaper headlines and machine technology, from her own struggles as a creative artist, from her relentless exploration of the "potential

Just as Isadora Duncan is firmly associated with the photographs of Edward Steichen, so is Martha Graham with those of Barbara Morgan. Her best known image of the dancer shows Graham in Letter to the World *(1940), choreography by Martha Graham and music by Hunter Johnson. The ballet is based on the life of poet Emily Dickinson, and excerpts from her poems are spoken in the performance.*

greatness" of the human body. In classes at her Greenwich Village studio, Graham built up a system of exercises that constituted her answer to the daily class of traditional ballet companies. Students began on the floor with stretches and leg extensions, then stood up for bends, lifts, hip swings, and turns in place, followed by jumping, walking, running, and skipping. Each class concluded with what she described as "a series of falls forward, side, and back. . . . In no fall does the body remain on the floor, but assumes an upright position as part of the exercise. My dancers fall *so they may rise.*"

Central to her technique was postural control, which began with close observation of the act of breathing. Dancer Jane Dudley remembers Graham telling her classes: "If you breathe out through your teeth as hard as you can and then notice what's happened to your shoulders and your pelvis and your back, that's what a contraction is. Then if you breathe in and see how the back straightens and centers itself, that is a release."

"Contraction" and "release"—the muscular activity independent of the act of breathing—became the bywords of the Graham technique. Neither had anything to do with relaxation; she believed that movement should always be emphatic, expressive, disciplined. In her opinion it took at least ten years of hard work to make a dancer.

Graham treated her trained dancers as her personal choreographic instrument; with few exceptions, no one else performed her dances. She created new pieces in the studio, demonstrating a

movement she wanted and expecting her dancers to pick it up the first time. Rehearsals were long and exhausting. Enlivened by gestures and poses adapted from the dances of Asia, Graham's technique exerted a powerful influence on her movement vocabulary. In time, many of her best dancers left her in search of more creative freedom, as she had once left Denishawn. But Graham herself continued to grow as an artist. After 1934, instead of setting dances to previously written music, she started collaborating with composers like Aaron Copland, Paul Hindemith, and Samuel Barber on new works; the next year she began a long collaboration with the sculptor Isamu Noguchi, whose enigmatic sets and props became as much a part of her dances as the dancers themselves.

In the late thirties she hired her first male dancers, the ballet-trained Erick Hawkins and the young and talented but largely untrained Merce Cunningham. With these new resources at her command, Graham fashioned a series of powerful "dance plays," often based explicitly or implicitly on the travails of women in Greek mythology. While more "theatrical" than her earlier works, these were hardly conventional narratives; what happened onstage was best understood as taking place in the mind of a suffering, struggling archetypal figure, who was invariably Graham herself. To expand the possibilities of storytelling through gesture, she borrowed the flexible staging of Asian dance drama forms like Nō, kabuki, and Chinese opera, where a few steps can indicate a journey, a few moments the passage of years.

One way to make sense of the history of modern dance in America is to read it as a family tree of creative parturition: after training in an established company, a dancer or group of dancers with a fresh personal vision moves on to form a new company. A few years after Martha Graham broke with Denishawn, two other mainstays of that school, Doris Humphrey and Charles Weidman, left to create a varied body of work that stressed movement initiated "from the inside out." Humphrey summed up her credo in the phrase "A movement without a motivation is unthinkable." Yet her repertoire ranged from rigorously formal exercises like *Two Ecstatic Themes: Circular Descent, Pointed Ascent* (1931) to humanistic "music visualizations" like *Passacaglia and Fugue in C Minor* (1938) to socially conscious pieces like *Inquest* (1944). Weidman is best known for his wryly humorous pantomime in autobiographical dances like *And Daddy Was a Fireman* (1943). Mexican-born José Limón, who emerged from the Humphrey-Weidman company after the Second World War, scored a success with his first major work, *The Moor's Pavane* (1949), which compressed the turbulent emotions of Shakespeare's *Othello* into the formal framework of a court dance.

Meanwhile, as modern dance's most prominent spokesperson, Martha Graham openly defied, in words and accomplishments, the primacy of ballet as the institutional center of the dance world. Her students taught the Graham technique to dancers around the world, and dancers and choreographers came

from Europe, Asia, and South America to learn it at the source. Her company was one of the first multiracial dance companies, with black, white, and Asian dancers performing together; from its ranks came an entire generation of outstanding choreographers, including Hawkins and Cunningham. Throughout her career, during which she created more than 170 dances, Graham played for the highest stakes; dancing, she wrote, "had its origin in ritual," which she defined as "the formalized desire to achieve union with those beings who could bestow immortality." She continued to tour and make dances up until her death in 1991. The angular, austere style of her most productive years so dominated the public perception of modern dance that it became almost a cliché: the barefoot dancer in black expressing herself onstage while an audience of insiders tries

bravely to figure out what it all means. But her career established once and for all that dance could be a vehicle of personal expression—not just for the dancer but for the choreographer.

The world of ballet was by no means insulated from this revolution of dance-makers. But in a world where dance is made within institutions—a company with a school attached—an innovative dance-maker has no choice but to come to terms with the tradition that the institution represents. The choreographers who figured prominently in the evolution of ballet in eighteenth- and nineteenth-century Europe—men like Jean Georges Noverre, Charles Louis Didelot, Auguste Bournonville, and Marius Petipa—were ballet masters of major companies. They did not have to reinvent dance from the ground up;

their innovations rejected some precedents from earlier times while building on others. This was the model envisioned by Mikhail Fokine when, at the time of Isadora Duncan's visit to Russia, he sent an artistic manifesto to the director of the Imperial Theaters. Fokine believed that the great classical tradition that the Russians had inherited from the French and lovingly nurtured for much of the century—since 1869 under the leadership of Marius Petipa at St. Peterburg's Maryinsky Theater—had gone stale. Fokine revered Petipa but he wanted to let in fresh air. His approach to reform was both aesthetic and scientific. In place of a loosely organized succession of "numbers," "entries," and so on, he called for a unified work of art whose performance would be uninterrupted even by pauses for leading dancers to acknowledge applause; in place of "mere gymnastics" and conventional gestures, he called for expressive dancing that would make use of the whole body down to "the last muscle." And, through careful research into the time and place in which each ballet was set, he believed that all elements of a production—"music, painting, and the plastic arts"—could be harmoniously blended to express a single, underlying theme.

The director of the Maryinsky Theater ignored this manifesto but permitted the precociously talented Fokine to dabble in choreography. Fokine had made his debut as a dancer in 1898 on his eighteenth birthday; at the age of twenty-two he was already teaching classical technique to the junior girls at the Imperial Ballet School. In the years following Duncan's visit, he pressed his

Costume sketch of a bacchante (Bronislawa Nijinska) and a young boétienne (Vera Fokina) by Léon Bakst for the Ballets Russes production of Narcisse (1911), choreography by Mikhail Fokine and music by Nikolai Tcherepnin.

campaign to reform the Russian ballet tradition. His first efforts to stage ballets with Greek themes and Duncanesque freedom of movement and costume—including bare feet and bare knees for the ballerinas—provoked opposition, and he was forced to compromise: in one ballet the dancers appeared in tights with toes and knees painted on. The radical nature of his ideas can be appreciated from the comments of a ballerina who, a few years later, danced barefoot for the first time in a Fokine ballet: "This gave me a strange sensation of nakedness, like walking in public in a nightgown."

But gradually barriers fell. In 1906 a production he put together for his students won praise from the recently retired Marius Petipa, whose own historical spectacles Fokine had criticized as "unauthentic." In 1908 he presented two precedent-shattering works. In *Une Nuit d'Egypte*, an erotic divertissement featuring Anna Pavlova and himself in the major roles, dancers turned their profiles to the audience in the style of Egyptian tomb paintings, which shocked traditionalists accustomed to the predominantly frontal display of the classical canon; as the hero, Fokine danced with bare knees showing below the border of his striped kilt; and the ballerinas bent and twisted their upper bodies in unconventional and provocative poses. For *Chopiniana* he adopted not only the serious music favored by Isadora Duncan but, according to some accounts, her fluid and expressive arm movements as well. Another possible influence on Fokine's plastic use of the arms was the appearance in St. Petersburg of a troupe of Siamese court

Yet another of those photographs (left) that have become indissolubly linked with a dancer: Anna Pavlova as The Swan, a solo dance that Mikhail Fokine choreographed for her in 1905 to music by Camille Saint-Saëns. Pavlova's tireless touring with her own company did much to stimulate worldwide enthusiasm for ballet. Like many modern dance-makers she had an interest in non-Western dance traditions. In London she met a young Indian art student named Uday Shankar; he helped her stage, and danced with her in, Radha-Krishna (1923) and other dances (below). Shankar (1900–77) became a forceful popularizer of Indian dance in the West; in his later years he worked to reinvigorate traditional dance forms in India.

dancers in 1900 . In 1905, he choreographed a brief solo for Anna Pavlova, called *The Swan*, in which her tremulous arm movements represented the last futile efforts of a dying creature to regain the freedom of flight it had once known; when Pavlova began touring the world with her own company after 1910, this became her signature piece.

For all the excitement provoked by Fokine's innovations, it is by no means certain that he could have realized the full range of his ambitious reforms within the tradition-bound Imperial Ballet. Serge Diaghilev gave him the opportunity he had dreamed of. As tsarist Russia slipped further into financial and political chaos, Diaghilev received permission to bring a troupe of Maryinsky principals to Paris in 1909, with Fokine as ballet master. Audiences in the West were astonished by the technical facility and expressive power of the Russian dancers, who included Pavlova and the nineteen-year-old Vaslav Nijinsky. The settings and costumes by Léon Bakst and Alexandre Benois blazed with color. And the ballets themselves, choreographed by Fokine, challenged preconceived ideas of classical dance.

In *Cléopâtre*, an adaptation of *Une Nuit d'Egypte*, the queen and her paramour made love on stage (discreetly hidden behind veils) while half-naked slaves and attendants cavorted orgiastically. *Schéhérazade* featured an even wilder orgy and a merciless massacre onstage.

For three years, triumph followed triumph, confirming Fokine's dictum that choreographic style should change from ballet to ballet in accord with theme and music. The same audiences that thrilled to Fokine's acrobatic "Tartar" dances set to music from Borodin's opera *Prince Igor* were deeply moved by the abstract Romanticism of *Les Sylphides*, a revised version of *Chopiniana*, which emerged as the first entirely plotless ballet. In 1911 Fokine collaborated with Igor Stravinsky on *Petrouchka*, a Russian folk tale, with Nijinsky in the title role; this character's jerky, mechanical movements and turned-in toes dramatized his helplessness as a puppet of fate.

Fokine broke with Diaghilev in 1912, and although he later returned to the Ballets Russes, he never again equaled

Enrico Cecchetti and Vaslav Nijinsky in the Ballets Russes production of Petrouchka *(1911), choreography by Mikhail Fokine and music by Igor Stravinsky. The ballet, inspired by St. Petersburg Shrovetide Fair puppet shows, revolves around a puppeteer—the Charlatan—and three of his puppets. Here, the Charlatan, played by Cecchetti, kicks the puppet Petrouchka into his desolate room, which is decorated only with a portrait of his master. There, the tormented creature begins to discover his soul.*

Ballet companies work together and play together. Right, dancers Leon Woizikovsky, Lydia Sokolova, and Serge Lifar of the Ballets Russes horse around on a beach in the 1920s, while Diaghilev watches. Below, Woizikovsky, Sokolova, and Lifar together again, this time in rehearsal. The ballet is the Ballets Russes production of Les Matelots (1925), choreography by Léonide Massine and music by Georges Auric.

Couturiere Coco Chanel and artist
Henri Laurens designed the costumes
and set respectively for the Ballets Russes
production of Le Train Bleu (1924;
below), choreography by Bronislawa
Nijinska and music by Darius Milhaud.
Picasso painted the curtain.

Seven years earlier, Picasso had created
costumes and sets for the Ballets Russes
production of Parade (1917), choreography by Léonide Massine and music by
Erik Satie, in a vivid application of Cubist
principles to stage design. The Ballets
Russes poster (top right) features the
character of the Chinese Conjurer, danced
by Massine, from Parade. This ballet is
inextricably entwined with the history of
twentieth-century art; in his program note
to the original production, French poet
Guillaume Apollinaire first used the term
"Surrealism." Parade has had a number
of revivals, all faithful to Picasso's decor.
Right, Gary Chryst dances the role of
the Chinese Conjurer in a Joffrey Ballet
production.

213

his innovative achievements during those first three Paris seasons. Diaghilev, whose financially shaky company needed a steady supply of novelties to attract audiences, was neither a choreographer nor a dancer nor a composer nor an artist of any kind. Yet he had a hand in every aspect of the works his company produced. It was his idea to present three short ballets in a single evening, a format which has become standard for ballet companies around the world. He hired, and fired, and rehired the Stravinskys and Saties, the Fokines and Nijinskys, the Baksts and Benoises, the Picassos and Cocteaus whose talents merged in such exciting and often surprising ways that the contributors fought bitterly for years over who deserved credit for which aspect of this or that ballet. All his ballet masters—Fokine, Nijinsky, Léonide Massine, Bronislawa Nijinksa (Nijinsky's sister), and George Balanchine—were extraordinarily

talented, and he rarely second-guessed them; but their average age when he took them on was under twenty-three. There was never any doubt about who was in charge. Ultimately, it was Diaghilev's taste that was reflected in the style and the content of the Ballets Russes; his unique company was his instrument of self-expression.

W hen Vaslav Nijinsky, the most acclaimed male dancer of his day, began creating innovative ballets for Diaghilev's Ballets Russes in 1912, it looked for a time as if the young Nijinsky might achieve the choreographic goal that had eluded Fokine: to mold a first-class ballet company into a means of personal expression.

Nijinsky was born in Kiev in 1890 of Polish extraction. His parents headed their own touring dance company in Russia; from an early age he and his

younger sister Bronislawa appeared onstage with their father, who was noted for his enormous leaps. At the age of ten, Nijinsky enrolled in the Imperial Ballet School in St. Petersburg, where his teachers recognized his natural talent almost immediately. On graduation in 1907 he danced a succession of important roles in such ballets as *Giselle*, *Swan Lake*, and The *Sleeping Beauty*.

His dancing offered a rare mix of strength and facility. Propelled by powerfully muscled thighs, his leaps were legendary not only for their height but for the impression he gave of pausing in midair at the top of the arc. In the words of critic Edwin Denby: "When he moves he does not blur the center of weight in his body; one feels it as clearly as if he were still standing at rest, one can follow its course clearly as it floats about the stage through the dance." He projected a vitality, a sensuality, that some saw as innocent, others as erotic.

Among his admirers was Serge Diaghilev, who sensed that a great ballet company could be built around this young dancer who combined a rigorous schooling in classical technique with an almost palpable emotional intensity.

The roles that Fokine choreographed for Nijinsky in the first three seasons of the Ballets Russes allowed the dancer to display the full range of his powers to wildly appreciative audiences in Paris and London. As the Poet in *Les Sylphides* he embodied an abstract Romanticism seen through the lens of nostalgia; as the Favorite Slave in *Schéhérazade* he was the devotee of sexuality for whom even death is a kind of orgasm; in *Le Spectre de la Rose* his leaping exit from the stage had the sensational finality of a record-setting broad jump; in *Petrouchka* he was poignancy itself. There was, it seemed, nothing he could not do, no role he could not

bring to life onstage. He always had trouble communicating in words, but when he danced, he spoke with his entire body. Is it any wonder that, prompted by Diaghilev, he decided to take the next step and try his hand at making dances?

Having mastered technique as few dancers before or since, Nijinsky apparently had no interest in devising ever-more-challenging exercises in the traditional mode. Instead, he took up where Fokine had left off—seeking to express something of himself through the artistic medium of a classically trained ballet company.

In *L'Après-Midi d'un Faune* (*Afternoon of a Faun*), the subject was sex—adolescent sex. As the Faun, Nijinsky (adorned with a small tail, golden horns, and pointed ears) tried to entice some passing nymphs into joining him for a frolic. Intrigued, frightened, they dallied, then fled. One dropped her

Vaslav Nijinsky in four Ballets Russes productions (from left to right): Schéhérazade (1910), choreography by Mikhail Fokine and music by Nicolai Rimsky-Korsakov; Le Carnaval (1910), choreography by Fokine and music by Robert Schumann; Petrouchka (1911), choreography by Fokine and music by Igor Stravinsky; and Jeux (1913), choreography by Nijinsky and music by Claude Debussy.

215

A scene from L'Après-Midi d'un Faune (1912), choreography by Nijinsky and music by Claude Debussy, from a famous series of photographs of the ballet by the Baron de Meyer. The faun gambols with a nymph, who has dropped her scarf.

Opposite: Among revivals of L'Après-Midi d'un Faune, the most faithful to Nijinsky's original was the Joffrey Ballet's of 1980 with Rudolf Nureyev. Nureyev, like Baryshnikov, studied at the Leningrad Choreographic School and made his debut with the Kirov Ballet. He moved to the West in 1961, at the age of twenty-three, and became the leading male dancer of the 1960s and early 1970s.

scarf. Like an animal playing with its prey, the Faun retrieved the scarf, draped it over a rock, and, throwing his head back in a soundless laugh, pressed out his longing against the smooth fabric. Those in the audience who were not shocked by this explicit mime of masturbation were outraged by the anti-classical movements that Nijinsky had devised for himself and the nymphs. The dancers moved back and forth across the stage like cutouts from a Greek frieze. Ballerinas who had spent years perfecting their turnout found it difficult to keep their feet parallel. Debussy's dreamlike music was no help in keeping time, as one dancer recalled: "[We] walked and moved quite gently to a rhythm that crossed over the beats given by the conductor. At every entrance one made—and there were several—one began to count, taking the count from another dancer who was coming off. For every lift of the hand or head there was a corresponding sound in the score."

Although Diaghilev toned down the ending at the insistence of the Paris police, he relished the outcry that the piece provoked; controversy generated publicity and sold tickets. For Nijinsky, the critical attacks hit closer to home: "The Faun," he said simply, "is me."

It had taken the young choreographer 120 rehearsals to prepare this twelve-minute ballet for its premiere. A year later, in May 1913, he presented two new ballets that set off an even greater furor. Today, the better known is Le Sacre du Printemps (The Rite of Spring) because of its propulsive score by Igor Stravinsky. It was Stravinsky's idea to create a ballet around a savage ritual from pre-Christian Russia, in which an adolescent girl dances herself to death as a sacrifice to the god of spring. Diaghilev turned to Nijinsky as choreographer only after Fokine, his original choice, had backed out over a monetary dispute.

To help Nijinsky set steps to the complex rhythmic structure of the music,

Diaghilev brought in an expert in eurhythmics, a method of matching body movements to musical rhythms invented by a Swiss music teacher, Emile Jaques-Dalcroze (1865–1950). The result was more "counting," as in *Faun*; but because there were many more dancers doing many more things onstage for a much longer time, the counts were much, much more complicated. Nijinsky did not dance in *Sacre*. On opening night he stood in the wings stamping his foot and counting out loud for the benefit of the dancers. But no one could hear him above the din of the orchestra and the disapproving shouts and whistles from the audience that began even before the curtain went up. A near-riot ensued. It was hard to tell which the protesters disliked more: Stravinsky's pounding, discordant music or Nijinsky's frenetic, knock-kneed choreography. Among the words that critics used to describe the ballet: "harsh," "raw," "bitter," "brutal," "undigested," "coarse," "frank."

As a *succès de scandale*, *Sacre* had no equal: It was the avant-garde event of the season, the decade, some might say the century. Within twenty years Stravinsky's music had entered the concert repertoire; its discordances and rhythmic innovations had become part of the musical language of its time. But the ballet itself received only six performances, and Nijinsky's choreography has been preserved only in the uncertain memories of those who were there. Attempts to restage the original work have met with no definitive agreement on whether the reconstructions represent what the original audience saw on opening night.

The other ballet that Nijinsky choreographed that spring, *Jeux* (*Games*), is almost entirely forgotten except by historians of dance. But in its own way, *Jeux* (set to a specially commissioned score by Debussy) was as radical as *Sacre*, and marked an important milestone in the evolution of ballet as an instrument of personal, rather than collaborative, creation. For perhaps the first time in the history of classical ballet the dancers portrayed characters who seemed to live in the same world as the spectators. The theme was sport—a game of tennis—but the subtext was sexual play, a three-way flirtation between Nijinsky and two female partners. All three dancers wore sports clothes only slightly modified from outfits that anyone in the audience might have worn the previous weekend. As in *Faun* the movements were angular, stilted; at times the principals looked more like silent-movie actors than dancers.

To dancers trained in classical technique, the poses and attitudes that Nijinsky specified (to be executed on three-quarter point) were punishing: "I had to keep my head screwed on one side, both hands curled in as in one maimed from birth," said one ballerina. In his diary the choreographer was explicit about the source of his inspiration: Diaghilev had been eager to have a young boy share their bed, an idea that Nijinsky rejected. Audiences were more puzzled than aroused by the encoded ménage à trois they saw onstage, but Nijinsky's artistic courage could not be faulted; in the words of Lincoln Kirstein: "Few dancers before had translated private tension into public parable."

But Nijinsky was unable to follow up

on this breakthrough. In August 1913 the Ballets Russes company sailed from Southampton, England, for a tour of South America that Diaghilev, always hard-pressed for cash, had arranged even though he was so terrified of sea voyages that he could not bring himself to go. (He had been told by a fortune-teller that death would find him at sea.) To many in the company, it was startling to see Nijinsky without Diaghilev at his side. What followed was a progression of tragicomic events that played like a darker sequel to *Jeux*. On the voyage Nijinsky spent all his time with Romola de Pulszka, the daughter of a famous and wealthy Hungarian actress, who had recently joined the corps de ballet. Shortly after their arrival in Rio, Nijinsky and Romola announced their engagement; they were married on September 10, 1913. When the news reached Paris, Diaghilev was furious. Seizing on the pretext that Nijinsky had breached his contract by refusing to dance one night in Rio, Diaghilev fired his rebellious protégé and appointed as ballet master in his place the seventeen-year-old Léonide Massine.

After the First World War began, Nijinsky was interned in Hungary as a Russian subject, only to be freed in 1916 by the string-pulling efforts of Diaghilev, who had secured a lucrative engagement for his company at the Metropolitan Opera in New York on the condition that Nijinsky dance. Although Nijinsky himself was already beginning to show signs of mental deterioration, the Metropolitan engagement in the spring of 1916 created a stir, and a second New York season was arranged for the fall of the same year, this time

George Balanchine with Tamara Toumanova and Natalie Shakhova in the Ballets Russes de Monte Carlo production of Cotillon *(1932), choreography by George Balanchine and music by Alexis Chabrier.*

with Nijinsky in full charge of the company. For a man who had trouble managing his own life, this was an impossible assignment. In addition, his contract stipulated that he produce two new ballets in three weeks for New York premieres. Only one was produced, a mimed narrative version of the German folk tale *Till Eulenspiegel*, set to Richard Strauss's tone poem. On opening night the second act was in such a raw state that the dancers had to improvise most of their steps.

After that, Nijinsky's mental decline was obvious to everyone. His last public appearance as a dancer was in September 1917. Over the next two years he planned a ballet to be set to the music of Bach and worked on an elaborate system of dance notation that he had invented. From 1919, when his condition was diagnosed as schizophrenia, until his death in 1950 he lived for the most part in a series of European asylums. After his departure from the scene, it became the fashion to denigrate his achievements as a choreographer, following the lead of Stravinsky and Fokine who claimed credit for most of Nijinsky's innovations. But other collaborators have testified to his hard work, high standards, and almost oppressive drive in bringing a dance to the stage. Just before his final mental breakdown he confided to a colleague: "I wish to work independently of other troupes of dancers in which intrigue prevents the creation of real art. I am planning to dance alone with a small company and achieve some interesting results."

As dreams go, this seems modest enough. For dancers who eschewed ballet and followed the path blazed by

Duncan and St. Denis, it would soon become the norm. But for Nijinsky it was a fantasy bred of madness. Even the greatest ballet masters had not enjoyed anything approaching artistic autonomy. During his four decades at the helm of the Imperial Ballet in St. Petersburg, Marius Petipa well understood the limitations within which he worked: an easily bored audience that demanded spectacles spiced with divertissements, court politics that often dictated which juicy parts went to certain favorites, and a prohibition (handed down from the sovereign himself) against unhappy endings that might suggest all was not well in the empire.

In the same year that Nijinsky voiced his dream, a young ballet student named Georgi Balanchivadze was trying to supplement his meager stipend playing the piano in silent-movie theaters in Petrograd (the new name given to St. Petersburg in 1914). The son of a

well-known composer from Georgia, he had entered the Imperial Ballet School in 1914 (when he was ten years old) and, after a miserably homesick first year, had become a star pupil. When Tsar Nicholas II abdicated in March 1917, the school was closed, and the students were left to their own devices while the Bolsheviks, who seized power in October, decided what to do with such a flagrant symbol of the old regime. Against all odds the new commissar of education, Anatoli Lunacharsky, a life-long balletomane, managed to get both the school and the theater reopened in 1918 under the auspices of the new Soviet state. With food, clothing, and fuel in short supply, hardship was the order of the day; the students cut trousers out of old draperies and burned chunks of the polished parquet floors to keep warm. But instruction continued without further interruption. In 1921 Balanchivadze graduated with honors and went on to three more years of study at the Conservatory of Music.

Jerome Robbins (above) rehearsing Maria Tallchief
for the first New York City Ballet production of
The Prodigal Son in 1950. George Balanchine is
standing behind the pianist. Tallchief was a member
of the Ballets Russes de Monte Carlo in the 1940s
and became one of the first principal dancers of the
New York City Ballet.

Right, Balanchine coaches Mikhail Baryshnikov in
the 1979 production of The Prodigal Son.

Although he was a talented enough pianist to consider a concert career, ballet held an even stronger appeal for him. At first it was the spectacle, the theatrical magic exemplified by the Maryinsky production of *The Sleeping Beauty*, in which he had made his stage debut, as one of the first-act garland dancers, at the age of eleven. He never forgot the beautiful garden setting with its "great cascading fountains," the grand coach of the wicked fairy Carabosse pulled by twelve rats, the flames that flared up from the floor when Carabosse was revealed in all her malevolence, the great trees and vines that enveloped the stage when the court fell into its hundred-year sleep. His interest in choreography surfaced early: "I had learned to dance, to move, I loved music, and suddenly I wanted to move people to music, to arrange dances." While still in his teens Balanchivadze composed a short ballet "in the Fokine style" for his fellow students; the students liked it, his teachers did not. To the budding choreographer the lesson was clear: "I saw immediately I should never be able to convince the management of the state theater to become interested in my work. I would have to present it myself."

In 1923 he put together several programs called "Evenings of the Young Ballet" with other recent graduates of the school who were dancing at the state theater; again his superiors expressed displeasure. Nevertheless, he received permission the following year to take a small troupe—four dancers including himself (average age: eighteen)—to Western Europe over summer vacation. After a successful tour of Germany,

Balanchivadze and his troupe were invited to Paris, where they auditioned for Diaghilev, who had been cut off from his main source of trained dancers by the Russian Revolution. He promptly hired all four dancers for his Ballets Russes, changed Georgi Balanchivadze's name to George Balanchine, and appointed him ballet master.

Balanchine has acknowledged his debt to Diaghilev as the second great influence on his artistic growth and development, after the training he received at the Imperial (now the Vaganova) Ballet School. Before Diaghilev's death in 1929, Balanchine created ten new ballets for the Ballets Russes. The most important of these were *Apollon Musagète* (*Apollo, Leader of the Muses*), set to a Stravinsky score in 1928, and *Le Fils Prodigue* (*The Prodigal Son*) in 1929, music by Sergei Prokofiev. Both were daring not in their rejection of classical tradition but in their affirmation of it.

The score for *Apollo* was originally commissioned by the U.S. Library of Congress. Having established a strongly personal, modern idiom, Stravinsky now chose to reassert his connection to the great tradition of European orchestral music. In a melodic piece for strings only, he paid homage to a long line of precursors from Bach and Lully to Glinka and Tchaikovsky. The result, to Balanchine's ears, had "a wonderful clarity and unity of tone" that taught him an important lesson about the making of dances:

"I saw that gestures, the basic material of the choreographer, have family relations, like different shades in painting and different tones in music. Some are incompatible with others; one must

work within a given frame, consciously, and not dissipate the effect of a ballet with inspirations foreign to the tone or mood one understands it must possess. . . .

"When I listen to a work by [Stravinsky] I am moved . . . to try to make visible not only the rhythm, melody and harmony but even the timbres of the instruments."

In the suite of dances that he made for Apollo and the three muses, Balanchine paid homage to *his* precursors, especially Marius Petipa. Apollo (danced by Serge Lifar) was an athletic embodiment of the creative principle. The choreography breathed new life into the classical style by treating it as living geometry—orderly, arbitrary, even artificial but, precisely because of that, intensely human. (Geometry, like art, is a human invention.) If Stravinsky's score was "about" music, Balanchine's choreography was "about" dance. Their pedigree notwithstanding, his freshly wrought combinations and permutations of standard steps and poses provoked laughter from some members of the audience.

The Prodigal Son made a different kind of statement about the relevance of the past. It was Diaghilev who suggested that Balanchine, a devout communicant of the Eastern Orthodox Church, base a ballet on the Biblical parable of the wayward son who returns as a penitent to his father and is forgiven for his sins. From the material in Luke 15, Balanchine created a work that showed how "old-fashioned" linear narrative could be reconciled with a modernizing temperament. With Prokofiev's forceful score and a vivid backdrop inspired by the designs of Georges Rouault, *The Prodigal*

Tamara Geva and George Church in the "Slaughter on Tenth Avenue" ballet from the musical comedy On Your Toes *(1936), choreography by George Balanchine and music by Richard Rodgers. Ray Bolger is in the foreground.*

Son remains a staple of the New York City Ballet. Among its many memorable moments of choreographic story-telling: the tavern debauchees who pair up, lock arms back to back, and scamper about the stage like four-legged mechanical insects; and the final tableau, in which the returning prodigal climbs up into the arms of his father who stands straight as a pillar of the Temple and lets his cloak fall protectively over his son's body in a majestic gesture of compassion.

After Diaghilev's death, Balanchine worked with the Royal Danish Ballet, helped launch one of the several successor troupes to the original Ballets Russes, and in 1933 founded his own company to put on new works. It was, in a sense, Balanchine's "declaration of independence," his first attempt to realize Nijinsky's dream. The seven ballets premiered by his new company aroused great interest. The financial future, however, was anything but secure. When the twenty-six-year-old Lincoln Kirstein, backed by the twenty-five-year-old Edward M. M. Warburg, met Balanchine in a London hotel room and invited him to come to the United States and form a major ballet company, the twenty-nine-year-old choreographer agreed, with one condition: "But first, a school."

All that Balanchine knew about America he had learned from the movies, but that was enough; he would be happy to visit any country, he told Kirstein, that could produce women like Ginger Rogers. From the beginning, he was in love with American female dancers. He loved their nervous energy, their no-nonsense manner. He liked

them young, tall, and skinny ("like toothpick"), with long legs and small heads. On January 2, 1934, the School of American Ballet opened in a loft on Madison Avenue and 59th Street that had once been Isadora Duncan's studio. The production of American ballet dancers to Balanchine's specifications had begun. The creation of a full-fledged company to perform his works took a little longer. An affiliation with the Metropolitan Opera foundered after two years because of artistic differences; conservative operagoers did not appreciate Balanchine's variations on conventional choreography.

To give heart to the young dancers and choreographers emerging from the school, Kirstein formed a touring troupe that premiered such all-American ballets as Lew Christensen's *Filling Station* (1937) and Eugene Loring's *Billy the Kid* (1938). To keep the school going, Balanchine hired himself out to create dance sequences for Broadway shows and Hollywood films; one of these, the jazz ballet "Slaughter on Tenth Avenue" for the 1936 musical *On Your Toes*, is now in the repertoire of the New York City Ballet. At a time when the standard onscreen credit for such efforts was "dance director," Balanchine insisted on "choreography by . . . ," to emphasize the creative aspect of dance making.

When the Second World War ended, Kirstein resumed his efforts to organize a company worthy of Balanchine's talents. The nonprofit Ballet Society that the two men founded in 1946 struggled along until 1948, when the New York City Center for Music and Drama asked them to establish a resident dance company. It was not quite the end of their

Maria Tallchief and Nicholas Mallanes (right) in a pas de deux from The Four Temperaments staged by George Balanchine for photographer George Platt-Lynes in c.1948. The ballet, as originally performed by Ballet Society in 1946 at the Central High School of Needle Trades auditorium in New York, had these costumes by Kurt Seligmann. When it was revived by the New York City Ballet in 1951, Seligmann's sets were dropped, and the dances wore plain leotards.

Balanchine's most fruitful musical collaborator was Igor Stravinsky. Below, they watch New York City Ballet principal dancers Diana Adams and Arthur Mitchell rehearse their ballet Agon (1957). In 1968, Mitchell became one of the founders of the Dance Theatre of Harlem, the first classically oriented ballet company in the United States with only black dancers.

223

Almost fifty years of Balanchine ballets performed by the New York City Ballet: Apollo (1928; opposite top right), music by Igor Stravinsky, with Peter Martins and, from left, Suzanne Farrell, Kyra Nichols, and Karin von Aroldingen; Serenade (1934; opposite bottom), music by Peter Ilyich Tchaikovsky; The Four Temperaments (1946; opposite top left), music by Paul Hindemith; and Vienna Waltzes (1977; below), music by Johann Strauss (the Younger), Franz Lehár, and Richard Strauss.

money worries; the newly christened New York City Ballet showed a deficit in its first year of $47,000, which Kirstein made up out of his own pocket. Balanchine, who was still receiving commissions for his stage and film work, took no salary. But the goal he and Kirstein had pursued for fifteen years was now within reach: an artistic home where, with some assurance of continuity, Balanchine could make dances as he saw fit. What the world could expect from this unparalleled venture had been foreshadowed two years earlier when a subscription audience of Ballet Society saw the first performance of Balanchine's *The Four Temperaments*, set to Paul Hindemith's *Theme and Four Variations for String Orchestra and Piano*.

Although Hindemith identified his four variations with the four medieval humors (melancholic, sanguinic, phlegmatic, and choleric), the choreography does not follow this scheme in a literal way. When working with a pre-existing score, like Hindemith's, Balanchine typically spent more time familiarizing himself with the music—trying to understand "what the composer had in mind musically"—than he did working out the steps. He played the piece over and over again on the piano; if no piano transcription existed, he made one himself. By his own testimony, when he came into the studio on the first day of rehearsal he had no definite idea of what steps he wanted. Nor did he ever write anything down. Yet Balanchine always remained in complete command:

"Often I try a step, or a series of movements, on a particular dancer and then I change it to something else.

I indicate the steps first and then the dancers repeat after me. . . . Sometimes I arrange the end of a ballet first; sometimes I commence in the middle. Rehearsal time is limited. . . . It has been my experience that dancers drop naturally into their parts; they gradually come to live them. Every detail is given; I show them every precise movement and the smallest mimed gesture and action."

Like most of Balanchine's work, *The Four Temperaments* is open to conflicting interpretations because it makes no attempt to represent anything outside itself and the music. To Suki Schorer, who danced in one of this ballet's pas de deux, the key to the choreography is that the male dancer is "manipulating . . . totally controlling the girl. The boy should appear to be strumming—playing—some sort of harp or cello. The girl is like an instrument."

To one critic, this same pas de deux looked as if the male partner were putting the ballerina "through an extraordinary sequence of precarious moves and off-kilter positions that render her totally vulnerable to his control. It is as if the man were experimenting with how far he could pull the ballerina off her own balance and still be performing classical ballet."

To another critic, the same sequence appeared to be "all about adagio—about where the woman places her legs and where the man holds her. The black and white practice clothes in which the ballet is now being done expose the mechanics of the pas de deux to make it quite sensual. There seems to be an extra weight, a lingering care, in the way the man clasps her waist, her thigh. The woman often has to lean back with her

whole body against him, and he carries her off folded against his chest, where she's so secure that she can extend her legs forward as she's carried out."

Still another observer has focused on the angular use of the arms, the syncopated steps, the jazz-inspired hip thrusts that recall Balanchine's work on Broadway with African-American dancers like the Nicholas Brothers, and his collaboration with Katherine Dunham in the 1940 all-black musical *Cabin in the Sky*.

Tanaquil LeClercq, an early product of the School of American Ballet who danced in the first performance of *The Four Temperaments* (and who was later Balanchine's third wife), has summarized the choreographer's instructions to his first cast: "It should look maximum, 100 percent everything: move 100 percent, turn 100 percent, stop dead. Kick legs as much as you can, straight knee, pointed toe. . . . You have certain steps to do in a certain amount of time and the certain steps give it a certain flavor. But you can't interpret because you'll be late, you won't be with the music."

In class as in the studio, Balanchine typically spoke to his dancers in concrete terms. "Hug a tree," he told them when he wanted to see their arms form the fullest possible circle in front of them. If he found they were making too much noise when they landed after a leap, he told them, "Come to ground like mother bird descending on her eggs." To get just the right combination of energy and impassivity in a particular sequence, he once told Schorer: "Let your legs and feet be going like mad, but up here you're just going to be talk-

ing to me and thinking about a martini with an olive." He hated sentimentality. Dancers who suffered from what he called "Gisellitis"—brooding over the interpretation of a role—were assured that the emotion was already in the choreography: "Don't think about it, just do it." When a dancer showed emotion onstage, he rebuked her: "This is serious theater. Not a music hall." His goal was "purified gesture—gesture with all the bugs taken out." "Be a cold angel," he told one ballerina.

The word most often applied to Balanchine's own temperament was "cool." But the word he preferred was "cold": "Some people are hot, some cold. Which is better? I prefer cold. I have never cried at a ballet. I never cry anytime. I don't have that type of reaction. Actually, when people cry they are only thinking of themselves. They think, I'm poor, I'm unhappy, I'm lonely, why did my girlfriend leave me?"

He disdained the pose of the angst-ridden artist, quipping that his muse worked on "union time." He created the original *Prodigal Son* in just ten days, the 1949 revival of *Firebird* in a week. His style is called neoclassical because the era of Marius Petipa is known in ballet history as the heyday of classicism; while Balanchine slimmed down and speeded up and occasionally turned inside-out the classical idiom, his primary concern, like Petipa's, was a felicitous match between steps and score, between structured movement sequences and musical structure. "The structure of a ballet must be tight, compact, like the structure of a building; good ballets move in measured space and time, like the planets," he said.

He also said that he never put anything of his own life into his ballets. In fact, he was married four times to ballerinas and romantically involved with several others; and those who knew him well said that they could tell the state of his private life from the dances he staged. His famous statement, "Ballet is woman," earned him the wrath of some feminist critics who saw his entire oeuvre as a glorification of the patriarchal order in which men elevate and display women for their own pleasure. Certainly, Balanchine treated his ballerinas as tools of his art; he referred to Suzanne Farrell, perhaps the quintessential Balanchine ballerina, as "my Stradivarius." But then he treated all his dancers, male and female, the same way—which was precisely the purpose for which the New York City Ballet was established: to give Balanchine a set of tools, and the freedom to wield them, that no other dance-maker in history had ever enjoyed.

All dance-makers engage in a creative dialogue between their impulse toward self-expression and the traditional forms of dance they inherit from the past; some reject more of the past than others. As we have tried to show by examining a few seminal figures and their work, Western theatrical dance in the twentieth century has seen an especially vigorous dialogue between individual creativity and tradition. The closer we come to our own time, the more difficult it is to sort out the seminal figures whose work will give rise to the traditions of tomorrow. This is especially true because the dialogue has become international in scope. There is virtually no continent, no country, no culture in which dance-makers are not reexamining their traditions, borrowing from other traditions, and looking within themselves for new ways of using the human body to communicate with other human beings.

The contributions of African-American and Afro-Caribbean dance to the contemporary dance dialogue are perhaps best exemplified by the work and influence of Katherine Dunham, who was born in 1909 in Chicago to a middle-class black family. She began studying dance while in high school and helped put herself through the University of Chicago by giving dance lessons in an abandoned storefront where she also gave recitals; at the age of twenty-two she formed her own dance company. Early on, Dunham conceived the idea of formulating a dance style that would connect with the roots of the black experience in the Americas. In 1934–35 she spent eighteen months in the Caribbean doing research for her master's thesis in dance anthropology, *The Dances of Haiti*. The dances she observed and participated in during this period formed the basis of the choreography that she developed for her own company on her return: "During the yonvalou we gravitated to partners, outdoing ourselves in undulating to low squatting positions, knees pressed against the knees of someone else without even realizing the closeness, each in his own transported world."

In 1938 Dunham described her long-range artistic goals as follows: "To establish a well-trained ballet group. To develop a technique that will be as important to the white man as to the Negro. To attain a status in the dance world that will give to the Negro dance-student the courage really to study, and a reason to do so." The recitals of her company received increasing attention, both in Chicago and in New York, but her career took a different turn when impresario Sol Hurok offered her the chance to reshape her work for the popular stage. In 1940 she appeared on Broadway in the all-black musical *Cabin in the Sky* (which she choreographed with George Balanchine). Between 1943 and 1965 the Dunham Company toured the United States and fifty-seven other countries in such productions as *Tropical Revue*, *Bal Nègre* and *Caribbean Rhapsody*. The dances in these shows ranged from "Shango," a reenactment

of a Trinidadian religious ritual, to a suite of "Plantation Dances" that included "Cake-Walk," "Juba," and "Ballin' the Jack." Among the many Hollywood movies she either appeared in or choreographed, the best known is probably *Stormy Weather* (1943). She became the first black choreographer to work at the Metropolitan Opera, when she choreographed its 1963–64 production of *Aida*.

In 1945 she had realized a long-held dream by opening the Dunham School of Dance and Theater in New York, which taught several generations of dancers and actors what scholar Brenda Dixon-Gottschild calls "the basic aesthetic principles of the African movement vocabulary." These involve the independent articulation of various parts of the torso so that, for example, the dancer "can play the pelvis against the rib cage in different rhythms and then offset that with a different pattern in the feet." To those who have studied it, the Dunham technique ranks with the Graham technique as one of the lasting achievements of twentieth-century dance.

Although Dunham's company made its last professional appearance in 1965, the Alvin Ailey American Dance Company revived fourteen of her works, including "Shango," in 1987 with the aid of a $100,000 grant from the Ford Foundation. Ailey himself did not study with Dunham, but his interest in dance was kindled when, as a junior high school student in Los Angeles, he saw a performance of her company. After attending UCLA, Ailey began dancing professionally with Lester Horton (1906–1953), who developed an influ-

ential school of modern dance on the West Coast. In New York, Ailey studied with such prominent teachers as Martha Graham, Doris Humphrey, Anna Sokolow, and Hanya Holm, a disciple of the pioneer of German modern dance, Mary Wigman (1876–1973). The multiracial repertory company that Ailey established in 1958 aimed at "providing art and entertainment, as well as institutionalizing modern dance by preserving works of the past and commissioning new ones." Ailey's best-known work is probably *Revelations* (1960), which is based on African-American spirituals. Since his death in 1989, the Ailey Dance Theater has continued under the direction of Judith Jamison.

As noted earlier, an important "family" of twentieth-century dance-makers can be traced back to Martha Graham's company. Merce Cunningham left Graham in 1945 to begin his experiments (often in collaboration with composer John Cage) in liberating dance from what he saw as the theatrical trappings that limited its freedom. These trappings include many of the elements that distinguished Martha Graham's later dance dramas: story-telling, character development, emotional expression, musical cues, and what might be called the "tyranny" of the choreographer.

While Cunningham typically works out movement sequences in some detail with members of his company, the order in which these sequences are danced may be left up to the performers themselves or deter-

Like Katherine Dunham, dancer, choreographer, and anthropologist Pearl Primus (left) has spent a lifetime exploring African and Caribbean dance and using these forms to create original works of her own. Here, she performs Fanga, based on a Liberian dance of welcome to honor a great chief. The occasion, appropriately, was a gala for the Alvin Ailey American Dance Company in 1978. Accompanying her dance are master drummers Alphonse Cimber (seated) and her son Onwin Borde.

Below, a scene from the Alvin Ailey American Dance Company's Revelations (1960), choreography by Alvin Ailey and music based on Afro-American spirituals. Here we see Donna Wood in the role that Judith Jamison had made famous: the umbrella-bearing leader of a group being baptised in cleansing waters, represented by billowing cloths of blue and white.

mined by a flip of a coin. Movements, score, and setting are created independently; often the dancers have not heard the music or seen the set before opening night.

As any statistician or gambler knows, the invocation of chance in a human undertaking does not necessarily preclude a sense of order. If a particular mood emerges during the creation of a piece, Cunningham may seal it with a title like *Summerspace* (1958) or *Winterbranch* (1964). Other titles are purely descriptive yet manage to capture some of Cunningham's process-oriented approach to dance-making, as in *How to Pass Kick Fall and Run* (1965). As for meaning, Cunningham has said: "If the dancer *dances*, everything is there. The meaning is there, if that's what you want. It's like this apartment where I live—I look around in the morning and ask myself, what does it all mean? It means: this is where I live. When I dance it means: this is what I am doing."

What the audience does at a Cunningham performance is its own business. In a piece called *Story* (premiered in 1963), an indeterminate number of dancers may perform all or any of eighteen choreographed sections on any given night; sets, costumes, even the choice of instruments is left up to the performers. But the "story" of the title, according to Cunningham, belongs to the audience: "The title does not refer to any implicit or explicit narrative, but to the fact that each spectator may interpret the events in his own way."

To the group of Cunningham-inspired dancers who came together at Judson Memorial Church in New York City in the early 1960s, even

Cunningham was too rigid in his approach to dance. While Cunningham's dancers did not move *to* music, there was music of some sort at his concerts, and many of his movements betrayed his familiarity with conventional dance techniques, including ballet and the Graham technique. His work conveyed the feeling that he was making "art," which was something different from life, something just a little bit privileged. At Judson, nothing was privileged—except perhaps the unencumbered human body "doing its thing." Music wasn't necessary. It wasn't even necessary to be a trained dancer. If someone protested that ordinary actions, like walking, standing, and sitting, done by ordinary people off the street, were not dance, the Judson pioneers asked: Why not? On what grounds can anyone say what is and isn't dance?

The experiments of people like Robert Dunn, Lucinda Childs, Steve Paxton, David Gordon, Yvonne Rainer, Simone Morris, Deborah Hay, Trisha Brown, and others were designed to jolt viewers out of unexamined preconceptions. One dance might consist of prerecorded instructions to move around the room to different locations. Another might begin with a dancer saying, "I've brought a dance and I will read it to you." Some dances were indistinguishable from adult parlor games. Admission to Judson concerts was by contribution. The choreographers were free to experiment in any way they chose. Yet poverty imposes its own limitations: Without a cohesive company of trained dancers to work with, a choreographer has no choice but to focus on dance that does

not require any special technique; in the long run, however, virtuosity extends the range of possibilities for dance-making.

This is evident in the career of Paul Taylor, who danced with both Merce Cunningham and Martha Graham while building a company of his own. His early choreography, under the influence of Cunningham and Cage, was resolutely avant-garde. *Duet* (1957) consisted of Taylor standing still while another performer sat motionless for four minutes. As a dancer with the Graham company, he created some of the major male roles in her most important Greek dramas during the late 1950s and early 1960s. For his own company, he has staged carefully structured ensemble pieces like *Esplanade* (1975), in which his dancers run, skip, and jump at such a furious pace and with such virtuosic intensity that they come across as superbly trained athletes oblivious to the physical danger they court at every moment. Some of these dances have entered the repertoires of contemporary ballet companies.

Because Taylor, like the dancers in *Esplanade*, keeps going off in different directions, his work has resisted critical pigeonholing: Is it modern, reactionary, ironic, moralistic, all (or none) of the above? An even greater restlessness marks the work of a former Taylor dancer, Twyla Tharp, whose entire life has been an adventure in eclecticism. A native of Indiana, she moved with her parents to southern California when she was eight years old. From a childhood filled with music, one of her earliest memories is "seeing dances in my head." She studied ballet, violin, baton twirling, and tap dancing after putting in a full day at school. She also took private lessons in acrobatics, flamenco, viola, drumming, typing, shorthand, French, and German. In her free time, she helped out in her parents' drive-in movie theater, selling tickets and refreshments and watching the films which were, she now says wryly, her only contact with the outside world.

She entered Pomona College in 1959 as a premed student, then switched to comparative literature. But dance was becoming more and more important to her, and in her sophomore year, she transferred to Barnard College in New York, a city where she could study ballet with former Maryinsky dancers, take classes with people like Merce Cunningham, Martha Graham, Erick Hawkins, and Alwin Nikolais, and see as much dance as she liked. What she liked best was the work of Cunningham, Graham, Balanchine, and Taylor. She also fancied "show-biz" dancing, from Broadway musicals to the Rockettes, because the dancers seemed to be having such a good time. After graduating from Barnard in 1963, she joined Paul Taylor's company because his own dancing and his easygoing personality appealed to her. (Her lifelong idol was George Balanchine, but she did not have enough ballet training to even consider trying out for the New York City Ballet.)

Two years later she left the Taylor company to start making her own dances. In her first solo effort, *Tank Dive* (1965), she combined ballet steps with a head-first slide across the floor that looked like something out of a sandlot baseball game. She spent the next five years doing what most other young choreographers in New York were doing—"reinventing dance" by exploring the fundamentals of bodies moving through space and time. While her experiments paralleled those going on at Judson Church (where she occasionally appeared), her approach was always a bit more theatrical, more open to the allure of emotion, of virtuosity. Together with the small company of dancers she had assembled, she rehearsed and performed in gymnasiums, social halls, schools, art galleries, parks, lofts, even theaters. Despite her lifelong "addiction" to classical music (Mozart, in particular), these pieces were unaccompanied, although they made imaginative use of props, such as the raw eggs that Tharp methodically dropped on the floor in a piece called *Re-Moves*.

One way to understand the agitation in the New York dance community in the 1960s is to compare it to the civil-rights agitation of the same era. The civil-rights activists were impatient to realize society's stated goal of providing equal opportunity for every American—an ideal guaranteed by law since 1868. The dance experimentalists were impatient to realize the long-stated ideal of modern dance: to clear away all rules, conventions, and habits that kept the body from being truly free in its movement. To do this, it was necessary to question not only assumptions from previous centuries—such as the idea that dance must be accompanied by music—but also more recent assertions that linked dance with self-expression or social action. Behind all the experimentation lay a simple hypothesis: Only when there is nothing that you *must* do, are you really free to do what you want—which may include thumbing your nose at the past or paying your respects to it.

In 1971 Twyla Tharp presented *Eight Jelly Rolls*, a dance accompanied by old jazz recordings of Jelly Roll Morton and his Red Hot Peppers. In fact, the dances in *Eight Jelly Rolls* had not been choreographed to the Morton music that the audience heard but to *other* early recordings. Nevertheless, the work represented something of a departure within an avant-garde dance community that was more accustomed to seeing works choreographed to minimalist music, weird sound effects, or unbroken silence. Tharp's newfound determination to please, even charm, her audience was also apparent in a show-stopping solo called *The Drunk*, in which she reeled and staggered around the stage like an inebriated clown, trying to keep up with a high-stepping drill team.

For many experimentalists of the 1960s, the 1970s were a time of reconsideration. When Robert Joffrey asked Tharp to make a dance for his ballet company, she went all out to communicate to a new audience. The music she chose was a medley of tunes by the Beach Boys. The steps she created for six of her dancers and fifteen members of the Joffrey Ballet ran the gamut from burlesque to frug, with references to ballet technique throughout. While subway graffiti artists created a new spray-painted backdrop during each performance, dancers from two different traditions struck sparks from one another on the crowded stage. In the words of critic Marcia Siegel, Tharp's witty maelstrom of nonstop movement was "neither

Members of Twyla Tharp's troupe (left) dance the Golden Section, the final segment of The Catherine Wheel *(1981), choreography by Tharp and music by David Byrne.*

Below, Twyla Tharp in Sue's Leg (1975), choreography by Tharp and music by Fats Waller.

Opposite top: The Paul Taylor Dance Company production of Esplanade *(1975), choreography by Paul Taylor and music by Johann Sebastian Bach.*

Opposite bottom: Merce Cunningham, seen here with his company in Exchange *(1978), has followed in the Ballets Russes tradition of working with important contemporary artists, among them Robert Rauschenberg, Jasper Johns, and Andy Warhol.*

Twyla Tharp (right) in When We Were Very Young *(1982), choreography by Twyla Tharp with texts written and recited by Thomas Babe, which was produced on Broadway by her own company on the eve of her fortieth birthday.*

Opposite: Mikhail Baryshnikov and Elaine Kudo in the opening movement of Twyla Tharp's Push Comes to Shove *(1976), music by Joseph Haydn and Joseph Lamb, in which the Russian dancer displayed a facility with movement vocabularies quite different from the classical style he had mastered at the Kirov. This was Tharp's first choreography for the American Ballet Theater, and the first major piece made for Baryishnikov by an American choreographer following his arrival in the United States in 1974.*

modern dance nor pop dance [but] a disciplined free-for-all of dancing that is reserved, competitive, exuberant, and stylistically unique." It was also, at times, sexy and silly and, in its unpredictable juxtapositions of balletic and show-biz conventions, laugh-out-loud funny.

Not at all coincidentally, Tharp's desire to communicate with a larger audience (even while some former colleagues in the avant-garde whispered "sellout") brought her to the attention of the grant-giving agencies that had begun to support dance in America. In 1963 the Ford Foundation had announced a series of multimillion-dollar grants to the School of American Ballet, the New York City Ballet, and other institutions committed to Balanchine-style neoclassical dance. In 1965 government support of the arts, including dance, was put on a continuing basis with the establishment of the National Endowment for the Arts and the New York State Council of the Arts; both agencies awarded grants to companies like Tharp's on the basis of decisions by panels of dancers, choreographers, and dance presenters.

Tharp went on to set dances to music as varied as that of Franz Joseph

Haydn, Frank Sinatra, and Philip Glass. She created a popular and critically acclaimed piece called *Push Comes to Shove* for Mikhail Baryshnikov and the American Ballet Theater; collaborated with Jerome Robbins on a new ballet, *Brahms/Handel,* for the New York City Ballet; and made dances for films, television, and Broadway. All in all, she has been perhaps the most visible manifestation of what is sometimes termed "crossover" dance—dance that rules out nothing, from ballet to boogaloo, from Bach to rock. Her own label for what she does is simply: dance.

The establishment of public funding agencies that support dancers and choreographers on the advice of other dancers and choreographers represents a significant break from the past. Despite the occasional threat of censorship by bureaucrats and legislators unhappy with "controversial" works, the dance world today probably has a greater control over its finances than at any time in history. One result has been a proliferation of small "experimental" dance troupes whose work appeals to a large number of small and diverse audiences. The newest generation of experimenters recognizes no boundaries—geographical or otherwise—in its search

for dance that speaks to contemporary audiences. This search is fueled by an unprecedented interplay of cultures and traditions on a truly global scale. Inevitably, most of the new dances that emerge from this creative ferment are quickly forgotten. Twyla Tharp, for one, cannot even remember some of her early works, a loss she characteristically refuses to mourn. She has compared the desire to preserve dances for posterity with the urge to prolong the pleasure from a mouthful of bubble gum: "You can keep on chewing for ten hours but after about a minute and a half you've got all the good out of it."

Despite the long and revered tradition in which he worked, George Balanchine also insisted that there was no sense in creating dances for posterity. He liked to compare ballets to flowers: "A flower doesn't tell you a story. It's in itself a beautiful thing." And as flowers do, he expected his ballets to fade over time: "I think ballet is NOW. Not about what will be. Because as soon as you don't have these bodies to work with, it's already finished. . . . I'm not interested at all that there will be some dancers who could do something of mine in the future. It wouldn't be right because I would have to do it myself."

Butoh is Japan's post–World War II experimental dance. It originated in 1959, when Hijikata Tatsumi (1928–86) resigned from the All-Japan Art Dance Association following an uproar over a performance that made use of a live chicken. With a number of collaborators, including Ono Kazuo, Hijikata developed a style of choreographic extremism designed to startle the Japanese into recognizing unpalatable truths about their society. The name given to their movement was ankoku butoh, which can be translated as "dance of the dark soul." Butoh has since evolved a more flexible aesthetic that makes room for lyricism and even humor alongside grotesquerie. Ono (above) can be seen in his Admiring la Argentina, a choreographic tribute to the Hispanic dancer La Argentina (c.1888-1936), who inspired him to a career in dance. Ono was seventy-nine when this photograph was taken in 1985.

Opposite: A member of the all-male butoh troupe Sankai Juku (top) is suspended from a rope high above Washington, D.C., in The Hanging Piece (1985). Bottom, members of Sankai Juku now perform the last segment of Kinkan Shonen in homage to Yoshiyuki Takada, a member of the troupe who died during a 1985 performance of The Hanging Piece in Seattle, Washington. Sankai Juku, which can be translated as "studio of mountain and sea," was founded in the mid-1970s by Ushio Amagatsu (hanging by his feet in the photograph), a leading member of the second generation of butoh performers.

Chapter 8
Dancing in One World

Because it cannot be detached from the people who make it, dance is "personal" in a way that poems, paintings, sculptures, and buildings are not. All these forms transcend their creators and the moment of their creation. Even the other performance arts, such as music and word-oriented theater, have a life apart from performance through scores and texts. But dance, even when recorded on film or video, exists in a personal here-and-now. We cannot watch a dance without being aware that someone is dancing—even when that someone is entirely covered with a costume or mask.

This means that every dance, no matter how ancient its pedigree, no matter how steeped in tradition, always says something about the present. The conscious preservation, in whatever form, of the dances of yesterday—Japan's bugaku and kabuki, the ballets of Petipa and Balanchine, the court dances of Java and west Africa, the devotional dances of India and Brazil, the formation dances of the Cook Islands, the ritual dances of Native Americans, the ballroom dances of the nineteenth century, and so on—is proof that we value the past in a way that goes beyond the restoration of old canvases, statues, and manuscripts or the construction of museums to house ancestral artifacts. The past comes alive in its dances, if only because someone alive today must feel the urge, the need, the duty to dance them. The fragility of these survivals from the past is a source of concern to many; a dance can be lost forever if a single generation fails to pass it on. No one knows what the dances of ancient Egypt and Greece looked like; historians argue over the exact shape of the minuet of Louis XIV's day; many of the movements and meanings of Hawaii's "ancient-style" hula have been forgotten.

Various systems of notation have been devised to capture dances for posterity on paper at least as accurately as music can be captured in a score.

The best known of these systems is Labanotation, invented by the Swiss theoretician and teacher Rudolf Laban (1879–1958). All such systems face the problem of reducing to static two-dimensional diagrams a dynamic three-dimensional form that changes in many different dimensions simultaneously. In our own century, film and videotape have come to the aid of dancers, choreographers, scholars, and others who are concerned with extending the life of today's dances into the future. As methods of dance notation, film and videotape are far from perfect: even multiple cameras cannot always be at the right angle at the right moment to capture every important gesture and nuance, especially when many dancers are performing at the same time. Inevitably, what gets recorded is a highly personal view of the dance as seen by the recorder.

And yet film and television have made it possible for vastly greater numbers of people than ever before to become acquainted with the dances of their day—both survivals from the past and contemporary dances from their own and other cultures; these include dances, such as the ones seen on music-video channels like MTV, that have been created with the latest electronic techniques. The extensive distribution of music videos and recordings of popular music, along with international air travel, has given rise to crossovers and fusions between long-separated traditions on a truly global scale. The videos of performers like Michael Jackson and Madonna are seen, appreciated, and inspire emulation the world over. Composer-performers like Paul Simon, Peter Gabriel, and David Byrne draw on African, Afro-Brazilian, and Afro-Caribbean sources in their rock videos; Johnny Clegg, a white South African, and his black South African band called Savuka mix American-style rock with Zulu music and dance; Yotho Yindi, a group of Australian aborigines, combine the traditional music and dance of their people with rock and country-and-western sounds; the heavy-metal recordings of Ingvie Malmsteen, a Swedish speed-guitar virtuoso, top the pop-music charts in Japan.

The live performances of the biggest rock stars are participatory events that might be mistaken by a visiting anthropologist from Mars with the devotional rites of a Dionysian religion. While the performer sings and dances to a propulsive, hugely amplified beat amid billows of stage smoke and computer-controlled barrages of lights, members of the audience shout out the familiar lyrics, dance in place, throw themselves into each other's arms, shake their fists in ragged unison, and, all in all, appear to be caught up in an atmosphere of ecstatic frenzy. Music videos began in the late 1970s as brief clips from live concerts; today, it is the electronically recorded images of these performers that fuel their global appeal. Some contemporary music videos are artfully assembled montages of shots from live perfor-

*Michael Jackson (below) in the music
video "Smooth Criminal" (1987).*

*Opposite: The Jets, choreographed
by Jerome Robbins, in the film version
of* West Side Story *(1961).*

mances that emphasize the audience's adulation of the performer. But the most acclaimed videos tend to be those that match specially crafted visual material, particularly dance sequences and high-tech electronic effects, to words and music; the result is an entirely new kind of aesthetic spectacle. In the words of Don Was, a producer and leader of his own rock group, "Video has become the art form, and the audio track is really just a part of the product."

One of the first performers to realize the potential of this new medium was Michael Jackson. His 1983 video "Beat It"—directed by Bob Giraldi and choreographed by Michael Peters—was a tightly plotted dance drama in which a young man from an inner-city neighborhood dares to show up at a gang confrontation in an abandoned warehouse. The lyrics leave some doubt about

the nature of his involvement in the impending battle, but the metaphorical thrust of the narrative is clear: communicating only through dance, Jackson pacifies the would-be combatants. When two gang leaders pull knives and start circling each other, Jackson steps between them and begins to strut in a hard, clean, "macho" style that pays homage to two sources: Jerome Robbins's street-gang choreography for the 1961 movie version of *West Side Story* and the break dancing that emerged from the black ghettos of North American cities in the late 1970s. Like the Giselles and sylphs of nineteenth-century ballet, the fierce-looking, rumble-minded gang members of "Beat It" cannot resist the lure of the dance; they fall in behind Jackson in an all-male wedge that turns muscular street moves—sudden leg thrusts, right-angled knee flexions,

pelvic lunges, march-like swaggering with bendable torsos—into fluid ensemble work.

To Michael Jackson's vast audience, there was nothing strange about the notion that dance could "speak" directly to the violence and anger of contemporary life. The irrepressible vitality of dance-as-self-expression had already been demonstrated by the phenomenon of break dancing. Unheralded even by the media that make it their business to keep up with the latest trends, self-taught dancer-choreographers set up radios or tape machines on city streets and dazzled passersby with innovative, acrobatic moves they had perfected in their own homes and neighborhoods: risky head- and shoulder-spins, "moon-walking" (a space-age shuffle in which the dancer seems to glide backward or forward without lifting his feet from the ground), eerie machine-like pantomime.

Jackson, like other black performers, had begun to incorporate break dancing into his live shows before "Beat It." The video uses street-derived moves to tell a story that parallels but does not depend on the lyrics of the song; a viewer would have no trouble following the action with the sound turned off. The originality of the concept is immediately apparent if the video is compared to the famous opening sequence of *West Side Story*, which tamed the violence of street life by transforming it into art. "Beat It" stays closer to its source; the gang members in the video look as if they had just stepped off the street; it is impossible to imagine these grizzled characters dancing along with Robbins's Sharks and Jets. Instead of reinventing street violence as an aesthetic experi-

ence, Jackson's video traps and displays it live—like the not-quite-tame lions and tigers that leap through their routines in an animal trainer's cage.

For all its innovative snap, however, "Beat It" looks old-fashioned by the music-video standards of the 1990s. Although conceived with television in mind, "Beat It" is essentially dancing bodies transferred to the screen. While the crisp editing contributes to the rhythm of the piece, the camera stays with individual shots long enough for the viewer to get a sense of the dancers as dancers; there are no special effects, multiple exposures, or electronic tricks. The focus, literally and figuratively, is on the dancing. But despite the fact that dancing has become a staple of music videos, few featured performers can move well enough to sustain an entire dance-oriented number. For singers who can't dance there are other options. With the right mix of quick cuts, camera angles, odd backgrounds and sets, and elaborate electronic doctoring, a video can be made to "move" even when its performers don't. In recent years, even bona fide dancers like Jackson, Madonna, M. C. Hammer, Paula Abdul, and (among the elder statesmen of rock) Mick Jagger have appeared in videos where dancing bodies (usually seen in brief shots that capture the "signature" moves of the stars) are only one element in a dazzling succession of images accessible only as a video experience.

In one sense there is nothing new about recorded images of dance that transcend (some might say violate) the reality of live performance. Georges Méliès, a professional magician, made over four hundred films in the late 1890s

and early 1900s that confounded viewers' expectations of reality; in a Méliès short called *The Ballet Master's Dream* (1903), the figure of a dancer breaks in half at the waist (like the sawed-in-half body of a magician's assistant) and the legs, still kicking, sail off into the air. In 1924 the painter Fernand Léger collaborated with filmmaker Dudley Murphy on a film called *Ballet Mécanique* (music by George Antheil) in which the repetitive movements of levers, gears, pulleys, pendulums, and eggbeaters were juxtaposed with repetitive human movements like an eye opening and closing; the resulting rhythms demonstrate that "screen dance" does not have to be limited to shots of dancers dancing. In Maya Deren's trail-blazing *Choreography for the Camera* (1945), dancer Talley Beatty begins a leap in the woods that ends inside a rehearsal room. More recently, Merce Cunningham, Alwin Nikolais, and Twyla Tharp are among the choreographers who have taken advantage of the freedom provided by film and video to make dances for the screen that cannot be duplicated in the studio or onstage. What's new about music videos is that, with the electronic tools now available, there is virtually nothing a director or choreographer cannot do with an image—up to and including making a nondancer look like a dancer.

But with all the tools of manipulation at its command, the pop-music industry is far from a media monolith capable of dictating taste to a captive audience. Especially where dance is concerned, the impetus for change often comes from the outside—as demonstrated by the advent of break dancing in the 1970s

and rap music and hip-hop in the 1980s. With its antiestablishment (and often crudely misogynistic) lyrics and its many-layered, infectiously danceable rhythms, rap is clearly a product of the street, not the executive suite. Like so many forms of pop music since the 1960s, rap vibrates with anger; its self-aggrandizing, in-your-face stance expresses the disaffection of young black urban males—a group whose greatest health risk, according to government statistics, is death by gunshot. Hearing the lyrics of groups like Public Enemy and 2 Live Crew for the first time is like encountering outspoken descendants of Ralph Ellison's Invisible Man. Yet as sales figures indicate, the appeal of rap extends far beyond the African-American ghettos where it was born. Anger (not necessarily aimed at a specific target) also informs the best-selling records and videos of white groups like Mötley Crüe and Guns 'n' Roses, who appeal primarily to white teenagers.

Just what messages are being exchanged across the laser lights separating performers from audiences these days is not easy to divine. Along with the macho posturing of the black rappers and the white heavy-metal groups, audiences also cheer the artfully formulated androgynous personae of many of rock's biggest stars. When Michael Jackson contorts his delicate features into a defiant snarl, when Madonna flexes her well-developed biceps and shakes her pointed bras, when the latest Mick Jagger clone dances around the stage in "shit-kicker" boots and fishnet stockings with pornographic tattoos showing through his sequined vest, it is tempting to speculate that: (1) the stars are acting out the fantasies of their fans, and (2) these fantasies are deeply ambivalent, at least by the standards of previous generations. When the 1960s raised the banner of "Do your own thing," it came across as a call to action, a manifesto that demanded nothing less than a rewriting of the social contract. Today, even the angriest rappers seem less concerned with changing society than with cutting out a small piece of turf where they (and those who share their vision) can be assured a piece of the action.

Pop music in the last decade of the twentieth century is a market-driven, dance-energized medium that simultaneously divides up its vast audience into antagonistic segments (black vs. white, men vs. women, young vs. old, haves vs. have-nots) and brings them together in an electronic "global village" where the old boundaries of nationality and gender have been redrawn to suit local needs. There are dance clubs frequented exclusively by Puerto Ricans or Filipinos or Haitians or Salvadorans or working-class whites. There are clubs where people do only the Texas two-step or ballroom dances like the waltz and the Lindy or the latest thrash dancing. There are also clubs where people of every ethnic background and sexual orientation dance side by side to a mix of music that combines influences from many different cultures. And the way people dance in all these clubs continues to influence the music and dance that appear on worldwide networks like MTV—and vice versa.

Are we entering a world where, in place of the courts, academies, and elites of the past, market forces alone will determine what people listen to and how they dance? Even so powerful a figure as Michael Jackson must occasionally bow to the dictates of public opinion—as he did when he removed a sequence that offended large numbers of viewers from his 1992 video "Black or White." The video, which ostensibly preached a message of interracial harmony, showed Jackson dancing with groups of black Africans, southeast Asians, Native Americans, and an Indian bharata natyam dancer. While the appropriation of ethnic dance for commercial purposes disturbs some defenders of intellectual and artistic "property" rights, these were not the sequences that got Jackson in trouble. Nor was there an outcry against the opening sequence in which a small boy who has been ordered to turn off his hi-fi takes revenge by literally blasting his father through the roof of the family home with an explosion of music. The sequence that offended enough viewers to prompt an apology from Jackson was the video's finale, in which he jumps on top of a car and, accompanied only by the sound of his own dancing feet, performs a vigorous solo while smashing the windows of the car and periodically caressing his crotch with his hand; in the final shot, he is seen zipping up his fly. In apologizing for any distress this sequence might have caused, Jackson said: "It upsets me to think that 'Black or White' could influence any child or adult to destructive behavior, either sexual or violent. I've always tried to be a good role model."

Monopolistic control over communication and information—whether governmental or commercial—is becoming increasingly difficult to sustain. In the successor regimes to the disbanded Soviet Union there has been a resurgence of once-banned rock-and-roll and a new interest in the distinct dance traditions of ethnic minorities that were formerly lumped together under an officially sanctioned "national" dance. Television networks that transmit via earth-orbiting satellites are no respecters of national boundaries. The early 1990s saw the start-up of two new satellite networks, one controlled by Asian, the other by Arab investors, to compete with the MTVs and CNNs of the West. Since music videos combine the power of television, the power of music, and the power of dance, we can expect to see the market for them continue to expand—and their influence continue to increase. Will this result in a new homogenization, in which local and ethnic differences are smoothed away to appeal to the largest possible audience? Or are we entering an era in which diversity will be the only norm? What is happening today may not be so different from the cultural turmoil that Walt Whitman confronted in 1871 when he wrote about the "new world" of which the United States was only a part. His visionary exhortation may be even more broadly applicable today:

" . . . not to create only, or found
   only,
But to bring perhaps from afar what is
   already founded,
To give it our own identity . . .
To . . . accept, fuse, rehabilitate,
To obey as well as command, to
   follow more than to lead,
These also are the lessons of our New
   World. . ."

Acknowledgments

**M**ore than most books, *Dancing* has been a collaborative effort. There could have been no book without all the scholars, performers, teachers, advisors, and researchers who gave generously of their time and insights. I would like to extend my personal thanks to Omofolabo Ajayi, Elizabeth Aldrich, Diane Apostolos-Cappadona, Karin Barber, Brenda Dixon-Gottschild, Peter Grilli, Pamela Takiora Ingram, V. Kaladharan, Elizabeth Kendall, Daniel Ampousah (Ko Nimo), Samuel L. Leiter, K. C. Manavendranath, Morton Marks, Maria Messina, Barbara Stoler Miller, Judy Mitoma, Cynthia Novack, Albert Opoku, Malavika Sarrukai, Suki Schorer, Louise Scripps, Allegra Fuller Snyder, Kapila Vatsyayan, and Anmol Vellani; and a special note of gratitude to the patient, thorough, and extraordinarily knowledgeable Joann Keali'inohomoku.

While deeply involved in their own creative work, the filmmakers were very helpful to me every step of the way. My sincere thanks to Orlando Bagwell, Ellen Hovde, Muffie Meyer, Mark Obenhaus, Stephanie Bakal—and to Geoff Dunlop, Sabita Kumari-Dass, and Jackie Unsworth, who made me feel welcome on their shoots in Ghana and India. Heartfelt thanks to David Wolff, Licia Hurst, Elisabeth Keating, and the staff at Thirteen/WNET; to Alexandra Truitt and Jerry Marshall for illuminating images; to Kris Dahl and staff at ICM; to the entire staff of *Dancing*; and to Eric Himmel, Paul Gottlieb, and the staff at Harry N. Abrams, Inc. Beth Pollack, the associate producer at *Dancing*, was a wonderful support and a good friend throughout the project.

The "onlie begetter" of *Dancing* was executive producer Rhoda Grauer, who is an extraordinary person to work with; her enthusiasm, stores of information, sense of humor, high standards, and passion for both dancing and *Dancing* were an inspiration from the start. The entire project has been a learning experience for me; through Rhoda I have learned more than I would have dreamed possible about the world of dance and the world of people who love dance. I would like to express my deepest gratitude to her for making it all possible—and for making it such a pleasure as well.

Having expressed my appreciation to so many for all the help and encouragement I received, let me add that any errors or omissions in the book itself are of course my own responsibility.

Gerald Jonas

For me, personally, *Dancing* has been an extraordinary adventure full of colorful places, fascinating people, problematic travel arrangements, deadlines, funding applications, many, many surprises, and amazingly few disappointments. The scarcity of disappointments I attribute to the generous support and backing of the more than one hundred people who have played a part in making this project happen. They include:

Members of my family—specifically my mom, Ethel Grauer, a fine musician and painter who sparked my earliest interest in the arts; my dad, Paul, who convinced me I could do anything I set out to do; my brother, Victor, who taught me to love music and appreciate cultural differences; and my sister-in-law, Holly—endlessly optimistic; and dear friends David Gordon, Valda

Setterfield, Twyla Tharp, Jeff Moss, Sheila Pickles, and Suzanne Weil, who, though they thought I was mad when I started, encouraged me nonetheless;

My colleagues at Thirteen/WNET and the BBC: Ella Baff, Bill Baker, Ruth Ann Burns, Harry Chancey, Nancy Dennis, Carmen Di Rienzo, Judy Kinberg, Bob Kotlowitz, Arnie Labaton, Bunny Lester, Bob Lockyer, Dennis Marks, George Miles, Robert Miller, Mel Ming, Hugh Price, Therese Steiner, David Wolff, and Alan Yentob who were on board and supportive from day one—and especially Jac Venza, who has made an enormous contribution to keeping the arts on television for more than twenty years; and

An array of outstanding professionals starting with my extraordinary associate producer, Beth Pollack, without whose consummate skills, talent, and friendship there would be no Dancing; Bill Murphy, our production comptroller, who has kept us on budget and on schedule and in good humor; and Cherie Fortis, our post-production supervisor who pulled all the threads together; and

All those who contributed to the project from the beginning: John Adams, Prudence Arndt, Diane Boardman, Gary Clare, Tara Delson, Rosie Fishel, Larry Greenblatt, Lyn Willis Harris, Herb Homes, Licia Hurst, Sally Klingenstein, Michael Kustow, Franc Martarella, Dorothy Pringle, Anita Shapiro, Ellen Sollod, Charisse Minerva Spencer, Linda Szmyd, Catherine Tatge and Dominique Lasseur, Arlene Whittick, Adrienne Wollman, and

All the scholars, artists, and writers who shared with an enormous spirit of generosity the research, insights, contacts and ideas that they have taken years to develop and refine. In many ways Dancing is really theirs. I would like to thank them all and apologize for any errors that may have found their way into the series and the book. Even scholars occasionally disagree. So, while many have contributed, the point of view presented in the series and the book are mine and those of the filmmakers and the book's author. Deserving of special thanks are Joann Keali'inohomoku, Diane Apostolos-Cappadona, Judy Mitoma, Elizabeth Kendall, Cynthia Novack, Allegra Fuller Snyder, and Elizabeth Aldrich. They are wonderful people and dear friends whose contributions to Dancing cannot be overestimated. Special thanks to the International Encyclopedia of Dance.

I owe a particular debt of gratitude to Lincoln Kirstein who may have done more for dance in this century than any other single person. Very early on in the process, Lincoln encouraged me to think globally and gave me the faith in myself that allowed me to proceed. I sincerely hope he will find some pleasure in the work he made possible.

Dancing has been supported by an extraordinary partnership of arts funding sources. At each agency, there were individuals who believed in Dancing and guided it through the often complicated application processes: Brian O'Doherty, Nigel Redden, and Sally Ann Kriegsman at the National Endowment for the Arts; Toby Quitslund and Candace Katz at the National Endowment for the Humanities; Jessica Chao of the Lila Wallace-Reader's Digest Fund; Don Marbury of the Corporation for Public Broadcasting; Melinda Ward and Barry Chase of the Public Broadcasting Service; Ruth Mayleas of the Ford Foundation; Alberta Arthurs of the Rockefeller Foundation; Rosalind P. Walter; Alfred Terlizzi of Ballet Makers, Inc.; and Patsy Tarr of the JCT Foundation.

The four teams of producer/directors who turned all of these resources into television are deserving of special thanks: Jane Alexander, Orlando Bagwell, Geoff Dunlop, Ellen Hovde, Muffie Meyer, and Mark Obenhaus. They are an extraordinarily gifted group of artists supported by film professionals of the highest quality: Stephanie Bakal, Susan Bellows, Smokey Forester, Sabita Kumari-Dass, and Jackie Unsworth. I am grateful to all of them.

Final thanks go to Gerry Jonas, the author of Dancing. Gerry has been the most amazing colleague. The enthusiasm and love for Dancing that Gerry brought to both the series and the book are contributions beyond quantifying. The amount of research, looking, and thinking that he has synthesized into the pages of this book is monumental. I hope the dance community will welcome this contribution to the growing field of dance scholarship.

Rhoda Grauer
Executive Producer, Dancing

Bibliography

The first part of this bibliography is a general selection of works relating to dance. Although dance scholarship, especially dance ethnology, is a young field, there is an important body of literature, much more copious than this selective bibliography. At the end of this section is a brief list of references and bibliographic sources, for those who wish to explore specific topics more intensively. The final part of this bibliography includes additional works specifically consulted in the writing of this book, and is organized by chapter.

Selected bibliography:

Adams, Doug, and Diane Apostolos-Cappadona, eds. *Art as Religious Studies*. New York: Crossroad Publishing Co., 1987.

———. *Dance as Religious Studies*. New York: Crossroad Publishing Co., 1990.

Ahye, Molly. *The Dance in Trinidad and Tobago*. Petit Valley, Trinidad & Tobago: Heritage Cultures Ltd., 1978.

Almeida, Bira. *Capoeira, A Brazilian Art Form*. Richmond, CA: North Atlantic Books, 1981.

And, Metin. *A Pictorial History of Turkish Dancing*. Ankara: Dost Yayinlari, 1976.

Anderson, Jack. *Ballet and Modern Dance: A Concise History*. Princeton: Princeton Book Co., 1986.

———. *The One and Only: The Ballet Russe de Monte Carlo*. New York: Dance Horizons, 1981.

Andrews, Edward Deming. *The People Called Shakers*. New York: Dover, 1963.

Arbeau, Thoinot [pseudonym of Jehan Tabourot]. *Orchesography* (1588). Translated by Mary Stewart Evans. New York: Kamin Dance Publications, 1948. Reprint, with a new introduction and notes by Julia Sutton. New York: Dover, 1967.

Ariès, Philippe. *Centuries of Childhood: A Social History of Family Life*. Translated by Robert Baldick. New York: Vintage Books, 1962.

Aristotle. *The Poetics*. New York: Bobbs Merrill, 1958.

Artaud, Antonin. *The Theater and Its Double*. New York: Grove Press, 1958 (Paris: Gallimard, 1938).

Ashihara, Eiryo. *The Japanese Dance*. Tokyo: The Japan Travel Bureau, 1965.

Bahti, Tom. *Southwestern Indian Ceremonies*. Las Vegas: KC Publications, 1970.

Balanchine, George, and Francis Mason. *Balanchine's Complete Stories of the Great Ballets*. Garden City: Doubleday, 1977.

Bandem, I Made, Frederik Eugene Deboer. *Kaja and Kelod, Balinese Dance in Transition*. Oxford: Oxford University Press, 1981.

Banes, Sally. *Terpsichore in Sneakers: Post-Modern Dance*. Boston: Houghton Mifflin, 1980.

Barnes, Sandra T., ed. *Africa's Ogun Old World and New*. Bloomington and Indianapolis: Indiana University Press, 1989.

Barney, Garold D. *Mormons, Indians and the Ghost Dance Religion of 1890*. Lanham, MD: University Press of America, 1986.

Barrère, Dorothy B., Mary Kawena Pukui, and Marion Kelly. *Hula: Historical Perspectives*. Honolulu: Bishop Museum, 1980.

Bastide, Roger. *The African Religions of Brazil: Toward a Sociology of the Interpenetration of Civilizations*. Translated by Helen Sebba. Baltimore: Johns Hopkins University Press, 1978.

Beckford, Ruth. *Katherine Dunham: A Biography*. New York: Marcel Dekker, 1979.

Benthall, Jonathan, and Ted Polhemus, eds. *The Body as a Medium of Expression*. New York: Dutton, 1975.

Binney, Edwin. *Glories of the Romantic Ballet*. London: Dance Books, 1985.

Birdwhistell, Ray L. *Kinesics & Context, Essays on Body Motion Communication*. Philadelphia: University of Pennsylvania Press, 1970.

Blacking, John A. R., ed. *The Anthropology of the Body*. New York: Academic Press, 1977.

Blacking, John A. R., and Joann Keali'inohomoku, eds. *The Performing Arts*. Worlds Anthropology Series. The Hague: Mouton Publishers, 1979.

Blasis, Carlo. *The Code of Terpsichore* (1828). Translated by R. Barton. New York: Dance Horizons, 1976.

———. *An Elementary Treatise upon the Theory and Practice of the Art of Dancing*. New York: Dover, 1968.

Boas, Franziska, ed. *The Function of Dance in Human Society: A Seminar on Primitive Society*. New York: The Boas School, 1944.

Bournonville, Auguste. *My Theatre Life*. Translated by Patricia W. McAndrew. Middletown: Wesleyan University Press, 1979.

Bowers, Faubion. *The Dance of India*. New York: Columbia University Press, 1953. New York: AMS Press, 1967.

———. *Theater in the East: A Survey of Asian Dance & Drama*. New York: Thomas Nelson & Sons, 1956.

Brainard, Ingrid. *The Art of Courtly Dancing in the Early Renaissance*. West Newton, MA: I.G. Brainard, 1981.

Brandon, James R. *Theatre in Southeast Asia*. Cambridge: Harvard University Press, 1967.

Buckle, Richard. *Diaghilev*. New York: Atheneum, 1979.

———. *George Balanchine: Ballet Master*. New York: Random House, 1988.

———. *Nijinsky*. New York: Simon & Schuster, 1971. Rev. ed. Harmondsworth, Eng.: Penguin, 1980.

Caldwell, Helen. *Michio Ito the Dancer and His Dances*. Berkeley and Los Angeles: University of California Press, 1977.

Chaffee, George. *The Romantic Ballet in London: 1821–1858*. Dance Index, Vol II. Nos. 9–12, 1943.

Chatterjee, Ahoke. *Dances of the Golden Hall*. New Delhi: Indian Council for Cultural Relations, 1979.

Chernoff, John Miller. *African Rhythm and Sensibility*. Chicago: University of Chicago Press, 1979.

Christout, Marie-Françoise. *Le Ballet de Cour de Louis XIV*. Paris: Editions A. et J. Picard & Cie., 1967.

Coe, Robert. *Dance in America*. New York: E.P. Dutton, 1985.

Cohen, Selma Jeanne. *Doris Humphrey: An Artist First*. Middletown: Wesleyan University Press, 1972.

———. *Next Week, Swan Lake: Reflections on Dance and Dances*. Middletown: Wesleyan University Press, 1982.

———, ed. *Dance as a Theatre Art: Source Readings in Dance History 1581 to the Present*. New York: Dodd, Mead and Co., 1974.

Cornazano, Antonio. *The Book on the Art of Dancing* (1465). Translated by Madeleine Inglehearn and Peggy Forsyth. London: Dance Books, 1981.

Craig, Edward Gordon. *The Art of the Theatre*. Introduction by Edward Gordon Craig and preface by R. Graham Robertson. Edinburgh and London: T.N. Goulid, 1905.

Croce, Arlene. *Going to the Dance*. New York: Knopf, 1982.

———. *Sight Lines*. New York: Knopf, 1987.

Crowley, Daniel. *African Myth and Black Reality in Bahian Carnival*. Los Angeles: UCLA, Fowler Museum of Cultural History, 1984.

Cunningham, Merce. *Changes: Notes on Choreography*. New York: Something Else Press, 1968.

Davies, J. G. *Liturgical Dance: An Historical, Theological and Practical Handbook*. Philadelphia: Trinity Press International, 1984.

De Bary, Wm. Theodore, ed. *Sources of Indian Tradition*. New York: Columbia University Press, 1958.

Demidov, Alexander. *The Russian Ballet: Past and Present*. Translated by Guy Daniels. Garden City: Doubleday, 1977.

de Mille, Agnes. *Dance to the Piper*. Boston: Little, Brown & Co., 1952. Reprint. New York: Da Capo Press, 1980.

Denby, Edwin. *Dancers, Buildings and People in the Streets*. New York: Horizon Press, 1965.

———. *Dance Writings*. New York: Knopf, 1986.

Devi, Ragini. *Dance Dialects of India*. London: Vikas Publications, 1971.

———. *Dances of India*. Calcutta: Susil Gupta Private Ltd., 1928.

Dixon, Brenda. "The Afrocentric Aesthetic." In *Black Choreographers Moving: A Dialogue*, edited by Halifu Osumare and Julinda Lewis. Berkeley: Expansion Arts Services, 1991.

———. "The Afrocentric Paradigm." *Design for Arts in Education* (January/February 1991).

Drewal, Margaret Thompson, ed. *Africa. The Drama Review* 118. Cambridge: MIT Press. 1988.

Duncan, Isadora. *Art of the Dance*. New York: Theatre Arts, 1928.

———. *My Life*. New York: Boni & Liveright, 1927; often reprinted.

Dunham, Katherine. *Dances of Haiti*. Los Angeles: CAAS/UCLA, 1983.

———. *Island Possessed*. New York: Doubleday, 1969.

Ekstrom, Parmenia Migel. *The Ballerinas: From the Court of Louis XIV to Pavlova*. New York: Macmillan, 1972. Reprint. New York: Da Capo Press, 1980.

Ellis, Havelock. *Dance of Life*. Boston: Houghton Mifflin, 1923.

Evans, Arthur. *The God of Ecstasy: Sex Roles and the Madness of Dionysus*. New York: St. Martin's Press, 1988.

Fergusson, Erna. *Dancing Gods: Indian Ceremonials of New Mexico and Arizona*. Albuquerque: University of New Mexico Press, 1966.

Fewkes, Jesse Walter. *Hopi Snake Ceremonies*. New Mexico: Avanyu Publishing Co., 1986.

Forster, Harold. *Flowering Lotus: A View of Java*. New York: Longmans, 1958.

Frazer, Sir James George. *The Golden Bough*. New York: Macmillan, 1963 (1922, 1950).

Frisbie, Charlotte J., ed. *Southwestern Indian Ritual Drama*. Albuquerque: University of New Mexico Press, 1980.

Fuller, Loïe. *Fifteen Years of My Life*. Boston: Small, 1913.

Fuze, Magema M. *The Black People and Whence They Came: A Zulu View*. Pietermaritzburg, South Africa: University of Natal Press, 1979.

Gardel, Luis D. *Escolas de Samba*. Rio de Janeiro: Livraria Kosmos Editora, 1967.

Garfias, Robert. *Gagaku: The Music and Dances of the Japanese Imperial Household*. New York: Theatre Arts Books, 1959.

Gautier, Théophile. *The Romantic Ballet*. Translated by Cyril W. Beaumont. Rev. ed. London: Cyril W. Beaumont, 1947. Reprint. New York: Dance Horizons, n.d.

Gorer, Geoffrey. *Africa Dances*. New York: John Lehmann, 1949.

Grigoriev, Serge L. *The Diaghilev Ballet 1909–1929*. Translated by Vera Bowen. London: Constable, 1953. Reprint. New York: Dance Horizons, n.d.

Guest, Ivor. *The Ballet of the Second Empire 1847–1870*. 2nd ed. Middletown: Wesleyan University Press, 1974.

———. *The Romantic Ballet in England*. 2nd ed. Middletown: Wesleyan University Press, 1972.

———. *The Romantic Ballet in Paris*. Middletown: Wesleyan University Press, 1966.

Gunji, Masakatsu. *Buyo: The Classical Dance*. Performing Arts of Japan Series. New York and Tokyo: Walker Weatherhill, 1970.

———. *Kabuki Guide*. Translated by Christopher Holmes. Tokyo: Kodansha, 1988.

Halford, Audrey S., and Giovanna M. Halford. *Kabuki Handbook: A Guide to Understanding and Appreciation*. Tokyo: Charles E. Tuttle, 1955.

Hall, Edward T. *The Dance of Life*. Garden City: Anchor Press/Doubleday, 1983.

———. *The Hidden Dimension*. Garden City: Doubleday, 1966.

———. *The Silent Language*. Greenwich: Fawcett Publications, 1959.

Hanna, Judith Lynne. *Dance, Sex and Gender*. Chicago: University of Chicago Press, 1988.

———. *To Dance is Human: A Theory of Nonverbal Communication*. Austin: University of Texas Press, 1979.

Harris-Warwick, Rebecca. "Ballroom Dancing at the Court of Louis XIV." *Early Music*. (February 1986): 41–49.

Haskell, Arnold. *Diaghileff*. London: Victor Gollancz, 1935.

Hauser, Arnold. *The Social History of Art*. Translated by the author and Stanley Godman. 2 vols. New York: Knopf, 1951.

Highwater, Jamake. *Dance: Rituals of Experience*. New York: A & W Publishers, 1987.

———. *Ritual of the Wind*. Toronto: Methuen Publications, 1984.

Hoff, Frank. *Song, Dance, Storytelling: Aspects of the Performing Arts in Japan*. Ithaca: Cornell East Asia Papers Number 15, 1978.

Holborn, Mark. *Butoh: Dance of the Soul*. New York: Sadev/Aperture Foundation, 1987.

Holt, Claire. *Dance Quest in Celebes*. Paris: Les Archives Internationales de la Danse, 1938.

Huet, Michel. *The Dance, Art and Ritual of Africa*. New York: Pantheon, 1978.

Humphrey, Doris. *The Art of Making Dances*. New York: Holt, Rinehart and Winston, 1959.

Ikema, Hiroyuki. *Folk Dance of Japan*. Tokyo: National Recreation Association of Japan, 1981.

Jenyns, Soame. *The Art of Dancing: A Poem in Three Cantos* (1729). Edited by Anne Cottis. London: Dance Books, 1978.

Jones, Betty True, ed. *Dance as Cultural Heritage, vol. 1. Dance Research Annual* 15. New York: CORD, 1983.

———, ed. *Dance as Cultural Heritage, vol. 2. Dance Research Annual* 15. New York: CORD, 1985.

Kaeppler, Adrienne. *Polynesian Dance, with a Selection for Contemporary Performances*. Honolulu: Edward Enterprises, 1983.

———. *The Structure of Tongan Dance*. Ann Arbor: University Microfilms, 1967.

Karsavina, Tamara. *Theatre Street*. New York: E.P. Dutton, 1931; Reprint. London: Dance Books Ltd., 1981.

Katz, Leslie George, Nancy Lassalle, and Harvey Simmonds. *Choreography by George Balanchine: A Catalogue of Works*. New York: Viking Press, 1984.

Katz, Ruth. "The Egalitarian Waltz." In *What is Dance?*, edited by Roger Copeland and Marshall Cohen. Oxford: Oxford University Press, 1983.

Kavanagh, Robert. *Theatre and Cultural Struggle in South Africa*. London: Zed Books, 1985.

Kawatake, Shigetoshi. *Kabuki, Japanese Drama*. Tokyo: Foreign Affairs Association, 1958.

Keali'inohomoku, Joann W. *Theory and Methods for an Anthropological Study of Dance*. Ann Arbor: University Micro films, 1976.

Kendall, Elizabeth. *Dancing: A Ford Foundation Report*. New York: Ford Foundation, 1983.

Khokar, Mohan. *Traditions of Indian Classical Dance*. London: Clarion Books, 1979.

Kincaid, Zoe. *Kabuki: The Popular Stage of Japan*. London: Macmillan and Co., 1925.

Kinkeldey, Otto. *A Jewish Dancing Master of the Renaissance*. New York: Reprinted from the A. S. Freidus Memorial Volume, 1929.

Kirstein, Lincoln. *Ballet: Bias & Belief*. New York: Dance Horizons, 1983.

———. *Dance: A Short History of Classic Theatrical Dancing*. Westport, CT: Greenwood Press, 1970.

———. *Four Centuries of Ballet: Fifty Masterworks*. New York: Dover, 1984.

———. *Movement & Metaphor: Four Centuries of Ballet*. New York: Praeger Publishers, 1970.

Klosty, James, ed. *Merce Cunningham*. New York: E.P. Dutton, 1975.

Knight, Arthur. *Dancing in Films*. Dance Index. Vol. VI, No. 8, 1974.

Kothari, Dr. Sunil, and Mohan Khohar, eds. *Bharata Natyam: Indian Classical Dance*. Bombay: Marg Publications, 1979.

———. *Uday Shankar: A Photo-Biography*. New Delhi: RIMPA and the Uday Shankar Festival '83 Committee, 1983.

Kriegsman, Sally Ann. *Modern Dance in America: The Bennington Years*. Boston: G.K. Hall & Co., 1981.

Kurath, Gertrude P. *Half a Century of Dance Research*. Ann Arbor: Cushing-Mulloy, 1986.

———. *Michigan Indian Festivals*. Ann Arbor: Ann Arbor Publishers, 1966.

———. "Panorama of Dance Ethnology." *Current Anthropology* 1(3): 233–254, 1960.

Laban, Rudolf. *Principles of Dance and Movement Notation*. New York: Dance Horizons, 1956.

Lacroix, Paul, ed. *Ballets et mascarades de cour de Henri III à Louis XIV*. Vol. IV. Geneva: Slatkine Reprints, 1968.

Lamb, Warren, and Elizabeth Watson. *Body Code: The Meaning in Movement*. Princeton: Princeton Book Co., 1979.

La Meri. *Dance Out the Answer: An Autobiography*. New York: Marcel Dekker, 1977.

————. *Total Education in Ethnic Dance*. New York: Marcel Dekker, 1977.

Langer, Susanne. *Feeling and Form*. New York: Scribner, 1953.

Laubin, Reginald, and Gladys Laubin. *Indian Dances of North America: Their Importance to Indian Life*. Norman, OK: University of Oklahoma Press, 1977.

Lauze, F. de. *Apologie de la Danse: A Treatise of Instruction in Dancing and Deportment* (1623). Translated by Joan Wildeblood. London: Frederick Muller, 1952.

Laws, Kenneth. *The Physics of Dance*. New York: Schirmer Books, 1984.

Leiter, Samuel L. *Kabuki Encyclopedia: An English Language Adaptation of Kabuki Jiten*. Westport, CT: Greenwood, 1980.

Lekis, Lisa. *Dancing Gods*. New York: Scarecrow Press, 1960.

————. *Folk Dances of Latin America*. New York: Scare crow Press, 1958.

Lloyd, Margaret. *The Borzoi Book of Modern Dance*. New York: Knopf, 1949. Reprint. New York: Dance Horizons, 1974.

Locke, Alain, ed. "The Negro and the American Theatre." In *The Black Aesthetic*, edited by Addison Gayle, Jr. New York: Anchor Books/Doubleday, 1972.

Lomax, Alan. *Folk Song Style and Culture*. Washington, D.C.: American Association for the Advancement of Science, 1968.

Lopoukov, Andrei, Alexander Shirayev, and Alexander Bocharov. *Character Dance*. London: Dance Books, 1986.

Magriel, Paul, ed. *Chronicles of the American Dance*. New York: Da Capo Press. Republication of 1948 original by Dance Index.

Malm, William P. *Music Cultures of the Pacific, The Near East and Asia*. New York: Prentice Hall, 1967.

Manor, Gloria, ed. *Israel Dance 1986*. Tel Aviv: Friends of the Dance, 1986.

Martí, Samuel, and Gertrude P. Kurath. *Dances of Anahuac: The Choreography and Music of Precortesian Dances*. New York: Aldine Publishing, 1964.

Martin, John. *The Modern Dance*. New York: A.S. Barnes & Co., 1933. Reprint. New York: Dance Horizons, 1965.

McGowan, Margaret M. *L'Art du Ballet de Cour en France 1581–1643*. Paris: Editions du Centre National de la Recherche Scientifique, 1978.

Mehrabian, Albert, ed. *Nonverbal Communication*. Chicago: Aldine Publishing Co., 1972.

Menestrier, Claude-François. *Des Ballets Anciens et Modernes*. Paris, 1682. Reprint. Geneva: Slatkine Reprints, 1972.

Miller, David Humphreys. *Ghost Dance*. Lincoln & London: University of Nebraska Press, 1959.

Money, Keith. *Anna Pavlova: Her Life and Art*. New York: Knopf, 1982.

Moore, Lillian. *Echoes of American Ballet*. New York: Dance Horizons, 1976.

————. *Artist of the Dance*. New York: Thomas Y. Crowell Co., 1938.

————. *Images of the Dance: Historical Treasures of the Dance Collection 1581–1861*. New York: New York Public Library, 1965.

Negri, Cesare. *Le Gratie d'Amore*. Milan: Ponti & Piccaglia. 1602. Reissued as *Nuove Inventione di balli*. Milan: Bordone. 1604/Facsimile reprint of 1602. New York: Broude Brothers, 1969; also Bologna: Forni, 1969.

Nevell, Richard. *A Time to Dance*. New York: St. Martin's Press, 1977.

Nijinska, Bronislava. *Early Memoirs*. Translated and edited by Irina Nijinska and Jean Rawlinson. New York: Holt, Rinehart & Winston, 1981.

Nketia, J.H.K. *Drumming in Akan Communities of Ghana*. Edinburgh: Thomas Nelson and Sons, 1963.

Novack, Cynthia J. *Sharing the Dance: Contact Improvisation and American Culture*. Madison, WI: University of Wisconsin Press, 1990.

Noverre, Jean Georges. *Letters on Dancing and Ballets* (1760). Translated by Cyril W. Beaumont. London: Cyril W. Beaumont, 1930. Reprint. New York: Dance Horizons, 1966.

Omari, Mikelle Smith. *From the Inside to the Outside: The Art and Ritual of Bahian Candomblé*. Los Angeles: UCLA, Fowler Museum of Cultural History, 1984.

Opoku, A. M. and Willis Bell. *African Dances: A Ghanaian Profile*. Legon: Institute of African Studies, University of Ghana, 1965.

Page, Jake, and Susanne Page. *Hopi*. New York: Harry N. Abrams, 1982.

Painter, Muriel Thayer. *The Yaqui Easter*. Tucson: University of Arizona Press, 1950.

————. *With Good Heart: Yaqui Beliefs and Ceremonies in Pascua Village*. Tucson: University of Arizona Press, 1986.

Palmer, Geoffrey, and Noel Lloyd. *A Year of Festivals: British Calendar Customs*. London: Frederick Warne and Co., 1972.

Pegg, Bob. *Rites and Riots: Folk Customs of Britain and Europe*. Poole, Dorset: Blandford Press, 1981.

Prabhavananda, Swami. *The Spiritual Heritage of India*. Garden City: Doubleday, 1963.

Prevots, Naima. *Dancing in the Sun: Hollywood Choreographers 1915–1937*. Ann Arbor: University of Michigan Research Press, 1987.

Pronko, Leonard Cabell. *Avant-Garde: The Experimental Theater in France*. Berkeley and Los Angeles: University of California Press, 1964.

————. *Theater East and West: Perspectives Toward a Total Theater*. Berkeley and Los Angeles: University of California Press, 1967.

Quirey, Belinda. *May I Have the Pleasure? The Story of Popular Dancing*. New York: Gordon Press, 1986.

Raftis, Alkis. *The World of Greek Dance*. London: Finedawn Publishers, 1987.

Reynolds, Nancy. *In Performance: A Companion to the Classics of the Dance*. New York: Harmony Books, 1980.

————. *Repertory in Review: Forty Years of the New York City Ballet*. New York: The Dial Press, 1977.

Roslavleva, Natalia. *Era of the Russian Ballet*. New York: E.P. Dutton & Co., 1966.

Rouget, Gilbert. *Music and Trance: A Theory of the Relations Between Music and Possession*. Translated by Brunhilde Biebuyck in collaboration with the author. Chicago: University of Chicago Press, 1985.

Rowse, A. L. *Court and Country: Studies in Tudor Social History*. Sussex: The Harvester Press, 1987.

Royce, Anya Peterson. *The Anthropology of Dance*. Bloomington, Indiana: Indiana University Press, 1976.

Sachs, Curt. *The World History of Dance*. Translated by Bessie Schöenberg. New York: Bonanza, 1937.

Saint-Léon, Arthur. *Letters from a Ballet Master*. New York: Dance Horizons, 1981.

St. Méry, Moreau de. *Dance*. New York: Dance Horizons, 1975.

Sam, Chan Moly. *Khmer Court Dance: A Comprehensive Study of Movements, Gestures and Postures as Applied Techniques*. Newington, CT: Khmer Studies Institute, 1987.

Schechner, Richard. *Between Theater and Anthropology*. Philadelphia: University of Pennsylvania Press, 1986.

Schlundt, Christena L. "Into the Mist with Miss Ruth." *Dance Perspectives* 46 (Summer 1971).

————. *The Professional Appearances of Ruth St. Denis and Ted Shawn*. New York: The New York Public Library, 1962.

————. *The Professional Appearances of Ted Shawn and His Men Dancers*. New York: The New York Public Library, 1967.

Scott, A. C. *The Theatre in Asia*. London: Weidenfeld and Nicolson, 1972.

Sharp, Cecil J. *The Dance: An Historical Survey of Dancing in Europe*. London: Halton & Truscott Smith Ltd., 1924.

Shattuck, Roger. *The Banquet Years*. New York: Harcourt, Brace, 1958.

Shaver, Ruth M. *Kabuki Costume*. Rutland, VT and Tokyo: Charles E. Tuttle Co., 1966.

Shawn, Ted. *Every Little Movement: A Book About Delsarte*. Pennington, NJ: Dance Horizons/Princeton Book Co., 1988 (Originally published 1954).

Shelton, Suzanne. *Divine Dancer: A Biography of Ruth St. Denis*. Garden City: Doubleday, 1981.

Siegel, Marcia B. *Days on Earth: The Dance of Doris Humphrey*. New Haven & London: Yale University Press, 1987.

————. *The Shapes of Change: Images of American Dance*. Boston: Houghton Mifflin, 1979.

————. *Watching the Dance Go By*. Boston: Houghton Mifflin, 1977.

Simmonds, Harvey, Louis H. Silverstein, and Nancy Lassalle. *Lincoln Kirstein: The Published Writings 1922–1977. A First Bibliography*. New Haven: Yale University Press, 1978.

Snyder, Allegra Fuller. "The Dance Symbol." *New Dimensions in Dance Research: Anthropology and Dance—The American Indian*. CORD Research Annual 6 (1974).

Sorell, Walter, ed. *The Dance Has Many Faces*. 2nd ed. New York: Columbia University Press, 1966.

————. *Dance in Its Time: The Emergence of an Art Form*. Garden City: Doubleday, 1981.

Sorley Walker, Kathrine. *De Basil's Ballets Russes*. New York: Atheneum, 1983.

Souriau, Paul. *The Aesthetics of Movement*. Amherst: University of Massachusetts Press, 1983.

Sparshott, Francis. *Off the Ground: First Steps to a Philosophical Consideration of the Dance*.

Princeton: Princeton University Press, 1988.

Spencer, Paul, ed. *Society and the Dance: The Social Anthropology of Process and Performance.* London: Cambridge University Press, 1985.

Steinberg, Cobbett, ed. *The Dance Anthology.* New York: New American Library, 1980.

Stratou, Dora. *The Greek Dances: Our Living Link with Antiquity.* Athens, 1966.

Strong, Roy. *Splendor at Court: Renaissance Spectacle and the Theater of Power.* Boston: Houghton Mifflin, 1973.

Svetloff, V. *Anna Pavlova.* New York: Dover, 1974.

Sweet, Jill D. *Dance of the Tewa Pueblo Indians.* Santa Fe, NM: School of American Research Press, 1985.

Sweet, Waldo E. *Sport & Recreation in Ancient Greece: A Sourcebook with Translations.* New York: Oxford University Press, 1987.

Swift, Mary Grace. *A Loftier Flight: The Life and Accomplishments of Charles Louis Didelot, Balletmaster.* Middletown: Wesleyan University Press, 1974.

Tateishi, Ryuichi. *Classic Dancing In Japan.* Tokyo: Tokyo Shobo Co., 1969.

Terry, Walter. *I Was There.* New York and Basel: Marcel Dekker, 1978.

Thompson, Robert Farris. *African Art in Motion: Icon and Act.* Berkeley: University of California Press, 1974.

———. *Flash of the Spirit: Afro-American Art and Philosophy.* New York: Random House, 1983.

Titon, Jeff Todd (ed.), James T. Koetting, David P. McAllester, David B. Reck, and Mark Slobin. *Worlds of Music.* New York: Schirmer Books, 1984.

Togi, Masataro. *Gagaku Court Music & Dance.* New York & Tokyo: Walker/Weatherhill, 1971.

Tracy, Robert, and Sharon Delano. *Balanchine's Ballerinas: Conversations with the Muses.* New York: Linden Press/Simon & Schuster, 1983.

Uralskaya, V. *Nature of the Dance.* Soviet Russia, 1981.

Utsuoka, Satoru. *Dance & Music in South Asian Drama.* Tokyo: Academia Music Ltd., 1983.

Van Zile, Judy. *The Japanese Bon Dance in Hawaii.* Hawaii: Press Pacifica, 1982.

Varadpande, M. L. *History of Indian Theatre.* New Delhi: Abhinav Publications, 1987.

Vatsyayan, Kapila. *Indian Classical Dance.* New Delhi: Publication Division, n.d.

———. *Ramayana and the Arts of Asia.* Tehran, Iran: Asian Cultural Documentation Centre, n.d.

———. *Traditions of Indian Folk Dance.* 2nd Edition. New Delhi: Clarion Books Associated Hind Pocket Books, 1987.

Vaughan, David. *Frederick Ashton and His Ballets.* New York: Knopf, 1977.

Vuillier, Gaston. *A History of Dancing from the Earliest Ages to Our Own Times* (1898). Reprint. Boston: Milford House, 1972.

Wallace, Carol McD., Don McDonagh, Jean L. Druesedow, Lawrence Libin, and Constance Old. *Dance: A Very Social History.* New York: The Metropolitan Museum of Art/Rizzoli, 1986.

Wallen, Lynn Ager, and Joan Acocella. *A Spectrum of World Dance.* New York: CORD, 1987.

Ward, John. "The English Measure." *Early Music* 14 (1986): 15–21.

———. "The Manner of Dauncynge." *Early Music* 4 (1976): 127–142.

———. "The Morris Tune." Reprint from *The American Musicological Society* Vol. 39, No. 2, 1986.

———. "The Relationship of Folk and Art Music in 17th Century Spain." From *Studi Musicali* Vol. 12. Florence: Leo S. Olschki Editore, 1983.

Warren, Larry. *The Dance of Africa: An Introduction.* Englewood Cliffs: Prentice Hall, 1972.

———. *Lester Horton: Modern Dance Pioneer.* New York: Marcel Dekker, 1977.

Weitz, Shirley, ed. *Nonverbal Communication.* New York: Oxford University Press, 1979.

Wenig, Adele R. *Pearl Primus: An Annotated Bibliography of Sources from 1943 to 1975.* Oakland, CA: Wendance Unlimited, 1983.

White, Joan W., ed. *Twentieth Century Dance in Britain.* London: Dance Books, 1985.

Wigman, Mary. *The Language of Dance.* Translated by Walter Sorell. Middletown: Wesleyan University Press, 1966.

Wilkes, Ivor. *The Ashanti in the 19th Century: the Political Struggle and Evolution of a Political Power.* London: Cambridge University Press, 1975.

Wolz, Carl. *Bugaku Japanese Court Dance.* Providence: Asian Music Publications, Brown University, 1971.

Wood, Melusine. *Historical Dances, 12th to 19th Century.* London: Dance Books Ltd., 1982.

Wosien, Maria-Gabrielle. *Sacred Dance: Encounter with the Gods.* New York: Avon, 1974.

Yates, Frances A. *The French Academies of the Seventeenth Century.* London: The Warburg Institute, University of London, 1947.

Youngerman, Suzanne. "Curt Sachs and His Heritage." *CORD News* 1. (1974): 6–19.

Zorn, John W. *The Essential Delsarte.* Metuchen, NJ: Scarecrow Press, 1968.

General References and Bibliographic Sources:

The Concise Oxford Dictionary of Ballet. 2nd ed. Horst Koegler. London: Oxford University Press, 1982.

Dance Abstracts and Index 1989. UCLA: Dance Database Project, 1989.

The Dance Encyclopedia. Rev ed. Edited by Anatole Chujoy and P.W. Manchester. New York: Simon and Schuster, 1967.

Dance Sources: UCLA Libraries and Archives.

Dictionary of Ballet Terms. Leo Kersley and Janet Sinclair. New York: Da Capo Press, 1981. (1979)

Dictionary Catalog of the Dance Collection. New York: The New York Public Library, 1974.

Encyclopaedia Britannica. Chicago: Encyclopaedia Britannica.

Encyclopedia Judaica. Jerusalem: Kefer Publishing House Jerusalem Ltd., 1972.

The Encyclopedia of Dance. Edited by Mary Clarke and David Vaughan. New York: G.P. Putnam's Sons, 1977.

Encyclopedia of Religion Vol. 4. Edited by Mircea Eliade. New York: Macmillan Publishing Co.

The International Encyclopedia of Dance. Edited by Selma Jeanne Cohen, et. al. Berkeley: University of California Press. Forthcoming.

Music and Dance Research of Southwestern United States Indians: Past Trends, Present Activities, and Suggestion for Future Research. Edited by Charlotte J. Frisbie. Detroit: Detroit Studies in Music Bibliography, No. 36, 1977.

Sources on African and African Related Dance. Edited by Margaret Thompson Drewal. New York: American Dance Guild, 1974.

What is Dance? Edited by Roger Copeland and Marshall Cohen. Oxford: Oxford University Press, 1983.

Additional works cited by chapter:

Chapter 1: The Power of Dance

Asante, Kariamu Welsh. "The Jerusarema Dance of Zimbabwe." *Journal of Black Studies* 15 (June 1985): 381–403

Blumenthal, Eileen. "Cambodia's Royal Dance." *Natural History* (April 1989): 55–63.

Bourguignon, Erika. *Religion, Altered States of Consciousness and Social Change.* Columbus: Ohio State University Press, 1973.

———. "Trance Dance." *Dance Perspectives* 35 (1968).

Brandon, James R. *Brandon's Guide to Theater in Asia.* Honolulu: University Press of Hawaii, 1976.

Cravath, Paul. "The Ritual Origins of the Classical Dance Drama of Cambodia." *Asian Theatre Journal* 3 (Fall 1986): 179–200.

Ingber, Judith Brin, ed. "Dancing into Marriage: Collected Papers on Jewish Wedding Dances." *Dance Research Journal* 17–2 (1985–86): 51–86.

Keali'inohomoku, Joann W. "An Anthropologist Looks at Ballet as a Form of Ethnic Dance." In *What is Dance?*, edited by Roger Copeland and Marshall Cohen. Oxford: Oxford University Press, 1983.

———. "The Hopi Katsina Dance Event 'Doings'." In *Seasons of the Kachina*, edited by John Bean Lowell. Hayward: Ballena Press/California State University, Hayward Cooperative Publications, 1989.

Mooney, James. *The Ghost Dance Religion and the Sioux Outbreak of 1890.* Ed. Anthony F. C. Wallace. Chicago: University of Chicago Press, 1965.

Moulin, Jane Freeman. *The Dance of Tahiti.* Papeete: Christian Gleizal, 1979.

O'Reilly, Patrick. *Dancing Tahiti.* Société des Océanistes Dossier 22. Paris: Nouvelles Editions Latines, 1977.

Chapter 2: Lord of the Dance

Backman, E. Louis. *Religious Dances in the Christian Church and in Popular Medicine.* London: Greenwood, 1952.

Drewal, Margaret Thompson. *Yoruba: Art in Life and Thought.* Victoria: African Research Institute, La Trobe University, 1988.

Drewal, Henry J., and John Pemberton III. *Yoruba: Nine Centuries of African Art and Thought.* New York: Harry N. Abrams, 1989.

Embree, Ainslie T. *Sources of Indian Tradition.* New York: Columbia University Press, 1988.

Herman, A. L. *A Brief Introduction to Hinduism.* Boulder, CO: Westview Press, 1991.

Iyer, K. Bharatha. *Kathakali: The Sacred Dance-Drama of Malabar.* New Delhi: Oriental Books Reprint Corp. London: Luzac and Co., 1955.

Johnson, Paul. *A History of Christianity.* New York: Macmillan, 1979.

Khokar, Mohan. *The Splendours of Indian Dance.* New Delhi: Himalayan Books, 1985.

Lawler, Lillian. *The Dance in Ancient Greece.* Middletown, CT: Wesleyan University Press, 1965.

Marks, Joseph E., III. *The Mathers on Dancing.* New York: Dance Horizons, 1975.

Massey, Reginald and Julia. *The Dances of India.* London: Tricolour Books, 1989.

Miller, Barbara Stoler. *Love Song of the Dark Lord: Jayadeva's Gitagovinda.* New York: Columbia University Press, 1977.

Sen, K. M. *Hinduism.* New York: Penguin Books, 1961.

Soyinka, Wole. *Myth, Literature and the African World.* Cambridge: Cambridge University Press, 1976.

Thapar, Romila. *A History of India.* New York: Viking Penguin, 1966.

Vatsyayan, Kapila. *Classical Indian Dance in Literature and the Arts.* New Delhi: Sangeet Natak Akademi, 1968.

Chapter 3: Dance of the Realm

Department of Information, Republic of Indonesia. *Indonesia 1990: An Official Handbook.*

Dodds, Maggie, ed. *Ghana Talks.* Washington: Three Continents Press, 1976.

Garrard, Timothy F. *Gold of Africa.* New York: TeNeues, 1989.

Hilton, Wendy. *Dance of Court and Theater: The French Noble Style 1690–1725.* Princeton: Princeton Book Co., 1981.

Jessup, Helen I. *Court Arts of Indonesia.* New York: The Asia Society Galleries of New York/Harry N. Abrams, 1990.

Kenny, Don. *On Stage in Japan.* Tokyo: Shufunotomo Co., 1974.

McLeod, Malcolm D. *The Asante.* London: British Museum Publications, 1981.

Morgan, Ted, ed. and trans. *The Age of Magnificence.* New York: Paragon House, 1990.

Murgiyento, Sal. "Basic Principles of Javanese Court Dance." *Dance Research Annual* 15 (1983): 180–184.

Nketia, J.H.K. *The Music of Africa.* New York: Norton, 1974.

Oliver, Roland, and J. D. Fage. *A Short History of Africa.* 3rd ed. New York: Viking Penguin, 1970.

Olsin-Windecker, Hilary. "Characterization in Classical Yogyanese Dance." *Dance Research Annual* 15 (1983): 185–193.

Rameau, Pierre. *The Dancing Master,* n.d. Translated by Cyril Beaumont. New York: Dance Horizons, 1970.

Soedarsono. *Wayang Wong: The State Ritual Dance Drama in the Court of Yogyakarta.* Yogyakarta: Gadjah Mada University Press, 1984.

Thompson, Robert Farris. "An Aesthetic of the Cool, West African Dance." *African Forum* 2 (2): 85–102.

Zarina, Xenia. *Classic Dances of the Orient.* New York: Crown, 1967.

Chapter 4: Social Dance

Aldrich, Elizabeth. *From the Ballroom to Hell: Grace and Folly in Nineteenth Century Dance.* Evanston: Northwestern University Press, 1991.

Berger, Morroe. "The Arab Danse du Ventre." *Dance Perspectives* 10: A Curious and Wonderful Gymnastic . . . (Spring 1961): 4–41.

Buonaventura, Wendy. *Serpent of the Nile: Women and Dance in the Arab World.* New York: Interlink Books, 1990.

Deaver, Sherri. "Concealment vs. Display: The Modern Saudi Woman." *Dance Research Journal* 10 (Spring–Summer 1978): 19–22.

Tannahill, Reay. *Sex in History.* Chelsea: Scarborough House, 1982.

Chapter 5: Classical Dance Theater

Bellah, Robert. *Tokugawa Religion.* New York: The Free Press, 1985.

Benedict, Ruth. *The Chrysanthemum and the Sword.* Boston: Houghton Mifflin, 1946.

Bowers, Faubion. *Japanese Theater.* Rutland, VT, and Tokyo: Charles E. Tuttle Co., 1974.

Brandon, James R., William P. Malm, and Donald H. Shively. *Studies in Kabuki: Its Acting, Music, and Historical Context.* Honolulu: University of Hawaii Press, 1978.

Ernst, Earle. *The Kabuki Theater.* London: Secker and Warburg, 1956.

Gerstle, C. Andrew. "Flowers of Edo: Eighteenth-Century Kabuki and Its Patrons." *Asian Theatre Journal* 4 (Spring 1987): 52–75.

Leiter, Samuel L. *The Art of Kabuki: Famous Plays in Performance.* Berkeley: University of California Press, 1979.

Lohr, Steve. "The New Face of Kabuki." *The New York Times Magazine,* May 30, 1982, p. 13–17.

Chapter 6: New Worlds of Dance

Emery, Lynne Fauley. *Black Dance in the U.S. from 1619 to Today.* 2nd, rev. ed. Salem, NH: Ayer Co., 1988.

Goldwasser, Maria Julia. "Carnival." In *Encyclopedia of Religion,* edited by Mircea Eliade. New York: Macmillan.

Guillermoprieto, Alma. *Samba.* New York: Knopf, 1990.

Hazzard-Gordon, Katrina. *Jookin': The Rise of Social Dance Formations in African-American Culture.* Philadelphia: Temple University Press, 1990.

Herskovits, Melville J. *The Myth of the Negro Past.* New York: Harper and Brothers, 1958.

Keali'inohomoku, Joann W. "A Comparative Study of Dance as a Constellation of Motor Behaviors Among African and United States Negroes." *Dance Research Annual* 7 (1976): 1–179.

Marks, Morton. "Popular and Ritual Dance in Brazil." In *International Encyclopedia of Dance,* edited by Selma Jeanne Cohen. Berkeley: University of California Press. Forthcoming.

Szwed, John F., and Morton Marks. "The Afro-American Transformation of European Set Dances and Dance Suites." *Dance Research Journal* 20 (Summer 1988): 29–36.

Stearns, Marshall and Jean. *Jazz Dance: The Story of American Vernacular Dance.* New York: Macmillan, 1968.

Tucker, Iantha Elizabeth Lake. "The Role of Afro-Americans in Dance in the United States from Slavery to the Present." In *African American Dance: Beauty, Rhythm, and Power.* Washington: National Museum of American History, 1990.

Chapter 7: Modernizing Dance

Daly, Ann. "The Balanchine Woman: Of Hummingbirds and Channel Swimmers." *The Drama Review* 31 (1): 8–21.

Jowitt, Deborah. *Time and the Dancing Image.* New York: William Morrow and Co., 1988.

Kendall, Elizabeth. *Where She Danced.* New York: Knopf, 1979.

Kirstein, Lincoln. "Beliefs of a Master." *New York Review of Books* (March 15, 1984): 17–23.

MacDougall, Alan Ross. *Isadora: A Revolutionary in Art and Love.* New York: Thomas Nelson and Sons, 1960.

Magriel, Paul, ed. *Nijinsky, Pavlova, Duncan.* New York: Da Capo, 1977.

McDonagh, Don. *The Rise and Fall and Rise of Modern Dance.* Pennington: A Capella/Chicago Review Press, 1990.

Sokolova, Lydia. *Dancing for Diaghilev: The Memoirs of Lydia Sokolova.* San Francisco: Mercury House, 1989.

Stebbins, Genevieve. *The Delsarte System of Expression.* 6th ed. 1902. Reprint. New York: Dance Horizons, 1977.

Chapter 8: Dancing in One World

Keali'inohomoku, Joann W. "Culture Change: Functional and Dysfunctional Expressions of Dance, a Form of Affective Culture." In *The Performing Arts: Music and Dance,* edited by John A.R. Blacking and Joann W. Keali'inohomoku. The Hague: Mouton, 1979.

Milward, John. "Still Rockin' (Sort of) After All These Years." *The New York Times,* March 4, 1992, p. C21.

Index

255

Photograph Credits